50 HIKES

IN WISCONSIN

50 HIKES

IN WISCONSIN

THIRD EDITION

John and Ellen Morgan

THE COUNTRYMAN PRESS

A division of W. W. Norton & Company

Independent Publishers Since 1923

An Invitation To The Reader
Over time, trails can be rerouted and signs and landmarks can be altered. If you find that changes have occurred on the routes described in this book, please let us know, so that corrections may be made in future editions. The author and publisher also welcome other comments and suggestions. Address all correspondence to:

50 Hikes Editor
The Countryman Press
500 Fifth Avenue
New York, NY 10110

The Countryman Press
www.countrymanpress.com

A division of W. W. Norton & Company, Inc.,
500 Fifth Avenue, New York, NY 10110
www.wwnorton.com

978-1-68268-090-2 (pbk.)

10 9 8 7 6 5 4 3 2 1

Because this is a guide to hiking trails, we have to recognize those who build them. These are the volunteers, friends' groups, park and forest employees, and other dedicated folks who literally move boulders, build stone stairwells, haul timbers, construct boardwalks and bridges, cut back invasive buckthorn, pull garlic mustard, clear fallen trees, install benches, plow park roads in the winter, and otherwise devote countless hours so that hikers can drive up, amble onto a trail, and enjoy a great hike. We must also recognize the citizens of Wisconsin and our elected officials and governments for continuing to value and trumpet the public health, conservation, and economic benefits of having parks, forests, and trails. To Wisconsin's trailblazers and advocates, thank you!

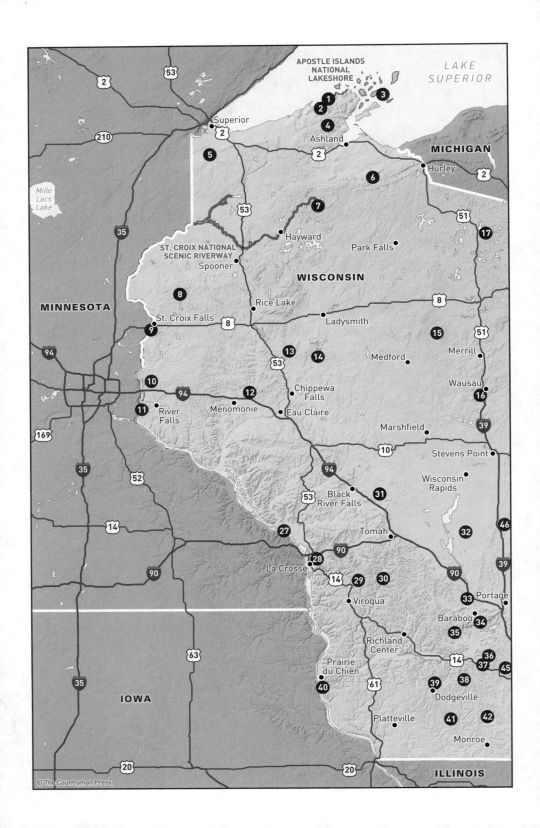

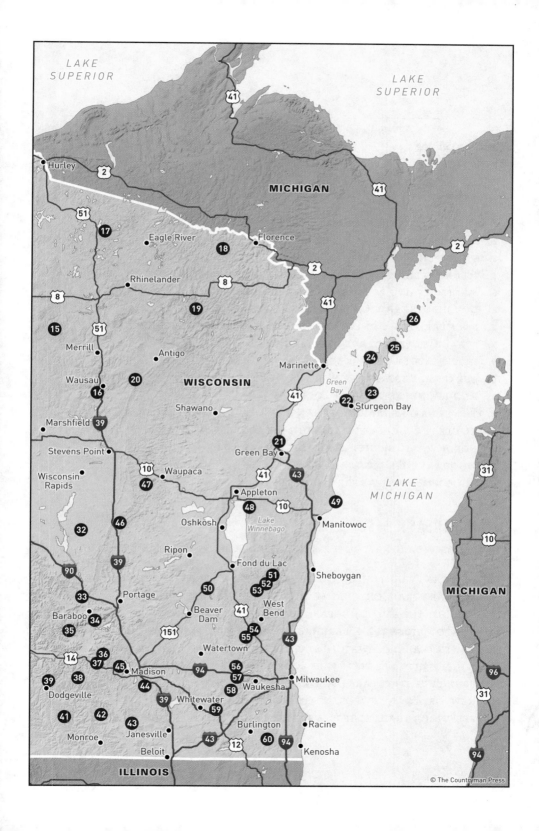

Contents

III. SOUTHWEST | 123

IV. SOUTHEAST | 207

Hikes at a Glance

Hike Name	Region	Distance (miles)	Difficulty
1. Lakeshore Trail, Apostle Islands National Lakeshore	NW, Cornucopia	3.8	3
2. Lost Creek Falls Trail, Bayfield County Forest	NW, Cornucopia	3	2.5
3. Stockton Island, Apostle Islands National Lakeshore	NW, Bayfield	4.2	3
4. Mount Valhalla, Chequamegon-Nicolet National Forest	NW, Washburn	2.25	3
5. Manitou Falls, Pattison State Park	NW, Superior	4.9	4.5
6. Doughboys Trail, Copper Falls State Park	NW, Mellen	2.5	3.5
7. Rock Lake Trail, Chequamegon-Nicolet National Forest	NW, Cable	4	2.5
8. Straight Lake, Ice Age Trail	NW, Luck	3.2	2
9. Interstate State Park Loop	NW, St. Croix Falls	5	3.5
10. Burkhardt Trail, Willow River State Park	NW, Hudson	3.3	3.5
11. Kinnickinnic State Park Loop	NW, Prescott	2.8	1.5
12. Tower Nature Trail, Hoffman Hills State Recreation Area	NW, Menomonie	2.7	3
13. Circle Trail, Chippewa Moraine Ice Age Reserve	NW, Bloomer	4.5	3.5
14. Nordic Trail, Brunet Island State Park	NW, Cornell	3	1.5
15. Wood Lake, Ice Age Trail	NW, Rib Lake	3	1.5
16. Rib Mountain State Park Loop	NW, Wausau	3.2	4.5
17. Fallison Lake Nature Trail, American Legion-Northern Highland State Forest	NE, Woodruff	2	1
18. Lost Lake Trail, Chequamegon-Nicolet National Forest	NE, Florence	4.5	3.5
19. Ed's Lake Trail, Chequamegon-Nicolet National Forest	NE, Crandon	3.5	2
20. Dells of the Eau Claire Park Loop, Marathon County	NE, Wausau	3	2
21. Meadow Ridge Trail, Barkhausen Waterfowl Preserve	NE, Green Bay	3.1	1.5
22. Tower Trail, Potawatomi State Park	NE, Sturgeon Bay	3.5	2.5

Good for Kids	Camping	Waterfalls	Scenic Views	Notes
			✓	Sea Caves
✓		✓		Snowshoeing
	✓		✓	Ferry Crossing Required
✓			✓	Nordic Skiing
	✓	✓	✓	Beach
	✓	✓	✓	Observation Tower
✓			✓	Nordic Skiing
✓			✓	Snowshoeing
	✓		✓	Beach
	✓	✓	✓	Scenic Overlook
✓	✓		✓	Nordic Skiing
			✓	Observation Tower
	✓		✓	Snowshoeing
✓				Nordic Skiing
✓	✓			Snowshoeing, Beach
			✓	Scenic Overlook
✓			✓	Snowshoeing
	✓		✓	Snowshoeing
✓			✓	Nordic Skiing
✓	✓	✓	✓	Beach
✓			✓	Nordic skiing
✓	✓		✓	Observation Tower

Hike Name	Region	Distance (miles)	Difficulty
23. Whitefish Dunes State Park Loop	NE, Jacksonport	2.8	1.5
24. Peninsula State Park Loop	NE, Fish Creek	4	3.5
25. Newport Loop, Newport State Park	NE, Ellison Bay	5	2.5
26. Fernwood Trail, Rock Island State Park	NE, Washington Island	3.5	2
27. Perrot Ridge and Brady's Bluff, Perrot State Park	SW, Trempealeau	3	4
28. Bicentennial Trail, Hixon Forest	SW, LaCrosse	3.7	3.5
29. Jersey Valley County Park Loop, Vernon County	SW, Westby	3.1	2.5
30. Old Settler's Trail, Wildcat Mountain State Park	SW, Ontario	2.5	3
31. Wildcat Mound Loop, Black River State Forest	SW, Black River Falls	4	2.5
32. Roche-A-Cri State Park Loop	SW, Friendship	3.7	3.5
33. Mirror Lake State Park Loop	SW, Wisconsin Dells	3.5	2
34. Devil's Lake, Ice Age Trail	SW, Baraboo	7	5
35. Natural Bridge State Park Loop	SW, Sauk City	2.5	2.5
36. Indian Lake County Park Loop, Dane County	SW, Cross Plains	3.5	3
37. Table Bluff, Ice Age Trail	SW, Cross Plains	4.1	3.5
38. Blue Mound State Park Loop	SW, Blue Mounds	5.1	3.5
39. Pine Cliff Trail, Governor Dodge State Park	SW, Dodgeville	5.5	3.5
40. Sentinel Ridge Trail, Wyalusing State Park	SW, Prairie du Chien	5	4.5
41. Yellowstone Lake State Park Loop	SW, Blanchardville	4.4	3
42. Havenridge Trail, New Glarus Woods State Park	SW, New Glarus	5.8	3.5
43. Magnolia Bluff County Park Loop, Rock County	SW, Evansville	2.4	2.5
44. Lake Kegonsa State Park Loop	SW, Stoughton	2.5	1
45. Picnic Point Trail, University of Wisconsin	SW, Madison	4.7	3
46. Mecan Springs, Ice Age Trail	SE, Coloma	5	3
47. Hartman Creek, Ice Age Trail	SE, Waupaca	8.5	4.5
48. High Cliff State Park Loop	SE, Kaukauna	4.8	3.5

Good for Kids	Camping	Waterfalls	Scenic Views	Notes
✓			✓	Scenic Overlook
	✓		✓	Scenic Overlook
	✓		✓	Nordic Skiing
✓	✓		✓	Scenic Overlook, Lighthouse
✓	✓		✓	Scenic Overlooks
			✓	Scenic Overlook
✓			✓	Beach
			✓	Scenic Overlook
✓			✓	Nordic Skiing
			✓	Observation Tower
✓	✓		✓	Beach
	✓		✓	Beach, Scenic Overlook
✓			✓	Scenic Overlook
			✓	Scenic Overlook, Nordic Skiing
			✓	Scenic Overlooks
	✓		✓	Observation Tower, Nordic Skiing, Swimming Pool
	✓		✓	Scenic Overlook, Beach
	✓	✓	✓	Scenic Overlooks
✓	✓		✓	Beach, Scenic Overlook
	✓		✓	Snowshoeing
			✓	Scenic Overlook
✓	✓			Beach, Nordic Skiing
			✓	Beach, Scenic Overlook
			✓	Scenic Overlook
	✓			Snowshoeing, Beach
	✓		✓	Observation Tower, Scenic Overlooks

Hike Name	Region	Distance (miles)	Difficulty
49. Point Beach State Forest Loop	SE, Two Rivers	5.5	2.5
50. Horicon National Wildlife Refuge Loop	SE, Waupun	4.5	2
51. Parnell Tower Loop, Kettle Moraine	SE, Plymouth	3.5	3.5
52. Butler Lake Loop, Kettle Moraine	SE, Dundee	3.1	2.5
53. Zillmer Trail, Kettle Moraine	SE, Dundee	5.4	3
54. Polk Kames, Ice Age Trail	SE, Slinger	3.6	2
55. Pike Lake Loop, Kettle Moraine	SE, Hartford	4.7	3.5
56. Nashotah Park Loop, Waukesha County	SE, Oconomowoc	3.5	1.5
57. Lapham Peak, Ice Age Trail	SE, Hartland	2.8	3.5
58. Scuppernong Trail Loop, Kettle Moraine	SE, Eagle	5.5	3.5
59. Nordic Trail Loop, Kettle Moraine	SE, Palmyra	3.7	3
60. Richard Bong State Recreation Area Loop	SE, Union Grove	4.2	2.5

Good for Kids	Camping	Waterfalls	Scenic Views	Notes
	✓		✓	Beach
✓			✓	Scenic Overlooks
	✓		✓	Observation Tower
✓			✓	Scenic Overlook
	✓		✓	Nordic Skiing
✓				Snowshoeing
	✓		✓	Observation Tower, Beach
✓				Nordic Skiing
	✓		✓	Observation Tower, Snowshoeing
			✓	Scenic Overlook, Nordic Skiing
✓			✓	Nordic Skiing, Scenic Overlooks
✓	✓			Nordic Skiing, Beach

QUIET BOARDWALKS TAKE HIKERS TO LAKE SUPERIOR SEA CAVES ON THE LAKESHORE TRAIL

Introduction

When it comes to hiking, Wisconsin rocks, and our goal for this guide over the past 12 years has been to celebrate and highlight the best trails and natural areas the Badger State has to offer.

Luckily for hikers, it's not hard to find great trails. The place is home to an immense 1.5-million-acre National Forest, it is bordered by two Great Lakes with more than 800 miles of shoreline, it has 66 state park units covering 60,000 acres, and there's another half-million acres of state forest. Add to this our county parks and forests, nature preserves, city parks, and more, and things are pretty kid-in-a-candy-store bountiful for hikers looking for trails.

And then there's our beloved Ice Age Trail. That's right, our state's own National Scenic Trail traces the 1,200-mile-long glacial moraine—essentially a serpentine hill—marking the farthest extent of the last glacier's path when it plowed down from the north, dumped its geological contents, and then receded 10,000 years ago. Many people don't know this, but the Ice Age Trail is one of four units of the National Park Service in Wisconsin. All four are featured in this book, the other three being the North Country Trail (which passes through on its path from North Dakota to New York), the Apostle Islands National Lakeshore, and the St. Croix National Scenic Riverway.

So revising this book and putting out a third edition is pretty easy stuff in a state like Wisconsin, where there are trails seemingly everywhere. We keep a list of possible hikes, and each time around we loop around the state, checking out new trails to add to each new edition of this guide, and the list feels endless. In terms of what's new this time around, there are five new hikes at new locations, including The Lakeshore Trail at the Apostle Islands National Lakeshore, The Lost Creek Falls Trail in the Bayfield County Forest, The Bicentennial Trail at Hixon Forest in La Crosse, The Nordic Trails in Kettle Moraine South, and the Natural Bridge State Park loop trail in the bucolic Baraboo Hills.

But wait, there's more! There are also 10 hikes from the last edition that either have completely new routes, were extended, or just plain needed fixing in some way. These include Devil's Lake (new route), Lapham Peak (new route), Pattison State Park (new route), Mirror Lake (extended), Point Beach (extended), Magnolia Bluff (rerouted), High Cliff State Park (extended), Picnic Point (rerouted and extended), New Glarus Woods (extended), and Indian Lake County Park (extended).

In the end, it's our hope that you, too, will enjoy exploring these great trails and have a great time hiking in the Badger State.

HOW TO USE THIS BOOK

The beginning of the book includes an "At a Glance" section that lists the hike name, the quadrant region it's in (along with the nearest town or city), the hike distance, the difficulty rating, and a listing of notable extras (good for kids, camping, waterfalls, etc.). In terms of "kids," we're basing the suitability for kids on whether a child up to around 10 years old would be able to handle a given hike.

As for the difficulty rating, we've made changes to how we've rated hikes this time around to have the ratings be relative to the hikes in the book. In this way, hikes that are very level and not very long are given a 1.0 or 1.5; as the hike encounters more length it will get into the 2.0 level; hills and increased distance will mean a 3.0 or 3.5; and significant elevation changes and significant distance will be indicated by a 4.0, 4.5, or 5.0.

The book's chapters for each hike include two main sections. First, a general introduction to the area puts the hike in perspective by including natural history, historical information about the area, and perhaps some explanation about the geology of the place. Next, there is a step-by-step walk-through of the trail itself that gives information on footing, terrain, scenery, elevation change, and difficulty.

Note: The chapter data gives a net elevation change—which is the difference between the lowest point and the highest point. Keep in mind that often these are roller-coaster hikes, and a hike that's listed as having a 70-foot net elevation change may actually take you on multiple ascents and descents, making the overall climbing several hundred feet total. We try to stress such things in the chapters.

For those of you who hike with your dog, we try our best to provide the most accurate information regarding rules for dogs. But, you should probably do a quick search for the place you're headed and maybe even call ahead of time to confirm. For the most part, dogs are allowed on nearly every hike in this book on a 6-foot-long leash. And a few places even have dog exercise or swimming areas, or both (Indian Lake County Park, Lake Kegonsa State Park, and Point Beach State Forest, to name a few). Dogs are never allowed on lookout towers and we take turns hanging out with the dog on ground level if we're interested in heading up.

Finally, a word about how we've titled hike names. There are some trails, like the Lost Creek Falls Trail, that are simple. There's only one trail at that location, it has a definite name, and it's intuitive and well marked. There are other situations and locations where the trail that we've defined is actually a combination of a few trails at a location and/or the trail we highlight doesn't even really have a specific formal name. In these cases, you'll see that we devise a route and add either "Loop" or "Trail" to the end of the hike title, which is usually based on the hike location (sometimes the hike is a loop, a lollypop, or an out-and-back trail).

Once you read the chapter and look at the map, you'll get the gist of what we're suggesting. A good example of a hike like this is the "Rib Mountain Loop," which is the combination of three trails to create a loop around the south side of the mountain. The state parks are particularly prone to having named trails that start at a common trailhead but end somewhere off in the middle of the park, with another trail starting at that point or intersecting it on its way past. So, a generic "Loop" title seemed to be the best solution for these hikes. Once you read about the trail in more detail, you'll find the precise names for the park trails that we stitched together.

MAPS

The maps found in each chapter are all completely new for the third edition, with many more details included regarding other trails in a given area, offshoots, etc., which will all hopefully make it much easier to follow the recommended route.

If you do a search for most of the trails, park, or forest included in the book, you will almost always find a link to a map at a county, state, national park, or forest website. Additionally, many trailheads and park offices highlighted in the book will have a kiosk or office with paper maps of these trails—not to mention updated information about trail conditions.

A note about the overall map of the state and the four regions: First, we divided the state into quadrants with the horizontal divider being 44° 30' latitude, which is a horizontal line drawn across the center of the state (this line basically starts on the west side of the state on the south end of Lake Pepin on the Mississippi River, heads east through the south side of Stevens Point, and then on through the center of the city of Green Bay). Then, for the middle vertical divider, we used highway US 39/51, which runs all the way from Hurley on the northern border south to Beloit. When numbering hikes, we tried our best to clump them together in groups of hikes in common areas.

VEHICLE PERMITS AND CAMPING

When entering a Wisconsin state park, forest, or recreation area—as well as the Chequamegon-Nicolet National Forest—you will be required to obtain either a daily or annual vehicle permit. You can do a search for permits online at the Wisconsin Department of Natural Resources website, www.dnr.wi.gov, and at the Chequamegon-Nicolet National Forest website, www.fs.usda.gov/cnnf. Nearly all sites have self-pay stations at trailhead parking areas.

Camping is available at many of the trail locations covered in this book, and the above websites will assist with this as well. Remote camping on the islands of the Apostle Islands National Lakeshore is also available. Find the National Park Service website for the Apostle Islands National Lakeshore online at www.nps.gov/apis for more information.

THE ICE AGE TRAIL

There are 17 sections of Ice Age Trail featured in this book. To learn more about the Ice Age Trail Alliance, the nonprofit group whose tireless volunteer efforts are making this 1,200-mile trail more of a reality each year, go to www.iceagetrail.org. You can become a member and even spend some time volunteering at a trail workday. There are also county trail chapters that host hikes and other events. The telltale Ice Age Trail marking is a rectangular bright yellow "blaze" (see photo on page 18). Blue blazes denote a spur trail, or an access trail from a parking lot to the main Ice Age Trail passing through nearby. White blazes denote loops that leave the main Ice Age Trail but return to the trail after completing a loop.

HUNTING IN WISCONSIN

In case you are new to Wisconsin, or new to exploring its parks and trails, you should note that there are several hunting seasons that begin in the fall months (and selected others in the spring). It is important to know that many state parks and forests, national forests, county parks, and recreational lands allow hunting in the same areas as trails or in adjoining areas at some point during the fall. The best idea is to inquire about any hunting in or near the area you are visiting to ensure a safe hike. Contact information is provided for each hike in this book and is as accurate as possible. It also doesn't hurt to include a blaze-orange hat and vest in your hiking wardrobe (there are also blaze-orange collars and vests for dogs, as well as bells they can wear).

HIKING HAZARDS

Wisconsin's outdoors brings with it certain hazards. The list of large mammals in this state includes black bears and grey wolves. We have never encountered either on a trail. It doesn't mean we won't, it just means that it's rare and also that there are steps you can take to be careful and minimize dangerous interactions. The Chequamegon-Nicolet National Forest has a webpage devoted to "Bear Country Awareness" if you're interested in reading up on their suggested dos and don'ts.

In terms of reptiles, there are two venomous snakes in Wisconsin—the

RECTANGULAR YELLOW BLAZES MARK THE PATH OF THE ICE AGE TRAIL

massasauga and timber rattlesnakes. Both are extremely reclusive and both are on the state list of protected species. The Wisconsin Department of Natural Resources has great webpages devoted to both of these snakes if you do a search for them. The bottom line is that it's rare to encounter one and bites are treatable (indeed, since 1900, only two deaths have been attributed to these snakes). Both species mostly reside in a range that more or less encompasses the southwest half of the state if you were to draw a diagonal line from Superior to Kenosha. Again, however, this isn't like in some western states where rattlesnakes out there are like deer for us. Most Wisconsinites will go their whole lives without ever seeing or hearing one. Check out the Wisconsin DNR website for more information.

The more pressing hazards at this point in Wisconsin's history seem to be both plant-based oils and tick-based bacteria. First, plants like poison ivy and wild parsnip are probably more likely to cause you distress than any animal. A web search for both will help you familiarize yourself with them. Wild parsnip is fast becoming ubiquitous. Brushing past it and getting its oils on your skin will leave you victim to an awful, blistering rash that is actually triggered as sunlight reacts with the oils, a phenomenon known as phytophotodermatitis.

Next, and quite seriously, perhaps the biggest potential menace for anyone spending any amount of time outdoors in Wisconsin is Lyme disease, and the microscopic bacterium that causes it, *Borellia bergorferi*. It lives in and is transmitted by the bite of the black-legged tick (more commonly known as the deer tick). According to the Centers for Disease Control, 94 percent of all Lyme cases occurred in 14 states,

Wisconsin being one of them. And if the northeast United States is the epicenter of the disease, Wisconsin (along with neighboring Minnesota) is a satellite runner-up. But there are steps you can take to lessen your risks of a tick bite, and, if you are bitten, Lyme is more easily treatable if detected early on. Untreated, longer-term effects can be life-altering and awful. To learn more about Lyme, and in particular how to prevent a tick bite and identify symptoms if you've been infected, go to www.cdc.gov/lyme.

Note: Dogs can also be afflicted with Lyme. Unlike humans, there is a vaccine for dogs and also several topical and even oral monthly tick preventions available. Our own vet recommends that our Labrador should be on tick prevention year-round because ticks can be active even on mild winter days.

In addition to the risk of deer ticks as outlined above, there are also biting flies, stinging bees and wasps, chiggers, and mosquitoes.

Also of note is weather. The National Weather Service reports that eight people were killed by lightning in Wisconsin between 2005 and 2014. See weather.gov for more information on protecting yourself from lightning. And be very careful hiking in high winds when branches or whole trees may fall.

In sum, this outlines *some* of the possible hazards you might encounter on the trail. While there's no way to totally eliminate all hazards, your interaction with them can be minimized by taking precautions.

HIKING GEAR

As the saying goes, "there's no such thing as bad weather, only bad gear." As hikers who are willing to hike just about

BOOT SPIKES AND METAL-TIPPED WALKING STICK FOR WINTER HIKING HAPPINESS

any day of the year and in any weather, we agree. While everyone has their own gear, here's our approach to gearing up for hiking in Wisconsin:

1. A daypack with a rigid internal frame with a padded waist belt is essential so that you can tug that belt tight and the bulk of the weight of the pack will rest on the tips of your hip bones, not on your shoulders and back.

2. A sort of "Must-Have Kit" in a big ziplock that includes some first aid supplies such as an ankle wrap; a small multi-tool; hand/feet warmers; an extra boot-length lace; and an extra big ziplock bag for phones, keys, and wallet, in case of rain.

3. We always have water for each of us and the dog if she's with us (as well as her collapsible bowl), and we always have snacks for us and treats for the dog, if only to use to redirect her when we see other hikers and dogs.

4. We each use a single telescopic and

shock-absorbing aluminum hiking stick with metal points. We find them invaluable for rocky and slippery ascents and descents. They're also great for pushing wild parsnips aside.

5. In winter and early spring, we nearly always hike with boot spikes. Because our part of Wisconsin tends not to get the big snows that warrant snowshoes, these spikes make hiking over slick ice a breeze. We also use another type that comes in more of a chain style and is useful in early spring mud and slush.

6. Finally, as for clothes and boots, we always wear long pants in the summer and tall socks to keep ticks at bay and to protect from poison ivy, wild parsnip, and thorns. If you carry backup clothes to wear after hiking, you can change so you won't have to sit around in socks and pants that may have ticks crawling on them. In winter, layer and shed clothes as you get warm and pull them back out of the pack as the sun goes down. We carry a couple of different thick-nesses of hats and gloves and a face shield. As for boots, well-made water-proof boots are a must. Buy from as close to the top of the line as you can and be sure to get boots that are bigger than your normal size, to account for thick socks and feet that swell up while hiking. A good out-doors store will help you get outfitted with boots. A useful tip is to go for a hike and *then* go to the store to try on boots while your feet are swollen and sore. You'll know what fits and feels good by doing this.

HIKING ETIQUETTE

We looked at several sources to confirm best practices when hiking. So, for the good of hiking order for all of us, here's some of what we found:

1. **Right of way.** First, downhill hikers should step off the trail to allow uphill hikers through. The reason for this is that uphill hikers don't have the field of view that downhill hikers have and they need to keep their momentum going. (We always move out of the way for trail runners, no matter what direction they're going.) Second, always yield to horses. Finally, from what we read, mountain bikers *should* yield for hikers, but it's often easier for hikers to yield the trail. *Note*: Both trail runners and mountain bikers should announce their presence well before passing hikers.

2. **Leave no trace.** Take out whatever you bring in. Period. We often pick up what others have left behind, hopefully by mistake. We have pockets on the back of our packs where we collect trash of all sorts—juice box straw wrappers, granola bar wrappers, water bottle caps, the little plastic ring below the water bottle cap, whole water bottles, cigarette butts, beer bottles, beer cans, knotted balls of fishing line, and, unfortunately, lots more.

3. **Be friendly.** A good rule of thumb is to say hi when passing people and to compare notes about trail conditions, etc. They may have information of use as you hike to where they've been and they also may be the people you need for help if you twist an ankle. Or they may need your help. Also, it's just nice to be nice out there.

4. **Passing.** Sometimes you may be moving a bit faster than the group in front of you. If so, well before you get to them, simply say, "Hello! Can we pass?" And also thank them as you go by. Some sources we looked at say to pass on the left. This seems less than

practical as a steadfast rule, since it may simply be easier for the group you're passing to step off to the left. The key should be to give notice and not barrel through while anyone is moving aside.

5. **Dogs.** This could be a chapter in itself, but here are some guidelines:

- Dogs should be on 6-foot-long leashes at nearly all locations in this book (note that some locations do not allow dogs).
- Police your dog's poop, particularly if your dog poops in the middle of the trail or just off it.
- Keep your dog to the far side of you when you're passing groups that are coming at you, or step off the trail and let them through. Remember that while you may be a dog person, other hikers you encounter may not be dog people. Read about "redirection"—having your dog sit or heal for treats or praise—when people pass or when you encounter others.
- Next, if your dog is dog-aggressive or people-aggressive, perhaps trails—which are confined avenues of traffic with constant interactions—just aren't comfortable places for your dog, and hiking may not be in the cards for them.

- On the flip side, if you're hiking *without* a dog and you encounter one, never go straight up to it, particularly if you don't know its demeanor. And never trust that the person with the dog has control of it. Sometimes dogs do unpredictable things and owners make mistakes.
- In the end, we are all out to have a good day on the trail; and, for some, our dog companions are very often a part of the experience. So it's just a matter of being courteous and conscientious if the dog is yours, and careful if it's not.

AUTHORS' NOTE

Finally, while the authors provide directions for and descriptions of the following trails—along with other advice and ideas—we stress that hiking is an unpredictable endeavor, as is any outdoor activity. We do not guarantee that following the advice offered in this book—or taking for granted any absence of information—will assure safety or prevent bodily harm of any degree or death. Hike these trails at your own risk, never explore unmarked offshoot trails on cliff edges, know your limits, and be safe.

I.

NORTHWEST

Lakeshore Trail, Apostle Islands National Lakeshore

TOTAL DISTANCE: 3.8 miles

HIKING TIME: About 2.0 hours

DIFFICULTY: 3.0

VERTICAL RISE: Minimal

TRAILHEAD GPS COORDINATES:
46°52'59.44" N, 91°02'50.78" W

Way up in the farthest outstretched reaches of Wisconsin and in the quiet corner of the Bayfield Peninsula is a wonderfully peaceful, ocean-like shoreline. So when you pull into the Meyers Beach parking lot, just off stunningly beautiful Mawikwe Bay, on a sleepy midsummer or fall day, it's hard to imagine that this place gets clogged with more than 15,000 visitors per day in the middle of winter with lines of cars stretching for a couple of miles down Highway 13 like a scene from Woodstock. But it's true: They come by the bushel. Their objects of desire? The crystalline ice caves bejeweling the Lake Superior shoreline. To make matters even more rare and exotic, the mob only appears in years that this awesome lake's surface freezes solid, creating a frozen footpath and treating visitors to a lake-level view of the otherwise elusive shoreline caves.

Indeed, around these parts, it's all about the shoreline. There are 21 islands and 12 miles of Lake Superior shoreline that comprise and are protected under the 70,000-acre umbrella that is the Apostle Islands National Lakeshore—one of four units of the National Park Service in Wisconsin (the three others, also highlighted in this book, include the Ice Age and North Country National Scenic Trails, along with the St. Croix National Scenic Riverway).

But for now, we're talking about a lake. A really big one. In fact, when it comes to surface area, it is the largest freshwater lake in the world. Its maximum depth is 1,333 feet, and it has a long list of ships and their sailors entombed in its depths. The history of the Apostle Islands lakeshore is a striking one, thanks to geological occurrences dating back a billion years to its delivery by ancient rivers of sand, that eventually morphed into the colorful dark

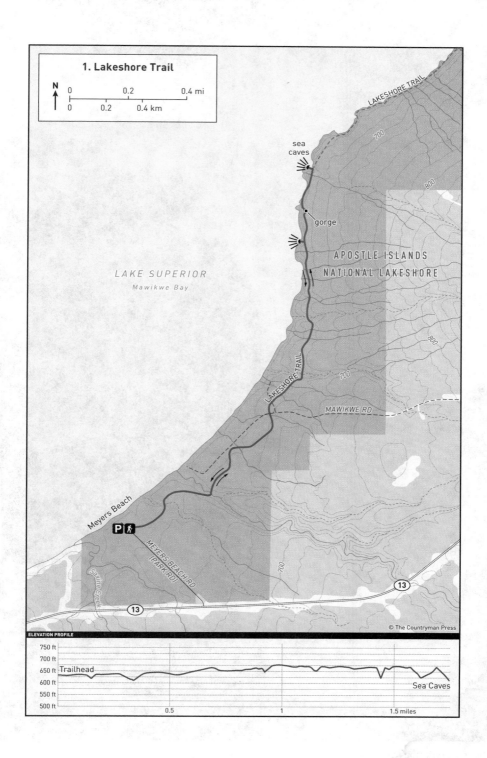

1. Lakeshore Trail

N

| 0 | | 0.2 | | 0.4 mi |
| 0 | 0.2 | | 0.4 km | |

LAKESHORE TRAIL

sea caves

gorge

APOSTLE ISLANDS
NATIONAL LAKESHORE

LAKE SUPERIOR
Mawikwe Bay

LAKESHORE TRAIL

MAWIKWE RD

700

800

800

700

Meyers Beach

P

MEYERS BEACH RD
(PARK RD)

Sailing Creek

13

13

700

© The Countryman Press

ELEVATION PROFILE

750 ft			
700 ft			
650 ft	Trailhead		
600 ft			Sea Caves
550 ft			
500 ft			
	0.5	1	1.5 miles

SEA CAVES ALONG THE EDGE OF THE LAKESHORE TRAIL ON LAKE SUPERIOR

red sandstone we see today—the same sandstone that makes up the sea caves. More recently glaciation bulldozed over that sandstone surface and left streams, rivers, and lots of glacial debris, like more sand and clay, in its wake when it retreated 10,000 years ago. It also left the meltwater that served as the beginnings of these immense Great Lakes.

This hike, along with the Stockton Island hike, takes you up close and personal with the Apostle Islands National Lakeshore. Starting at the Meyers Beach parking lot, the trail follows a 3.8-mile out-and-back trek to the site of one of the main sea cave locations from trailside height, 50 feet above the lapping water below. Much of the hike is along a really impressive wooden boardwalk, built to get you past perpetually wet areas and across the innumerable streams running east to west into the lake. These crossings formerly required fording, and so the boardwalks and bridges have made the hiking both very unique and much friendlier. Overall, in terms of terrain and length, this hike is not overly taxing, although there is a lot of repetitive up-and-down hiking as you cross several ravines, and so the overall elevation gain adds up. Also of note is that the boardwalks will be slippery when wet.

It should also be stressed that this is one of the most dangerous hikes in this book. While much of the hike is in the serene confines of a boggy forest, you will emerge about halfway into the hike on the edge of a sea cave cliff. Children must be monitored and kept very close, and if you can't do that—or they're not fans of being monitored—this hike isn't for them. Much of the cliff edge is cordoned off with timber railings, but much is not, and so it left up to you to stay back from the edge. Due to their hourglass shape you never want to be anywhere near the top edge of a cliff of a sea cave. You could slip and fall, or the cliff edge could give way, because there's often nothing below it offering support. Indeed, the first thing you see when you emerge at the main cave from the trail is a bright orange life preserver hanging next to a warning sign. Overall, it's a great hike and is a must-do if you're seeking to visit the geological highlights of Wisconsin. Just be very careful on this one. (Also, technically, you can bring your dog. Keep in mind that the boardwalks are very narrow and, again, the same issues with the cliff edges apply to dogs. Our vote would be to leave Fido at home for this one and visit Mount Valhalla instead, where there are wide ski trails to enjoy.)

HOW TO GET THERE

From Bayfield, take US 13 west for 17 miles to Meyers Beach Road (look for the sign for Park Service, too). Turn right and head down the road that ends at the parking area. A daily fee is required and is payable at a kiosk as you pull in. The well-marked trailhead is on the east side of the parking lot. From the west, out of Cornucopia on US 13, go 4 miles to Meyers Beach Road and take a left and follow the directions above.

THE TRAIL

The trail begins at the kiosk on the east side of the lot. There's a sign that points to the Sea Cave Overlook. Follow that into the woods and onto the first of many boardwalks. In fact, nearly half of the hike will be on this incredible assembly of massive timber bridges, walkways, and up-and-down steps.

It seems like overkill to some degree to say it, but with spring meltwater, things around here could be very wet. And, even on a fall day, if you look off to the sides you'll see that things are very boggy, particularly deep in the woods where the trail is located. Indeed, while termed the "Lakeshore Trail," most of this hike is in the woods away from the lake as you work your way uphill and curve toward the shoreline.

Eventually, you'll come to a very impressive steel-and-wood bridge that takes you across a stream ravine, formerly one of the slippery and wet crossings. On the other side and up a few steps is a bench looking back on the ravine and bridge. From here you'll turn a bit north and begin to ascend for about a quarter-mile before descending and emerging from the woods briefly as you pass a grassy park road opening. Back into the woods, and you'll see a sign for the overlook on a now-narrower boardwalk and then onto a dirt trail and uphill.

You will cross several small streams via footbridges before the trail buttonhooks steeply downhill on riser steps to the northwest. Things can get slick here, and a pile of timbers suggests that park officials are at work on replacing this with new boardwalk. Again, though, these wooden boardwalks will all be slippery when they're wet. You'll descend to a streambed and head steeply uphill via risers before the trail turns north and becomes much sandier. From here, there will be several downs and ups before you cross several streams via bridges and one gorge that is fairly deep. Eventually, you'll start turning northeast, and you'll notice more light filtering through the trees ahead. There will be one more gorge crossing and a steep uphill before you arrive at the shoreline high atop the lake at about 1.5 miles into the hike. There is a volunteer offshoot trail that will take you quickly to the cliff edge and doesn't seem to be an official overlook. Be very careful here and on or near the other small offshoot trails as you continue.

Continue on northeast and you will soon hike into a pine grove. You will come to a warning sign saying that the cliffs are 100 yards ahead, and beyond that you'll soon see the bright orange life preserver ring hanging on the kiosk. This deep crevasse extends nearly 100 yards inland from the shore in a 50-foot-deep V. Don't go anywhere near the edge; any land bridges that look like they cross to the other side are not meant for people to cross. Hike to the right, to the east, following the timber railings to a bridge that takes you over the tip of the V. Looking back out to the lake, the view here is spectacular as you get a sense of the force of water, listening to the gurgling and grumbling below. Follow this path to the other side of the gorge, where you'll find yourself on a small cliff-top peninsula with views, both of the gorge you just crossed and the next cliff to the north.

Note: Sea kayakers often visit these caves from below, so never throw rocks or anything into the water from up here.

This area is perfect for a rest and to take in the sights before heading back. It's a great snack or lunch spot. From here, the trail continues northeast to the campsite another 2 miles away, but the trail gets much less defined and thus even more dangerous on the cliff edges, so we used this area as our turnaround point. After a rest, head back around the gorge via the bridge, past the life preserver, and start the backtrack to the trailhead.

BOARDWALKS AND FOOTBRIDGES ESCORT HIKERS OVER SEVERAL CREEKS AND BOGS

Lost Creek Falls Trail, Bayfield County Forest

TOTAL DISTANCE: 3.0 miles

HIKING TIME: 1.5 hours

DIFFICULTY: 2.5

VERTICAL RISE: 200 feet

TRAILHEAD GPS COORDINATES:
46°49'57.81" N, 91°06'12.55" W

There are great hiking trails, and there are also scenic waterfalls, yet they aren't always in the same place. But they coexist wonderfully at Lost Creek Falls just south of Cornucopia on County Road (CTH) C. After hearing about this hike from some fellow hikers while hiking the Lakeshore Trail one blazingly gorgeous fall morning, we made a mental note to visit it some other time we were up this way. We finished our hike and headed down to Ehlers General Store in Corny for some lunch. While checking out, we got to talking hiking with the clerk at the register, who said we should definitely hike the Lost Creek Falls Trail while we were in the area. At this point, it became hard to ignore. And thank goodness for that. It's a wonderful trail and a great little falls.

Everything on the Bayfield Peninsula is about water. You're surrounded by it on the west, north, and east, and any stream, creek, or river is running from points as high as nearly 1,400 feet at places like Mount Valhalla (see Chapter 4), to places such as where the Lost Creeks (there are three of them) collectively empty into Lake Superior at 600 feet. And any time water is running downhill, particularly on a peninsula made of ancient rock, there's going to be waterfalls; and in this neck of the woods, there's lots of them.

This trail offers a 3-mile out-and-back through a quiet forest with a visit to the falls at the midpoint. Not an overly strenuous hike, it's still a 200-foot descent to the falls over those 1.5 miles, which means climbing gradually back up on the return trip. The trail tread itself is impressively well built and, like the Lakeshore Trail, it has a well-designed system of small bridges and boardwalks. There are lots of waterfalls in this area, but not necessarily lots of trails of this length that take you well

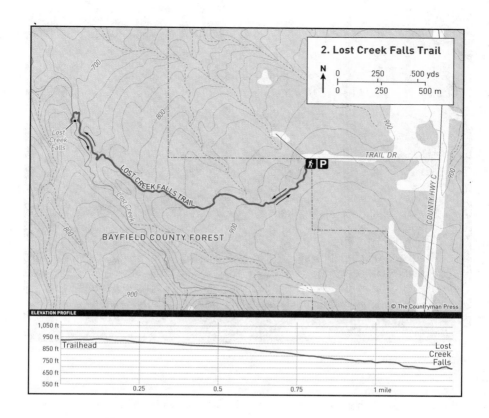

2. Lost Creek Falls Trail

N

| 0 | 250 | 500 yds |
| 0 | 250 | 500 m |

ELEVATION PROFILE

1,050 ft				
950 ft				
850 ft	Trailhead			Lost
750 ft				Creek
650 ft				Falls
550 ft				
	0.25	0.5	0.75	1 mile

into the quiet wilderness of the Bayfield Peninsula to see them. Kudos to Bayfield County for this trail; it's a must-visit.

HOW TO GET THERE

From the southwest, take WI 13 into Cornucopia and turn right onto CTH C, which will leave town to the south. Go about 1 mile to Trail Drive (there's actually a roadside sign for Lost Creek Trail) and turn right, west, and take it to the parking area on the left, about a half-mile down Trail Drive. From the southeast, take WI 13 north from Ashland to Washburn. Take a left, west, on CTH C and take it about 19 miles to a left, west, on Trail Drive and follow the directions above. From Bayfield, take WI 13 to Cornucopia and follow the directions above.

THE TRAIL

The trail begins next to a great little kiosk on the west side of the parking area next to the "Falls Hiking Trail" sign. You'll start off on crushed gravel and pass a sign for "Lost Creek Falls, 1½ Miles." The trail winds its way through the woods and almost immediately begins a very slight decline. You'll pass over the first of many small boardwalks, coming off those onto a packed dirt trail along a small ridge. The forest is mostly newer here but still very densely wooded, with a mix of maples and pines, some of which are towering old-timers.

Trailside ferns escort you along, and you occasionally have to hopscotch between a few rocks and roots. Soon a long boardwalk takes you south and

SERENE AND SECLUDED LOST CREEK FALLS

swings southwest on a swooping curve. Eventually, at about the 0.5-mile mark, you will pass a logging road that's probably a snowmobile trail in the winter, then you cross another boardwalk as it bends from the northwest to west. The trail will widen a bit as you head downhill on the edge of a valley. You'll cross the first of a few small bridges and begin a long, steady decline before things level out and you take a 90-degree turn to the left, southwest, for a few paces before heading uphill and button-hooking to the right, northwest.

Up on the top of the spine of a long ridge, you'll now find yourself meandering along the Lost Creek below and able to hear it babbling its way toward the falls. After about 0.25 mile the trail will take a sharp turn to the left and switchback quickly down toward the creek. You will come to a sign pointing to Lost Creek

Falls to the left (with the snowmobile trail and picnic area to the right). Hike down the trail to the edge of the creek, where you will see and hear the falls to the south. If the water isn't high, there are several areas from which you can access the falls (just be careful on slick rocks) and take photos, or take a break and just enjoy the solitude. The falls themselves are about 15 feet tall, but they are very picturesque. And because they drape over the rock ledge and there's open room behind them, they seem to carry a bigger presence in the little creek valley as their water splashes its way to Lake Superior.

After time at the falls, head back onto the trail from the east creek bank and hike back to the split in the trail with the picnic area. Stay right and head back to the southeast and the trailhead, 1.5 miles away.

3

Stockton Island, Apostle Islands National Lakeshore

TOTAL DISTANCE: 4.2 miles

HIKING TIME: 2 hours (see notes about time constraints)

DIFFICULTY: 3.0

VERTICAL RISE: Minimal

TRAILHEAD GPS COORDINATES:
46°54'46.65" N, 90°32'58.41" W

Lake Superior is perhaps Wisconsin's most visible remnant of the most recent Ice Age. The largest freshwater lake in the world—with an average depth of 500 feet and plunging to 1,300 feet at its deepest—it is what's left over when a mile-thick and hundreds-of-miles-wide block of ice melts.

Should you decide to venture out away from a protected bay for some swimming, you'll find yourself in waters that never get above 40 degrees Fahrenheit—cold enough to cause hypothermia within minutes and death in half an hour. Average summer weather around the islands is cool, with lows in the upper 40s and highs seldom in the 80s—and temperatures below freezing in the summer are not unheard of.

Gichigami—as Lake Superior is referred to by the Ojibwe—is teeming with shipwrecks that are entombed inside this icy coffin. In fact, as you stride along the exceptionally beautiful and tranquil beach at Julian Bay, you'd never guess that the wreck resulting from the fiery demise in 1904 of the *Noquebay* schooner is lying just offshore in 10 feet of water.

No longer crowded with schooners, the waters around the Apostle Islands are dotted with sailboats and ferries now. Stockton Island, the largest island included in the national lakeshore, contains more than 10,000 acres of wilderness. There are no cars, roads, phones, restaurants, or lighted sidewalks here. This is wilderness.

So it's here that you'll find a rich diversity of hundreds of species of plants and animals ranging from trailside flowers to towering hemlocks, and from tiny toads to black bears. In fact, Stockton holds the distinction of having

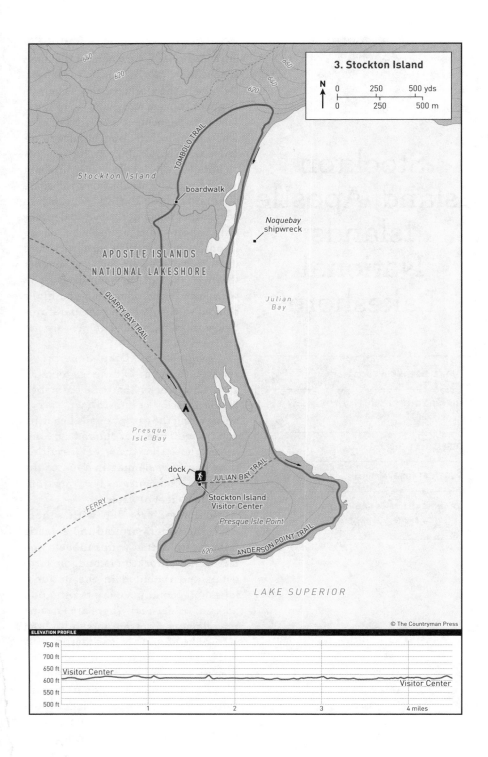

3. Stockton Island

N

| 0 | 250 | 500 yds |
| 0 | 250 | 500 m |

TOMBOLO TRAIL

Stockton Island

boardwalk

Noquebay shipwreck

APOSTLE ISLANDS
NATIONAL LAKESHORE

QUARRY BAY TRAIL

Julian Bay

Presque Isle Bay

dock

JULIAN BAY TRAIL

Stockton Island
Visitor Center

Presque Isle Point

620

ANDERSON POINT TRAIL

LAKE SUPERIOR

© The Countryman Press

ELEVATION PROFILE

| 750 ft |
| 700 ft |
| 650 ft | Visitor Center |
| 600 ft |
| 550 ft |
| 500 ft |
| | 1 | 2 | 3 | 4 miles |

Visitor Center

BOARDWALKS ALONG THE TOMBOLO TRAIL ON STOCKTON ISLAND

one of the densest concentrations of black bears in North America, so know your bear interaction etiquette before heading to Stockton and check in with the ranger about any problematic bears being monitored. Indeed, on our last trip to Stockton, a short visit with the ranger was mandatory after disembarking the ferry. Be sure to mention that you are there to hike the Tombolo Trail during the layover.

HOW TO GET THERE

As of 2016, the National Park Service concessioner for shuttling people to the islands in the Apostle Islands National Lakeshore is Apostle Islands Cruises. Called *The Stockton Island Dayhiker*, the layover is 2 hours (this differs from the 2.5 hours in this book's first edition).

Also, a great place for information regarding visiting any of the islands is the Apostle Islands National Lakeshore headquarters in Bayfield.

THE TRAIL

This clockwise loop is a combination of the Tombolo and Anderson Point trails that complete a loop past Julian Bay on the southeast corner of the island. Head up the boardwalk off the dock and up to the map kiosk outside the visitor center and restrooms. A boardwalk heading northeast out of this kiosk area will take you up to the trailhead.

Turn left and head northwest along the Quarry Bay/Tombolo Trail toward the campground on the shore of Presque Isle Bay. You will travel behind these campsites, among tall pine trees and on a soft pine-needle bed, for about 0.5 mile before coming to the turnoff for the Tombolo Trail. Take this to the right (north) and head deeper into the woods of the island. The trail is narrow, but the footing is pretty good. You will even pass over a few boardwalks.

Eventually, you will emerge from the woods and approach a long boardwalk taking you across a wetland that is just west of Julian Bay. In fact, from the boardwalk you can see the beach and the bay to your right.

Head back into the woods and follow the path through a pretty boggy, now-wooded area. There is also a boardwalk through a sometimes-wet section back here, and the footing stays quite good. Eventually, you will turn to the right (south) and head up toward a small dune, a path that will take you over to the beach. The trail is the beach itself, in fact. Looking all the way to the end of the beach shows you where you're headed, where the sand meets the woods about 1 mile to the south.

Soon after starting along the beach, you'll be in the exact place where the *Noquebay* perished and its crew came ashore. You may need to make a short water crossing. When we visited, a small inlet forced us to cross about 10 feet of knee-deep water, and the ranger mentioned that until recently it had been passable without wading. Keep in mind, this is an ever-changing island environment, and you will want to confirm things like the overall passability of this trail before heading off to hike it.

Eventually, you will find yourself back at the woods, where you will begin a very different hike. As you duck into the woods, you will pass the Julian Bay Trail to the right (west). Take this if you think you're running out of time (be sure to bring a watch!). The Anderson Point Trail will head left (southeast); if there's time, take this along the shore. It is a remarkable setting as you hike amid towering old-growth hemlock and amble over huge sheets of the brownish-red sandstone, called brownstone. Eventually, this quiet, wooded path will take you back to the Julian Bay Trail. Take it left (west) a few steps back to the visitor center and down toward the dock.

Hiking at an above-average pace—but certainly nowhere near jogging and not making too many stops—we finished the hike in 1.75 hours, leaving very little time before the ferry departed (obviously, this would have been quicker if we had taken the Julian Bay Trail shortcut). It all depends on your willingness to roll the dice with regard to the timing and schedule and the fact that unpredictable things can happen. Regardless, this remote hike in one of the most pristine and protected wilderness areas of the state is well worth a visit. Just don't forget to call ahead.

Mount Valhalla, Chequamegon-Nicolet National Forest

TOTAL DISTANCE: 2.25 miles

HIKING TIME: 1 hour, 15 minutes

DIFFICULTY: 3.0

VERTICAL RISE: 250 feet

TRAILHEAD GPS COORDINATES:
46°43'18.08'' N, 91°02'40.67'' W

The trails at Mount Valhalla were designed for Nordic skiing and are so attractive that they were once used as a training ground for the United States Olympic Nordic Ski Team. And as you meander along this wide trail and roll up and down the side of Mount Valhalla, you'll understand quickly why an Olympic team would value the terrain. The trails are great for hiking, too, and the trail highlighted here is actually one of several in the Mount Valhalla system, which includes the Teuton and Valkyrie trails.

The area is one of many trail systems in the immense Chequamegon-Nicolet National Forest, which includes more than 1.5 million acres and stretches all the way from Bayfield County in the west to Florence County in the east, including parts of 11 total counties along the way. Included in this natural masterpiece are tens of thousands of nonmotorized and wilderness-designated areas and thousands of miles of trails.

And thanks to the large expanse of forest, these are long, uninterrupted trails that take hikers, mountain bikers, skiers, horseback riders, snowmobilers, and ATV riders deep into the woods. In a farsighted move, the planners of this exceptional recreational area thought to give each group not only their own trails, but also often their own areas. So in the winter, this also means untold miles of Nordic ski trails separated from the equally impressive snowmobile trails.

The trailhead highlighted here is a base for mountain bikers, trail runners, and hikers during the warmer months and is a destination for Nordic skiers in the winter. This hike follows Loop B of the Teuton Trail System and is a 2.25-mile, 250-foot climb up the wooded west

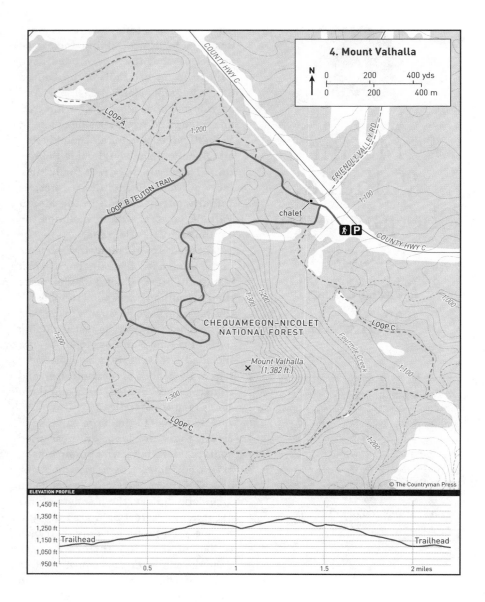

4. Mount Valhalla

N

| 0 | 200 | 400 yds |
| 0 | 200 | 400 m |

ELEVATION PROFILE

1,450 ft				
1,350 ft				
1,250 ft				
1,150 ft	Trailhead			Trailhead
1,050 ft				
950 ft				
	0.5	1	1.5	2 miles

side of Mount Valhalla to the top of the old downhill ski hill.

Note: The Valkyrie Trail system is on the other side of CTH C.

HOW TO GET THERE

From the southeast and east, take CTH C west out of Washburn and travel about 8.5 miles to the trailhead, which is marked with a large national forest sign for the Teuton and Valkyrie trail system, on the left. Formerly there were two parking lots and two entrances, now there is just one and it comes up quickly on the left as you round the bend on CTH C (you'll see a road sign marking a hiker crossing).

From the north, take CTH C south, east out of Cornucopia about 11.5 miles to the trailhead on the right. Again, it comes up fast and the former parking lot is tricky because it comes up first but doesn't actually offer parking and is now an ATV crossing. Take the second entrance down the hill a few hundred feet.

From the southwest, take US 2 to the junction with WI 13 outside of Ashland. Turn left (north) on WI 13 and take it 6.7 miles to CTH C in Washburn. From there, follow the directions from the southeast/east above.

Note: All the parking areas in the Chequamegon-Nicolet require either a day or seasonal parking pass. For more information, contact the Chequamegon-Nicolet National Forest, Washburn Ranger District. Many trailheads have self-registration stations, too.

THE TRAIL

Loop B of the Teuton Ski Trail is a counterclockwise trail that leaves the trailhead parking area's northwest corner—you'll see a small chalet up there, which is the trailhead. In tune with Nordic skiing, the trail is measured in kilometers at 3.6 km, which is approximately 2.25-miles and it meanders uphill along the backside of Mount Valhalla.

Perfect for skiing, this wide trail begins by taking you into the young maple and birch forest, alive in the summer with bright green leaves and pale bark emerging from a fern-covered forest floor. In the fall, you'll enjoy a forest ablaze with oranges and yellows. Soon after starting, you will come to an intersection with another trail, Loop A—but you will follow the trail to the left, which is marked with a sign for the Benchmark and is Loop B.

From here, you will curve to the southwest, and the trail will head up a steep slope as you charge up some of those 250 feet of elevation. Again, you will converge with the return intersection of Loop A, but head straight and continue slightly uphill along Loop B. Eventually, the trail will turn southward as you begin to descend just slightly. The trail gets a bit grassier here, but there is usually a good path running through the middle of the grass.

Again, you will pass a trail intersection, this time with Loop C heading off to the right. Stay straight and begin the more prominent downhill section. The trail, obviously a ski trail, will begin to zigzag its way downhill, now among some larger trees. This is a perfect place to round a bend and come upon a deer munching on grass in the open. The edge habitat is also great for wildflowers and spotting birds.

The trail will make its final turn eastward and down a steep decline through a stand of red pines. You will meet back up with Loop C before heading left (north) back to the trailhead and then south back to the main parking area where you started.

This great little hike along a great ski trail system is perfect for scouting out your winter Nordic skiing or stretching your legs while visiting the Chequamegon Bay area. And, if you or someone you're with is a fat tire fanatic, these trails are also home to some of the best mountain biking in the area.

5

Manitou Falls, Pattison State Park

TOTAL DISTANCE: 4.9 miles

HIKING TIME: 3.0 to 3.5 hours

DIFFICULTY: 4.5

VERTICAL RISE: 365 feet

TRAILHEAD GPS COORDINATES:
46°31'19.00'' N, 92°7'38.64'' W

There are good hiking trails and there are great ones. This is a great one. It's an out-and-back hike in Pattison State Park to two of Wisconsin's greatest waterfalls, making it one of the state's best waterfall hikes. The trail starts at Little Manitou Falls (the 35-foot-tall gushing little sibling) and then meanders along the bank of the Black River, past Interfalls Lake, over a catwalk where the river leaves the lake, and to both the top of Big Manitou Falls—a towering 165-foot-tall bruiser and the fourth-highest falls east of the Rockies—and finally down a plummeting descent below the falls to the river's exit out of the park. All told, the hike includes a 365-foot descent before turning back and hiking back along a river and a hike that often actually feels more like a setting in the Rockies than from the Dairy State.

According to the park literature, the reason for the unique landscape here is thanks to the area's geological history and the combination of forces that make this place what it is today. First, while it may be hard to picture, the area was covered in lava nearly a billion years ago, the aftermath of which is the rugged dark brown igneous basalt rock you see today. Then there is the Lake Superior Sandstone—a trademark building material used around the region—which was left over from the sand and silt of great ancient oceans that once covered the region. Next, there is actually a fault—the Douglas Fault—that thrust itself upwards at a 50-degree angle and left behind breccia, an angular quartzite rock. Finally, nearly seconds ago, geologically speaking, were the glaciers—the most recent one receding just 10,000 years ago and leaving behind its own sedimentary deposits. In the end, the rugged, rocky landscape is wonderfully unique and

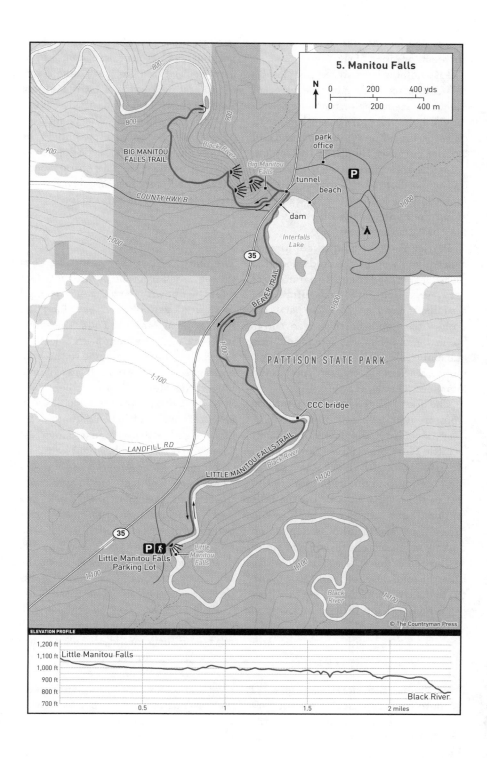

5. Manitou Falls

N

| 0 | 200 | 400 yds |
| 0 | 200 | 400 m |

BIG MANITOU FALLS TRAIL

Black River

Big Manitou Falls

park office

P

COUNTY HWY B

tunnel

beach

dam

Interfalls Lake

35

BEAVER TRAIL

PATTISON STATE PARK

1,000

1,100

CCC bridge

LANDFILL RD

LITTLE MANITOU FALLS TRAIL

Black River

1,100

35

P

Little Manitou Falls Parking Lot

Little Manitou Falls

1,100

Black River

© The Countryman Press

ELEVATION PROFILE

1,200 ft				
1,100 ft	Little Manitou Falls			
1,000 ft				
900 ft				
800 ft			Black River	
700 ft				
	0.5	1	1.5	2 miles

leaves you feeling like you're walking out west for much of the hike.

Also notable here are the people who called the place home. After the retreat of the most recent glacier, nomadic people moved here. Several Native American cultures, including the Archaic and Old Copper cultures, inhabited the region. Later, the area supported a trading post and was a hotbed for copper mining. Eventually, a logging camp was built along the banks of the Black River by Martin Pattison (1841–1918).

Pattison's wealth allowed him to stealthily buy up all the land needed to thwart a proposed complete damming of the river, which would have eliminated the falls. Today this 1,400-acre park, way up in Wisconsin's northwest corner, is home to more than 200 species of birds and mammals, including timber wolves, moose, black bears, eagles, ospreys, and lots more. Thanks Marty!

The hike outlined here is a new route from previous editions of the book. A 4.9-mile-long out-and-back hike, it starts at Little Manitou, rambles downstream along the bank of the Black River, passes Big Manitou, and finally plummets 200 feet to the river's bank below the falls (optional but worth it). It's a big hike and can take at least three hours, depending on how much picture taking and sightseeing you're doing. If you do the whole hike, the total descent, from Little Manitou to the river bank below Big Manitou, is 365 feet, with lots of ups and downs on the way there.

HOW TO GET THERE

From the north or northwest, take WI 35 south from Superior; the main park entrance is about 12 miles outside the city. Skip the main entrance and head to the south parking lot about a mile later.

Look for the sign for Little Manitou Falls parking lot and the park road on the left (southeast). From the south, take WI 35 to the first park road for Little Manitou Falls on the right, as described above.

Note: You will need a Wisconsin state park sticker or day permit to park in the Little Manitou Falls lot. If you don't have one, stop at the main park entrance and park office before heading down to the Little Manitou Falls parking lot.

THE TRAIL

The hike starts at the trailhead across the park road from the parking lot. Just a few feet down the trail you're treated to the first overlook of dozens along this hike, at Little Manitou Falls. The scene in the autumn is aflame with color and offers a wonderful welcome to the hike and a great vantage point from which to view Little Manitou Falls, which itself is a great display of hydrogeology in action. There's a little bench that's actually perfectly situated for a goodbye rest when you return in a few hours.

Moving along, there's actually a second overlook just a little way down the trail that is easy to miss. You'll then begin descending to the river's edge before turning north. A smaller falls and rapids located at this corner ushers you downstream. The trail rambles along the river, crossing small footbridges across little creeks that empty into the river. Thickly forested, the trail is lined with cedars, maples, pines, and oaks, which offer good shade in the summer and are alive with color in the fall.

The trail will come to a bend in the river and turn east, offering an incredible view upstream back up toward Little Manitou. There is a bench and overlook, too. Then you head uphill before turning away from the river a bit and eventually

LITTLE MANITOU FALLS ON A COLORFUL FALL AFTERNOON

returning to the river bank and arriving at a footbridge across the river. Stay on the south side of the river and follow the sign to Big Manitou Falls, which is 1 mile away.

Not too far upstream from here, you can get another great look at the bridge. You'll then ascend a bit along the edge of a large hill to the left, as the trail snakes between the base of the hill and the riverbank. The trail will head down to the river's edge again, coming to a 90-degree turn left to the west away from the river, across a small wooden bridge, and then heading uphill by way of some big riser steps. You'll then turn north again and descend back toward the river, where you'll come to a bench and another overlook pointed back upstream.

Eventually, you'll emerge at Interfalls Lake as you skirt along the western shoreline. The view across the lake back to the south is a great one, and it's the place where you might see an eagle or osprey. You'll undoubtedly hear the road traffic on the highway. And you'll need to cross to get to Big Manitou, but luckily there's an ingenious way to get there by going under the road. But first, once you come out of the woods on the shore of the lake, head straight for the small dam. Hard to see at first, the metal catwalk does take you across the dam. Then continue to the underpass tunnel (watch for slippery areas that get wet in the tunnel) and emerge on the other side.

There's a footbridge to the left, which is where you'll be going, but you can head to the two overlooks on the north side of the falls by heading straight and up the paved path. There will be two overlooks over here. (A trail continues after the second one, but doesn't lead anywhere.)

Double back to the wooden footbridge and cross to the other side of the falls. Head up to County Road B where there will be a sign for the picnic area and south overlooks. Hike along the road's gravel shoulder for just about 30 yards and duck back off the road. Follow the paved path past the rustic toilet (that looks like a chalet) and down to the first overlook. You'll immediately note that this side of the falls is much more scenic. And if you think this view is good, wait until you get to the second overlook. It's even better and it also happens to be where the cover photo for this edition of *50 Hikes in Wisconsin* was taken.

At this point, you're headed downhill. The trail crosses a bridge and then descends quickly toward the river's edge, 200 feet below the falls. After winding its way down, the trail will give way to some wooden stairs that emerge at water level. A trail will take you to the bank. The view is worth the trip, because it's yet another taste of the diversity of the place. The steep sandy and rock valley walls here are very unique to this area of the state. There are places to take a break here or have a snack break and enjoy the serene Black River before turning back up.

To head back, you'll turn around and retrace your steps, back up to the top of Big Manitou, through the tunnel, over the dam catwalk, past Interfalls Lake, and upstream back to Little Manitou. What's fun about this out-and-back, too, is that the view back upstream is so different from the view on the way out, really offering a great second look at this incredible park. Finally, you'll arrive at Little Manitou and that bench that's been waiting for your return, for a last contemplative rest after a wonderful waterfall hike.

Doughboys Trail, Copper Falls State Park

TOTAL DISTANCE: 2.5 miles

HIKING TIME: 1 hour, 30 minutes

DIFFICULTY: 3.5

VERTICAL RISE: 160 feet

TRAILHEAD GPS COORDINATES:
46°22'18.54'' N, 90°38'34.38'' W

While the most notable part of Wisconsin's geological past may be the most recent glacier, the state's geology had actually been affected earlier by another unstoppable force: the flow and deposition of miles-thick layers of lava. Due to this diverse history, there are now places where leftover lava rests next to sandstone, shale, clay, and granite that was deposited later. Quite conveniently, many of the geological changes that have occurred in Wisconsin, from eons ago to the present day, are etched in history at Copper Falls State Park.

Here, at the junction of the Bad River and the Tyler Fork of the Bad River, great displays of geological past and present collide with tremendous force. Standing atop a wooden overlook, it's possible to feel the thunder of the water as it cascades over the red-and-black lava rock of the falls before passing through conglomerate, sandstone, clay, and shale. This rocky, exposed river valley—bordered by rushing water and an amazing mix of towering maple, hemlock, and birch—is almost unreal in its beauty.

Almost as amazing as the area's geology is the state park located here. While it may have originally been tempting to run a road right up to the falls, this is a hiking park. The trails are incredibly well maintained and meticulously groomed. For the majority of this hike along the Doughboys Trail you are actually on either a stone path or a wooden plank walkway. The rest of the trail is smooth gravel or packed dirt.

The park itself is immaculately maintained, and thanks to the stone buildings and paths and massive beams used for overlook railings, the place

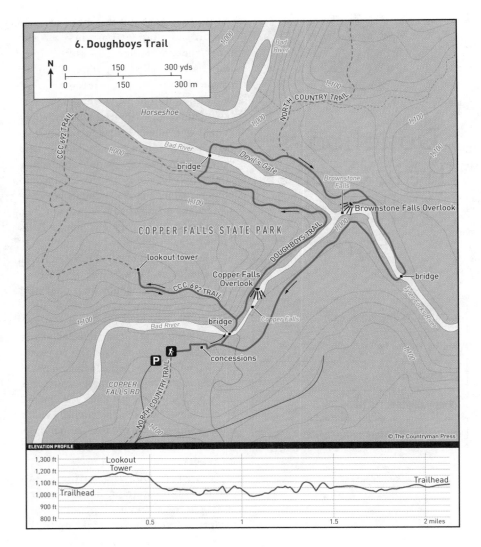

6. Doughboys Trail

N

| 0 | 150 | 300 yds |
| 0 | 150 | 300 m |

Horseshoe

Bad River

bridge

Devil's Gate

NORTH COUNTRY TRAIL

Bad River

Brownstone Falls

Brownstone Falls Overlook

CCC 692 TRAIL

COPPER FALLS STATE PARK

DOUGHBOYS TRAIL

lookout tower

Copper Falls Overlook

CCC 692 TRAIL

bridge

Tyler Forks River

Bad River

bridge

Copper Falls

concessions

P

COPPER FALLS RD

NORTH COUNTRY TRAIL

© The Countryman Press

ELEVATION PROFILE

| | Lookout Tower | | | | Trailhead |

1,300 ft / 1,200 ft / 1,100 ft / 1,000 ft Trailhead / 900 ft / 800 ft — 0.5 — 1 — 1.5 — 2 miles

resembles a national park. But don't let this utopia of a park and trail fool you. While relatively short in length, this trail makes up for it in vertical rise and fall. The valley of the Bad River is much more than a hundred feet deep, and this trail—through a series of steps, risers, and hills—takes you up and down the valley more than once. The stone steps aren't like the steps in your house, either. Like Morse code, they are an awkward combination of long and short, deep and

shallow. And, on a wet day, the rock gets pretty slick.

But the hike is a beautiful one. On a sunny day, the shimmering water, the crashing falls, and the trees overhead are breathtaking. And on top of the stunning river valley is a panoramic view of much of Ashland and Iron counties and Lake Superior's Chequamegon Bay—compliments of the treetop lookout tower, 227 steps up and high above the trail.

ENJOYING THE SUNSET OVER CHEQUAMEGON BAY ATOP THE COPPER FALLS LOOKOUT TOWER

HOW TO GET THERE

From the south, take Main Street east out of Mellen to WI 169. Turn right (north) on WI 169 and take it for 1.6 miles just past Loon Lake. Turn left at the park entrance and continue past the park office to the north parking lot and picnic area near the falls.

From the north, take WI 13 south from Ashland for about 23 miles to WI 169. From there, turn north on WI 169 and follow the directions above.

From the east, take WI 77 west from Upson for about 11.5 miles to WI 169. Go north on WI 169 and follow the directions above.

THE TRAIL

After parking, head past the concessions area to the trailhead. To do a clockwise hike, take the Doughboys Trail left (north) over the river via the impressive timber-beam bridge across the picturesque Bad River. Once across, steps will take you up to the base of the lookout tower offshoot trail. The trail will climb steeply and wind westward along the side of the hill as it approaches the tower. And, as with any tower, you'll have several more steps before the top. It's a phenomenal view from up there, and in the fall there is a sea of brilliant color below if you time your visit

COPPER FALLS FROM THE DOUGHBOYS TRAIL

right. From here, double back down to the main trail and turn left toward the Copper Falls overlook. This marks a great spot for a break before moving on. There are several scenic stopping points and benches along the trail, offering good rest stops and picture-taking opportunities.

Continuing on, the trail will make a sharp turn west just opposite Brownstone Falls. Then, soon after, a long series of steep steps will take you down to the bridge next to Devil's Gate. Head across the bridge and up the other side along another series of steep stone steps. Awaiting you soon after is both a bench and a boardwalk that heads out to an overlook just down from Brownstone Falls.

Note: If you're lucky enough to have nabbed the only backpacking site in the park, you'll head to the north, off the main trail here.

Staying along the main trail, you will turn southwest and amble along the river and back toward the parking area, parallel to the disabled-access trail. There are also several areas here for resting and taking pictures. Eventually, the trail will head down some stone steps across from Copper Falls, and you will emerge at the trailhead behind the concessions area.

7

Rock Lake Trail, Chequamegon-Nicolet National Forest

TOTAL DISTANCE: 4.0 miles	
HIKING TIME: 1 hour, 30 minutes	
DIFFICULTY: 2.5	
VERTICAL RISE: Minimal	
TRAILHEAD GPS COORDINATES: 46°11′54.22″ N, 91°8′6.10″ W	

Each winter, thousands of skiers from around the world flock to take part in a famous ski race, the American Birkebeiner. While the race began its tradition here in 1973, it dates back nearly 800 years to Norway and the heroic efforts of a group of skiers who smuggled an infant prince to safety. These skiers were known as Birkebeiners due to the birch-bark leggings they wore. The rescue of the prince—who later became King Hakon Hakonsson IV—forever altered the course of European history.

This piece of distant Norwegian history has also altered the history of Wisconsin, with thousands of skiers, from novice to world-class, descending on this very quiet corner of the state each winter to commemorate the efforts of the Birkebeiners. While they are no longer charged with the need to save a boy's life, they are often called upon to save their own! This grueling, 51-km race, which takes hours to complete, pushes the human body to its limits as the trail winds its way up and down hills from Cable to Hayward.

Resembling a plate of spaghetti, the Hayward-Cable region is strewn with trails. In the summer and fall, these trails are very popular with both mountain bikers and hikers.

The Rock Lake Trail system is located in the Chequamegon-Nicolet National Forest and offers miles of skiing, hiking, and mountain bike trails—meandering over glacial hills, down shallow valleys, and around pothole lakes. This hike takes you along one of these loops and around one of those lakes: Rock Lake.

HOW TO GET THERE

From the west or south, take CTH M out of Cable approximately 7.5 miles to the

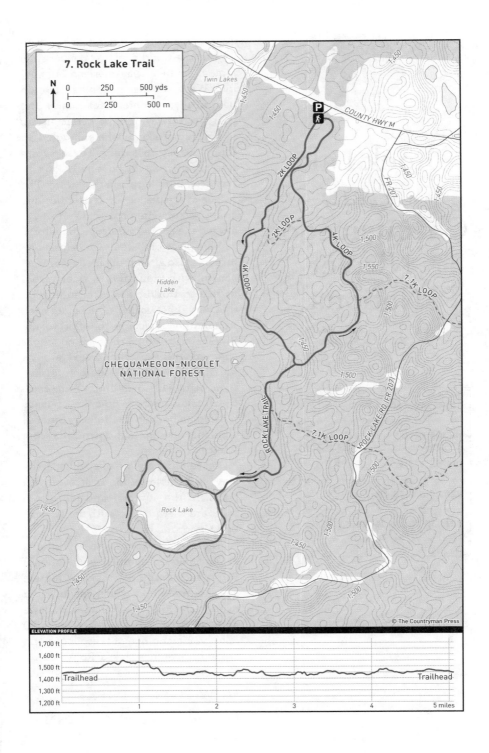

7. Rock Lake Trail

N

| 0 | 250 | 500 yds |
| 0 | 250 | 500 m |

Twin Lakes

1,450

1,450

COUNTY HWY M

P

FR 207

1,450

1,450

2K LOOP

2K LOOP

4K LOOP

1,500

1,550

7.1K LOOP

4K LOOP

1,500

Hidden
Lake

1,450

CHEQUAMEGON–NICOLET
NATIONAL FOREST

1,500

ROCK LAKE TRAIL

7.1K LOOP

ROCK LAKE RD (FR 207)

1,450

Rock Lake

1,500

1,450

1,450

1,450

1,500

© The Countryman Press

ELEVATION PROFILE

| 1,700 ft |
| 1,600 ft |
| 1,500 ft |
| 1,400 ft | Trailhead | | | | Trailhead |
| 1,300 ft |
| 1,200 ft |
| | 1 | 2 | 3 | 4 | 5 miles |

MEANDERING AMONGST THE PINES AT ROCK LAKE

trailhead on the right, marked with a large sign.

From the north, take US 2 west out of Ashland about 6 miles to US 63 south. Turn left (south) on US 63 and follow it almost 20 miles to Cable. In Cable, turn left (east) on CTH M and follow the directions above.

From the east, take CTH M west out of Clam Lake and go approximately 12 miles to the trailhead parking lot on the left.

For more information, contact the Chequamegon-Nicolet National Forest, Glidden office.

THE TRAIL

The trail begins just behind the kiosk at the northeast corner of the lot. Take it, following the 4 km loop next to the road before turning south. You will actually cross the return route of the 4 km loop while doing a sort of figure eight; so stay to the right or pretty much straight.

Soon after passing the first trail crossing, you will also pass an access road. Be aware that this area of the trail gets a bit jumbled with all the trails that crisscross here. There are several Cable Area Mountain Bike Association (CAMBA) trails, too. But all the trails are well marked, and if you follow the hiking trail signs, you should have no problem.

Just after passing the access road, you will come to a turnoff for another trail. Follow the arrow and sign for the Rock Lake Trail to the left and continue on a steep uphill climb. At the top, the 4 km loop will turn left and head back to the lot, while the Rock Lake Trail will head right. Go right and past another access road. Soon you will come to the 7.1 km loop turnoff to the left; ignore it and stay on the Rock Lake Trail, heading down into a valley before turning west toward the lake. This is a very scenic area, and the trees transition to less hardwood and more old-growth pines towering overhead.

Soon you will come to the lake itself. Turn left at the lake loop trail, to go clockwise around the lake (although you can go either way). Hiking amongst towering pines, you will pass a small opening and fire ring before turning more westward. At the southwest corner of the lake, you will pass the turnoff for the 11.5 km and 16 km ski trails to the left. Stay next to the lake and follow the Rock Lake Trail. You will pass some more towering pines as you climb a bit, enjoying a great view of the lake, before descending to a boggy area and a short boardwalk on the western side of the lake.

As you head along the northern edge of the lake, the trail is bordered by the lake on the right and a deep valley to the left. From here, hike up to the lake loop turnoff and head left (northeast). You will actually be doubling back, as you retrace about 0.5 mile of the trail. You will pass those huge white and red pines again, as well as the 7.1 km turnoff. At the 4 km turnoff, turn right and head northeast. Awaiting you will be the steepest and longest uphill stretch of the hike. Eventually, you'll level off and meet up with the 7.1 km loop before beginning a steady downhill and a sharp turn to the left. You will meet up with the 2 km Trail and pass a CAMBA mountain bike trail and an access road. Just stay straight on the hiking/skiing trail, and you will end up back at the lot.

8

Straight Lake, Ice Age Trail

TOTAL DISTANCE: 3.2 miles

HIKING TIME: 1 hour, 30 minutes

DIFFICULTY: 2.0

VERTICAL RISE: Minimal

TRAILHEAD GPS COORDINATES:
45°36'44.14" N, 92°25'43.72" W

No bustling beach, no boat launch, no jet skis, no campers or RVs. Nope. There are loons. And there is solitude. For now, other than wilderness, there is a trail that meanders through the woods, skirts a peacefully remote lakeshore, and then meanders off into the woods again. Straight Lake State Park is perhaps the most unusual of all Wisconsin state parks.

By a complete stroke of luck—and this will seem counterintuitive—the property was once owned by a paper company. But this company never logged it much. Eventually it was sold to the state, and it became a wilderness state park. An untouched, wild oasis that will forever be preserved.

A footpath, a segment of the Ice Age Trail that bisects the park diagonally, is the only human development so far. The entire segment is a 7.4-mile round-trip hike, or you can hike to the lake from either of the parking lot trailheads on the western or eastern end and do about half as much—about 3.0 miles from the west and 4.0 miles from the east, total. On a hot summer's day, the hike can be a bit taxing, and you'll be escorted by bloodthirsty insects of every kind. On a mild autumn day, you will be treated to a collage of color. The hike from the west trailhead is more rolling, while the hike from the east trailhead is much hillier, with a total climb of 100 feet and many ups and downs to get you there. For the sake of this guide we picked the western approach and what's outlined here is an easy hike along the lake's edge. Park at the northwest trailhead on 280th Avenue and do a round-trip hike to the southeast corner of the lake and back—about 3.2 miles total.

Alternatively, if you want to keep going, the whole segment from 280th

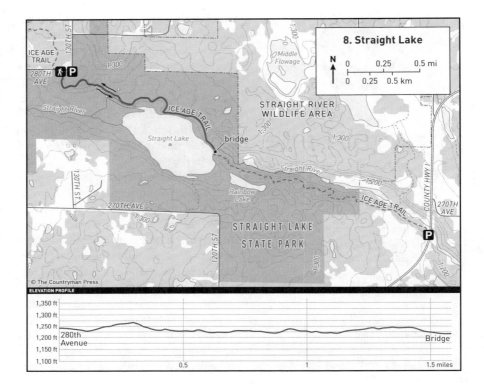

Avenue to CTH I is 3.7 miles. It's a great section to do with two cars and then hike end to end. Or, hiking the whole section out and back would be 7.4 miles. Either of these options would treat you to the much more rambling and hilly terrain along the Straight River Valley.

Note: Some maps show a white-blazed loop on the eastern half of the hike, but none existed in 2012 nor when we visited recently in 2016.

HOW TO GET THERE

From the north or south, take WI 35 to 280th Avenue. Take 280th Avenue east 2.75 miles to the trailhead on the south side of the road. From the west or east, take US 8 north to WI 35 and follow the directions above.

THE TRAIL

The hike leaves the parking lot trailhead to the south in relative lowland, which is a bit marshy in the wetter months. You'll cross a small footbridge and begin winding your way toward the lake, climbing slightly. You first will see the far western corner of the lake through the trees, where it is mostly bog. There is also a small creek running through the area. The entire hike is wooded, with various woodland plants, like ferns and bloodroot, carpeting the ground.

The trail will turn a bit to the east and head uphill into a pine stand. Soon you will turn more toward the lake and emerge on a slight hill on the lake's north shore. There is a nondescript offshoot trail over to the lake's edge. It's mostly grassy in this area, and there are even open spots where the sun leaks through and light-purple-colored prairie bergamot wildflowers bloom in summer. From here, you get a good look at the lake and the small island in the middle—and don't be surprised to see loons here in the summer. Perhaps they are summer residents.

Continue east and the trail will descend a bit into another boggy area where the Straight River begins from the lake. Two footbridges get you across the gurgling water. From the last footbridge, in the far northeast corner, the trail will emerge at the foot of a small bluff on this edge of the lake. There is another small pine stand here, which makes for a picturesque spot to take in the scenery before turning back (or before pressing on for a longer hike to the eastern trailhead on CTH I and back to your start— 7.4 miles total).

QUIET SUMMER MORNING AT STRAIGHT LAKE

9

Interstate State Park Loop

TOTAL DISTANCE: 5.0 miles

HIKING TIME: 2 hours

DIFFICULTY: 3.5

VERTICAL RISE: 250 feet

TRAILHEAD GPS COORDINATES:
45°23'40.48'' N, 92°38'57.07'' W

While it isn't a bad idea to live in the present, it's also not a bad idea to frame what is happening today in a historical context. And so while many of us show up to Wisconsin's state parks and hop on trails, it is worthwhile to stop a second and consider why a place was preserved as a park in the first place.

It becomes obvious this is a special place when you stand perched above the St. Croix River on the rocky terrain of the Pothole Trail, more than 100 feet above the glistening water below, and see nothing but majestic, towering bluffs on either side of the river. But by scratching the surface further, you realize that it is as remarkable from a geological perspective as much as from an aesthetic one. The formation on which you are standing is the result of a wild tale of billion-year-old mountains, lava flows, erosion, and then a glacier that retreated from here a mere 10,000 years ago—essentially a nanosecond in geological time.

This hike takes you on a geological history roller-coaster ride up and down a series of bluffs to places like Summit Rock, Horizon Rock, Echo Canyon, and eventually around a lake. It's a tough, rather long hike that seems a bit improbable at first glance on the trail map, which lists various trails' distances at 0.5 mile, 0.7 mile, 0.3 mile, and so on. But as you start connecting these hikes, it becomes possible to link together a great 5-mile hike that in the fall is accompanied by an explosion of autumn color.

Of special note at Interstate State Park is the fact this is the western terminus of the Ice Age Trail (the eastern endpoint resides at Potawatomi State Park in Door County, also in this book). It includes two federal designations as a National Scientific Reserve (the Dalles of the St. Croix as well as the Potholes).

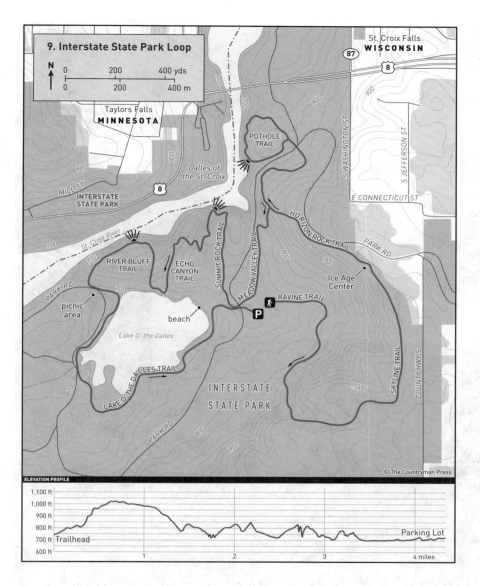

9. Interstate State Park Loop

N

| 0 | 200 | 400 yds |
| 0 | 200 | 400 m |

Taylors Falls
MINNESOTA

St. Croix Falls
WISCONSIN

POTHOLE
TRAIL

Dalles of
the St. Croix

**INTERSTATE
STATE PARK**

MILL ST

St. Croix River

RIVER BLUFF
TRAIL

ECHO
CANYON
TRAIL

SUMMIT ROCK TRAIL

MEADOW VALLEY TRAIL

HORIZON ROCK TRAIL

PARK RD

Ice Age
Center

picnic
area

RAVINE TRAIL

P

beach

Lake O' the Dalles

LAKE O' THE DALLES TRAIL

**INTERSTATE
STATE PARK**

PARK RD

SKYLINE TRAIL

COUNTY HWY S

S WASHINGTON ST

S JEFFERSON ST

E CONNECTICUT ST

PARK RD

© The Countryman Press

ELEVATION PROFILE

| 1,100 ft |
| 1,000 ft |
| 900 ft |
| 800 ft |
| 700 ft | Trailhead |
| 600 ft |

Parking Lot

1   2   3   4 miles

It is also the oldest state park in Wisconsin and home to the Pothole Trail, the oldest hiking trail in the state—both park and trail established around 1900.

on WI 35 to the park entrance. And from the north, take WI 87 to St. Croix Falls, turn left (east) on US 8 to WI 35 and south to the park entrance.

HOW TO GET THERE

From the south, take WI 35 to the park entrance, about 1 mile south of US 8. From the west or east, take US 8 south

THE TRAIL

To get to the trailhead, follow the park road past the interpretative center and wind your way past the small Pothole

HIGH ABOVE THE DALLES OF THE ST. CROIX ON THE POTHOLE TRAIL

Trail parking lot downhill to the beach. There's a small lot on the right, but there's also a much bigger one across from the beach on the left. Park there.

As the hike leaves the northeast corner of the lot, follow the access road past the stone shelter. You will see a sign marking the Ravine Trail. You'll take off to the south and into the open woods on a fairly rolling path. Soon the trail begins a series of switchbacks—including some stairs—that will take you up a tight, single-track trail to the northeast. You will cover some serious elevation here as you crawl up the ravine.

At the top of the ravine, you will eventually meet up with the Skyline Trail. Turn left (north) on it, and begin hiking along this wide crest trail toward the interpretative center. You will actually pop out at the interpretative center. Simply hike across its front yard and head into the woods again on the other side, where there is a sign for the Horizon Rock Trail.

You will soon emerge at one of many highpoints, Horizon Rock, and a landscape that looks a lot more like high desert than western Wisconsin. Head down the rocky bluff and into a cool ravine before crossing the road to the Pothole Trail. (There's no well-established pedestrian crossing here. Be careful for cars!)

The Pothole Trail, Wisconsin's oldest, will take you on a short, very rocky loop out to the first overlook over the Dalles of the St. Croix River. We hiked it counterclockwise. The potholes themselves are very unusual remnants from the force of meltwater, which created these "drainpipes" in the rock. Be careful here, too! Some potholes are small, but some are really big—as in feet wide and many feet deep. They are completely unmarked.

After passing the potholes, you will come to the western terminus of the Ice Age Trail, marked with a large boulder and plaque and overlooking the river far below. Looking south at the bluffs on the east side of the river, you will see where you are soon headed.

Head back to the beginning of the Pothole Trail and again cross the road (being careful as you do so). Continue through the woods and up to Horizon Rock, this time turning right (south) down toward Meadow Valley. You will head deep into this rock-walled valley and past a small pond before emerging at your original trailhead parking lot, this time from the north side.

Turn right and go to the main park road. Cross it carefully and turn right, hiking up to the small parking lot on the left (west) side of the road. There will be a trailhead for the Summit Rock Trail. This trail again will wind its way upward through a rocky valley and up to perhaps the most impressive overlook in the park. From here you can look north toward the Pothole Trail bluff and the Old Man of the Dalles rock formation across the river in Minnesota.

From here you will continue south down into Echo Canyon, past an immense rock wall, back toward the river, and up the River Bluff Trail. The trail will wind gradually up again to the final ascent and another viewing area before turning south and heading down a steep, gravel trail toward the picnic area below. The trail proper will give way to a grassy picnic area. Hike east toward the lake and you will rejoin the trail and loop around the lake counterclockwise. The trail will eventually emerge at the beach house and the main parking lot where you started, just to the east of it and across the park road.

Burkhardt Trail, Willow River State Park

TOTAL DISTANCE: 3.3 miles

HIKING TIME: 1 hour, 45 minutes

DIFFICULTY: 3.0

VERTICAL RISE: 130 feet

TRAILHEAD GPS COORDINATES: 45°1'41.84" N, 92°40'1.99" W

Rivers often flow with as much history as they do water. Willow River's legacy includes two remarkable, yet very different, wars. The Battle of the Willow River occurred in 1785 and pitted the Chippewa against the Sioux over rights to rice lakes.

More than 100 years later, another battle occurred and it, too, had everything to do with water. When a local club of outdoorsmen sought to fence off the Willow River and claim it as their own, Frank Wesley Wade, a brave Civil War veteran, paddled right past. After being arrested, he kept paddling to the Wisconsin Supreme Court—and won a landmark case protecting public waterways. As the park newsletter states, "The next time you go swimming, fishing, boating or are enjoying the beauty of one of Wisconsin's many lakes and rivers, be sure to think of Frank Wesley Wade and how he fought to make it all possible for future generations."

This hike follows the Burkhardt Trail and takes you along the river and through restored prairies. It also meanders through some of the woods in the park and then onward to the Willow Falls overlook. Since the first edition of this book was published, a new stairwell takes you from the overlook to the bridge below the falls, but there remains the original horseshoe trail that allows you to loop deep into the woods and then downhill to the falls—a longer and very scenic route.

HOW TO GET THERE

From the east, take I-94 west to the US 12 exit. Turn right (north) on US 12 and take it about 1.6 miles to CTH U. Turn left on CTH U and follow it 0.3 mile to where it ends at CTH A. Continue straight on A, past the main park entrance, for about 3.1 miles to CTH I. Turn left on CTH I (west)

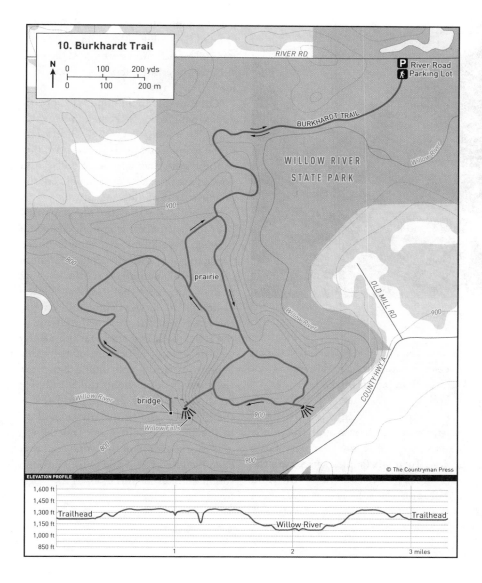

10. Burkhardt Trail

N

| 0 | 100 | 200 yds |
| 0 | 100 | 200 m |

RIVER RD

River Road
Parking Lot

BURKHARDT TRAIL

WILLOW RIVER
STATE PARK

Willow River

900

800

prairie

Willow River

900

OLD MILL RD

COUNTY HWY A

Willow River

bridge

Willow Falls

800

900

900

© The Countryman Press

ELEVATION PROFILE

| 1,600 ft |
| 1,450 ft |
| 1,300 ft | Trailhead | Trailhead |
| 1,150 ft | Willow River |
| 1,000 ft |
| 850 ft |
| | 1 | 2 | 3 miles |

and go 0.5 mile to River Road. Take a left on River Road, and the parking lot will come up pretty quickly on the left.

From the south, take WI 35 north out of River Falls about 8.5 miles to CTH N. Turn right on CTH N and go 0.4 mile to US 12. Turn left (north) on US 12 and follow the directions above.

From the north, take WI 64 west out of New Richmond 1 mile to CTH A. Turn left (south) on CTH A and follow it 8 miles to CTH I. Turn right on CTH I and follow the directions above.

THE TRAIL

The Burkhardt Trail heads out of the River Road parking lot and down toward the river. You'll turn west and meander along the river in this marshy area full of

THE THUNDERING WILLOW FALLS

may be some offshoot trails, this hike is shaped like a large hourglass. So stay left and loop around the edge of the prairie, ignoring the offshoots and the signs for Willow Falls.

Continue along the edge of the prairie with aspens, oaks, hickories, and maples to the left and a great mix of wildflowers to the right. The area is in constant flux in the spring and summer months, and you may see pockets of pink phlox or the purple spikes of blue vervain.

Eventually, you will work your way over to the first of two overlooks. Continue on the trail for only a few hundred yards to get to the falls overlook. There is a stairwell leading from this overlook to the water, more than 100 feet below—although we suggest continuing along the trail. You will find an offshoot to the left, which is a trail leading all the way down to the bottom of the falls. When returning, continue north from the turnoff point along the Burkhardt on the edge of the prairie and back to the T where you originally turned off to the southeast. Turn left (northeast) and backtrack along the same trail that brought you up. Head downhill, through the marshy area, and back to the River Road parking lot.

tall grasses and wildflowers. It's a good place to look for birds, and there may be waterfowl on the slow water.

Follow the trail until it peels away from the water and into the woods. A short, steady incline through the woods takes you out into another very large prairie. Turn left (southeast) where the trail comes to a T. This trail to the right is your return loop. Basically, while there

Kinnickinnic State Park Loop

TOTAL DISTANCE: A 3.2-mile loop on hiking trails

HIKING TIME: About 2 hours

DIFFICULTY: Easy

LOCATION: Jenny Wiley State Resort Park, 3 miles northeast of Prestonburg

MAPS: USGS Lancer and Jenny Wiley State Resort Park Visitor's Guide

River valleys are gorgeous things. When you find yourself at the confluence of two rivers like the Kinnickinnic and the St. Croix, the landscape is breathtaking and also provides a perfect opportunity for natural areas to flourish. But this part of western Wisconsin, now essentially a far eastern suburb of the Twin Cities, has become inundated with people. And so the incredible generosity and forethought of a few local landowners in the 1960s—assuring that this unique riverine landscape and its varied ecosystems were preserved as a state park—was more important than they may have guessed at the time.

While this piece of invaluable property could have easily ended up as a network of huge lawns owned by a handful of private landowners, seeing the park crawling with people on a warm, sunny day truly makes you appreciate public lands. And while this park does receive a lot of attention, the trails are not at all congested—probably due to the fact that the most popular hike is the short but steep downhill jaunt to the sandy shores of the St. Croix.

This hike takes you through the many habitats of the park—from the hardwoods near the overlook, out into the open prairie, and back again. This hike is actually a combination of three of the park's trails, pieced together to form a nice loop from the main parking lot. While this is not necessarily a long hike, nor a very hilly one, meandering through an open prairie on a hot day can be pretty taxing. Expect to be out and exposed to the sun for the majority of the hike, and don't expect many shady stops or any water along the way. However in warmer months expect to see a variety of plants and wildlife.

Prairies are among the most dramatic and diverse ecosystems around, with

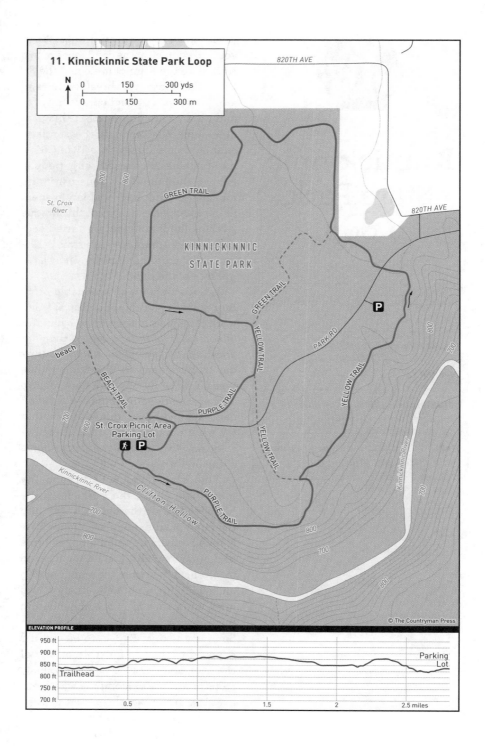

11. Kinnickinnic State Park Loop

N

0 — 150 — 300 yds
0 — 150 — 300 m

820TH AVE

GREEN TRAIL

820TH AVE

St. Croix
River

KINNICKINNIC
STATE PARK

GREEN TRAIL

P

YELLOW TRAIL

PARK RD

beach

BEACH TRAIL

YELLOW TRAIL

PURPLE TRAIL

YELLOW TRAIL

St. Croix Picnic Area
Parking Lot

Kinnickinnic River

Kinnickinnic River

Clifton Hollow

PURPLE TRAIL

700

800

700

© The Countryman Press

ELEVATION PROFILE

950 ft
900 ft
850 ft
800 ft
750 ft
700 ft

Parking
Lot

Trailhead

0.5   1   1.5   2   2.5 miles

red-winged blackbirds battling for territories, tall grasses reaching for the sky, and insects hopping around like jumping beans just about everywhere. As a bonus, much of this hike follows the edge of the woods and the prairie, a habitat perfect for a rich diversity of plants and animals.

HOW TO GET THERE

From the east, take I-94 west to exit 2, CTH F. Turn right on CTH F (east) and go 9 miles to 820th Avenue (you'll see park signs). Turn right and go 0.3 mile to the park entrance on the left. Follow the park road all the way back to the St. Croix Picnic Area parking lot.

From the north, take CTH F out of Hudson and follow the directions above.

From the south, take WI 29/35 north out of Prescott about 1.2 miles to CTH F. Turn left on CTH F and go 4.1 miles to 820th Avenue. From there, follow the directions above.

THE TRAIL

Once in the St. Croix Picnic Area parking lot, hike to the picnic benches and grills in the southwest corner. As you drive in, this is directly to your left. Eventually, you will see a small sign marking the beginning of the Purple Trail and an opening in the woods. Here's your trail.

Head southeast through woods full of cedars, aspens, and oaks. This trail winds up and down, very gradually, along the edge of the Kinnickinnic River Valley. Eventually, you will come to the turnoff for the Orange Trail; go past that and up to the Yellow Trail turnoff to the

OVERLOOKING THE ST. CROIX RIVER

right. Take this turnoff and follow the Yellow Trail northward toward the small parking lot near the road on the left. This area of prairie, interspersed with trees, makes for good bird viewing.

After passing the parking lot, you will follow the Yellow Trail as it turns left (west) and goes across the park road. Soon after crossing the road, you will come to the intersection with the Green Trail; turn right and take it north. This is your last turn for a while as you begin the long loop around the open prairie.

The trail continues southward from here before dodging across a tree line and along a long ridge before ducking back into the woods. Eventually, you will join back up with the Yellow Trail. Take it to the right (south) to the Purple Trail very soon thereafter. Take a right on it as it meanders through the woods downhill. You will pop out onto the paved Beach Trail; take a left and head uphill to the east and back to the parking lot.

Tower Nature Trail, Hoffman Hills State Recreation Area

TOTAL DISTANCE: 2.7 miles	
HIKING TIME: 1 hour, 15 minutes	
DIFFICULTY: 3.0	
VERTICAL RISE: 110 feet	
TRAILHEAD GPS COORDINATES: 44°56'38.92'' N, 91°46'57.48'' W	

Take miles of hiking, skiing, and snow-shoeing trails, and then add prairies, woods, wetlands, and an observation tower atop one of the highest points in Dunn County and you have just about the perfect park for silent sports. The only noticeable noise you hear may be the birds in the.summer, the crunch of leaves in the fall, or the yells coming from the sledding hill in the winter.

Although it has only been an official state property since 1980, Hoffman Hills State Recreation Area seems as though it was planned as a park long ago. The wide, well-maintained trails wind through the park's 700 acres, and a disabled-access trail spans 1 mile through the wetland area. The relatively new observation tower also looks as though it was always meant to be there.

The hike highlighted here, the Tower Nature Trail, meanders through the park in a counterclockwise loop. The first half dips up and down small hillsides while it makes its ascent to the tower. The trail is very well marked with small metal tower signs and offers a good sampling of what the area has to offer in terms of diverse habitats, elevation changes, and wildlife viewing.

HOW TO GET THERE

From the north, take WI 40 south out of Colfax for about 5 miles to CTH E. Turn right on CTH E and go 3.3 miles to 740th Street. Turn right on 740th (be careful, it comes up quickly) and take it 1.5 miles to the park entrance on the right, at the intersection with 730th Avenue.

From the south, take I-94 west from Eau Claire approximately 11 miles to WI 29/40. Take WI 40 north for about 3 miles to CTH E. Turn left on CTH E and follow the directions above.

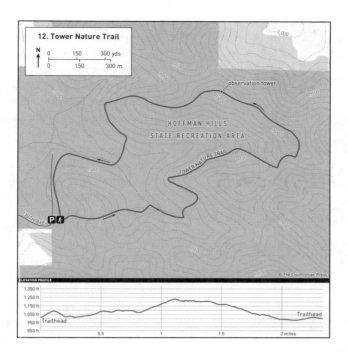

From the west, take US 12/WI 29 east out of Menomonie about 3 miles to CTH E. Turn left on CTH E and follow it for about 5 miles to 740th Street. Follow the directions in the first paragraph above.

THE TRAIL

The trail begins from the east side of the parking lot. After you hike up the grassy hill to the right of the trail kiosk, you will be greeted rather abruptly by a significant ascent, followed by a steep descent. The trail will wind its way toward the group camp area.

The trail will then bend from west to east and pass through a pine plantation before working its way first down and then up a long, steep ascent to the crest of the tower hill. Once atop the hill, you will have about a 0.5-mile break from climbing (while walking along the level ridge) before you reach the tower.

From the tower, the rest of the hike is mostly downhill. The trail leaves the ridge to the southwest along a wide trail bordered by aspen and alongside a deep valley. Be sure to follow the tower signs, as there will be other trails joining and leaving the tower trail. After turning more southward, the trail will meander up and down through some small valleys before emerging next to the woods.

You will hike west along a prairie for about 0.5 mile. The trail will bend south again, past the overflow parking lot and up into the woods along a slight ascent before descending into the grassy picnic and playground area next to the parking lot.

This trail offers a great variety of habitats and terrain and makes for a somewhat challenging hike. The view from the top is remarkable. Thanks to the Hoffman family for sharing this beautiful land with the rest of us.

Circle Trail, Chippewa Moraine Ice Age Reserve

TOTAL DISTANCE: 4.5 miles	

HIKING TIME: 2 hours

DIFFICULTY: 3.5

VERTICAL RISE: 120 feet

TRAILHEAD GPS COORDINATES:
45°13'24.93'' N, 91°24'50.79'' W

If you didn't know better, after looking at this trail, you would think the Wisconsin Department of Natural Resources scientists and engineers got together and built a 4,000-acre model of exactly what a glacier leaves in its tracks. They included a sweeping, several-mile-wide moraine, and then they peppered the landscape with all sorts of little hummock hills and kettle lakes. On top of that, literally, they placed the most remarkable visitors center—overlooking the entirety of their masterpiece to the south, atop a long hill covered in prairie plants. Giggling like kids in a candy store, they threw in some of the best trails in the state, exceptionally good trail markings, backcountry campsites accessible only by foot or canoe, and a heron rookery. The Chippewa Moraine Ice Age Reserve is even open year-round so that you can stop by and check out one of their pairs of snowshoes in the winter. It's an Ice Age paradise.

Thankfully, the place isn't fiction—it exists. All that was needed was legislation by Congress in 1964, which created the Ice Age National Scientific Reserves. Nine of these units are found around the state and seek to ensure the "protection, preservation, and interpretation of the nationally significant values of Wisconsin continental glaciation." Whether it's done by perusing the interpretive center, going on a guided hike, checking out a backpack full of nature identification materials, or simply tromping along the trails, these reserves are inimitably successful at teaching as well as preserving.

But getting out onto the trails reveals that much of what was preserved geologically is playing a critical role biologically. The dry hills and wet valleys of the hummocks and kettles support an incredible array of life—from tiny

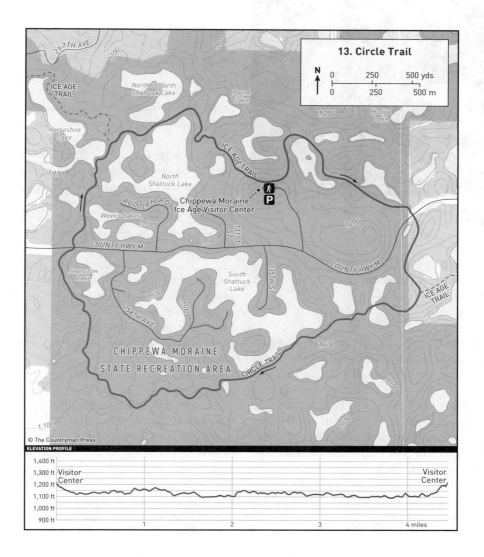

microorganisms to all sorts of reptiles and amphibians, all the way up to black bears. The very fact that a loon called in the distance on our visit to this glacial wonderland is evidence of what can exist in protected areas.

This hike, the Circle Trail, leaves the nature center and follows a seemingly endless series of ascents and descents along the shores of several small kettle lakes as it completes a 4-mile circuit of the reserve.

HOW TO GET THERE

From the north, take US 53 south out of Chetek for about 7.5 miles to CTH M. Take CTH M east through New Auburn for about 8.3 miles to the Chippewa Moraine Ice Age Unit visitors center entrance on the left.

From the south, take US 53 north to Bloomer. Take WI 40 north out of Bloomer for 11.7 miles to CTH M. Turn right on CTH M and follow it for about 2

WINDING BETWEEN THE LAKES AT CHIPPEWA MORAINE

miles to the Chippewa Moraine Ice Age Unit visitors center entrance on the left.

THE TRAIL

The trail begins just off the interpretive center parking lot to the north. As you enter the woods and start the trail you will come to a T intersection immediately, where you will head to the right (east), starting a clockwise route. The trail will pass along the shore of a lake and head downhill, where you will cross a road, CR M. At the foot of this hill is the entrance trail to one of the remote campsites, right on the shores of this secluded lake.

After crossing CTH M, you will soon pass by another lake before descending to the offshoot of the Ice Age Trail to the east. Stay right, on the Ice Age Loop, and continue westward. This marks the beginning of a long stretch of wooded trail that traverses bogs and wetlands and meanders up and down alongside several kettle lakes and ponds.

Eventually, the trail will turn more northward and the landscape will get a lot grassier and more open as you make a few final dips and climbs back toward CTH M. The trail will emerge just across the road from the gravel parking lot at the roadside trailhead. Cross the road and continue northward. The trail seems more open here, and there are more conifers. Also, the strange, steam engine–like noises you might hear coming from the other side of the lake to the left are the fascinating sounds of the heron rookery.

The trail then passes over a bridge and portage area before beginning its final loop eastward. It was right around here where we heard the wail of a loon in the distance. You'll pass yet another bridge and the entrance to another remote campsite before skirting along the edge of Payne Lake. From here you will wind back up a long and steep ascent, exploring a fern-laden amphitheater of a valley as you climb to the top of the trailhead hill.

Nordic Trail, Brunet Island State Park

TOTAL DISTANCE: 3.0 miles

HIKING TIME: 1 hour

DIFFICULTY: 2.0

VERTICAL RISE: Minimal

TRAILHEAD GPS COORDINATES:
45°10'47.98'' N, 91°9'43.17'' W

"Three Gifts of a Glacier," boasts a Wisconsin Department of Natural Resources informational pamphlet on Chippewa County recreation areas. And as far as Lake Wissota State Park, the Chippewa Moraine Ice Age Reserve (also included in this book), and Brunet Island State Park are concerned, the boasting is very appropriate. While there are several areas in the state that pay homage to the most recent Ice Age, the Chippewa County area devotes a very respectable amount of attention to its glacial history. Most notable is a collection of several glacial lakes and their drainage via many creeks and rivers into the Chippewa River—whose ultimate destination is the Mississippi River.

An island park flanked by the Chippewa and Fisher rivers, Brunet Island offers visitors a variety of options. While the bulk of the activity—beach, boat dock, campsites, and fishing pier—resides on the island, the best hiking is found on the "mainland." As a result of the last Ice Age, the park includes a wide range of plants, terrain, and wildlife. Activities at the park include several biking trails, canoeing, fishing, and swimming at a 200-foot sand beach.

The real gems of Brunet Island State Park are coniferous ones, though. Old-growth hemlock trees, a very rare find in Wisconsin, loom overhead and surround the trails throughout the park. While several of the trees were lost to a tornado a few years ago, there are still many left, both on the island and in the Nordic Trail section. A ranger at the park notes that it may be one of the best stands of hemlock remaining in the state.

The best uninterrupted hiking trail at Brunet Island is found on the Nordic Trail. This loop takes you away from the park office to the east, and then up and down a series of small glacial hills

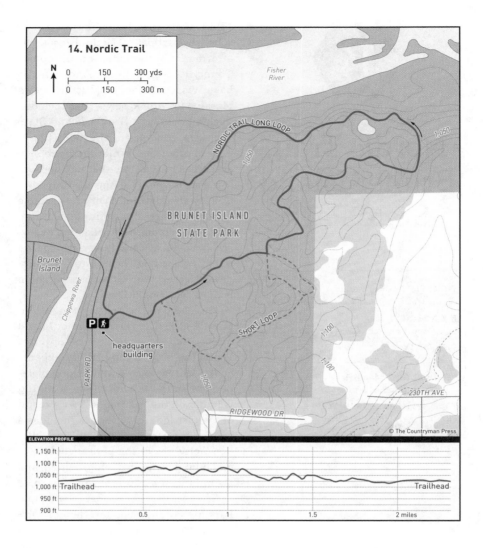

14. Nordic Trail

N

| 0 | 150 | 300 yds |
| 0 | 150 | 300 m |

Fisher River

NORDIC TRAIL LONG LOOP

1,050

1,050

BRUNET ISLAND
STATE PARK

Brunet Island

Chippewa River

SHORT LOOP

1,100

1,100

headquarters
building

PARK RD

1,050

230TH AVE

RIDGEWOOD DR

© The Countryman Press

ELEVATION PROFILE

| 1,150 ft |
| 1,100 ft |
| 1,050 ft |
| 1,000 ft | Trailhead | | | Trailhead |
| 950 ft |
| 900 ft |
| | 0.5 | 1 | 1.5 | 2 miles |

and valleys and past several small ponds. The trail then turns north before heading along the shore of the Fisher River to the west. It is along this segment of the trail that you pass the giant hemlocks before turning south and heading back to the park office.

HOW TO GET THERE

From Eau Claire to the southwest, take US 53/WI 124 north. Stay on WI 124 when the two split, and follow it 2 more miles to WI 29. Take WI 29 east about 12 miles to WI 27. Head left (north) on WI 27, through Cadott, and then about 15 miles farther to Cornell. At the stop sign, turn left on CTH CC. Take the first right under the railroad bridge—a crossing point of the Old Abe Bike Trail, which is accessible from the park. Follow the entrance road into the park. Park at the lot next to the headquarters building on the right. The trail begins off this lot.

If coming from the south or southeast, take WI 27 out of Augusta (approximately 10 miles from Osseo and I-94). Take WI 27 north through Cadott, about 20 miles farther, and follow the directions above.

From the north and northwest, take US 53 south to WI 64, just north of Bloomer. Head east on WI 64 for approximately 25 miles to where it crosses the Chippewa River. The road to the park will be the first road on the left after the bridge.

From the north and northeast, take WI 27 south out of Ladysmith to Cornell, about 22 miles. Head straight through town, but do not turn left out of town. Instead, head straight under the railroad bridge, toward the river, and take the first right after the railroad bridge and before the river.

THE TRAIL

The trailhead is found just off the park office parking lot. You will see a kiosk on the north side of the lot. Head east from the trailhead and begin a counterclockwise trip around the trail. There are two loops: a long loop and short loop. The long loop is about 3 miles long and takes about an hour. (This trail is also groomed for classic Nordic skiing in the winter.)

To follow the long loop, stay on the main trail through a rambling section filled with ferns and birch trees. An offshoot of the short loop will come up quickly on the right; head straight for the long loop. You'll come to another map kiosk and the convergence of three trails. Stay left on the long loop. The trail starts climbing from here and makes a few cutbacks as it heads up to its highest point.

Through this area you will pass several small ponds as you meander underneath birches, aspens, oaks, and a few hemlocks that start to make the scene. Eventually, the trail will make a left turn and head north toward the Fisher River. It passes between the Fisher and a picturesque large pond on the left. On sunny days, this may be the only sun you see on this tree-covered hike. As you follow along the river, the trail traces the top of a long esker, or ridge of glacial debris, before heading back up in elevation and past the best concentration of hemlocks in the park. These cinnamon-colored giants loom over the trail, and on rainy, overcast days this area resembles a rainforest, making it hard to believe that you are in the middle of Wisconsin.

The trail then pops out of the woods into a power-line opening and makes a quick left, taking you south back toward the parking lot.

Wood Lake, Ice Age Trail

TOTAL DISTANCE: 3.0 miles	

HIKING TIME: 1 hour, 15 minutes

DIFFICULTY: 1.5

VERTICAL RISE: Minimal

TRAILHEAD GPS COORDINATES:
45°20'16.04'' N, 90°4'57.90'' W

There are a few pockets of the state that are somewhat unassumingly tucked away. The roads that get you there contain long stretches between towns, past century-old cutover farms and tiny settlements. Mostly, you will just see a lot of trees.

If you look at the Wood Lake region, and all of Taylor County, on a gazetteer map, you'll see a lot of green. A lot. There's national forest, state wetlands, county forests and parks, and a small smattering of lakes. If you've wondered where Wisconsin's bears and wolves live, just look at places like this.

And so the whole experience of simply getting to a place like Wood Lake County Park can feel like an expedition, with roads in the area named "Wilderness" and "Bear." In the midst of it all, there is a quaint park on a little knoll above a nice beach, overlooking serene Wood Lake. Other than a small campground just south of the beach and in the woods, there is no settlement around the lake, which gives it a pristine and remote feel. The park offers a water pump along with changing rooms for the beach, restrooms, and an open grassy area.

The hike around the lake isn't overly long, nor is it overly taxing, although the footing is not great—particularly on the white-blazed loop section that is not Ice Age Trail—and a certain degree of bushwhacking is required in summer (along with bug swatting) but it really makes for a good little trek. There are no sweeping vistas and, in fact, the lake is hard to see for much of the hike. But ambling along the open woods on the north side of the loop, with forest grasses flopped over like a great green shag carpet, really is serene. And to be clear: if you are hiking in the summer, you will most likely slog through several sections of

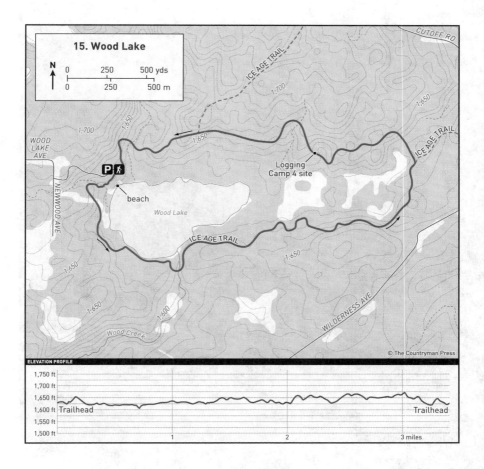

15. Wood Lake

ELEVATION PROFILE

quicksand-like mud while being bombarded with incessant and ubiquitous insects ecstatic to see you. Sound fun? Ah, summer hiking in Wisconsin's Northwoods!

Also of note in this region is the fact that you're just south of Timm's Hill County Park (which is about 10 miles to the northwest), noteworthy as the highest point in Wisconsin and the site of a tall observation tower. And, according to Mike Svob's *Paddling Northern Wisconsin,* you can also paddle on the nearby Jump, Yellow, Black, and Big Rib rivers. In fact, here at little Wood Lake, you could have a good time paddling a canoe or kayak and dropping a line

before or after a hike. Not to mention the fact that there are more segments of the Ice Age Trail to sample in what is definitely the most remote landscape the trail traverses.

HOW TO GET THERE

From the north or south, take WI 13 to WI 102 east. Take this approximately 9 miles to Wood Lake Avenue. Take this all the way to the park entrance and follow the signs for the beach parking lot.

From the west or east, take US 8 to WI 13 south at Prentice. Then follow the directions above.

CROSSING QUIET WOOD CREEK IN THE REMOTE WOODS OF TAYLOR COUNTY

For more information, contact the Taylor County Parks Department.

THE TRAIL

The hike begins at the picnic area/beach parking lot. Head across the grassy area from the parking lot past the shelter, in line with the water pump, and you'll come to the trailhead. Starting here, the loop will be a counterclockwise trip.

You will pass below the camping area, but you'll leave this quickly—and then cross the road to the boat launch. From here, welcome to wilderness. The trail ambles around wooded bogland and heads away from the lake a bit before turning back inward to go closer to the shore. Again, in the thick vegetation of summer, you won't see much of the lake, other than glimpses filtered by trees. In the fall, things are much different, as the leaves blaze with color.

Eventually you will come to a small offshoot trail to the left that takes you about 10 or 20 yards toward the shore; otherwise, the trail will turn right (south) and you'll head along Wood Creek until turning left (east) and crossing it at a small bridge.

From here, you will turn north again back toward the lake before peeling away to the east—essentially, this will be the last you'll see of the lake until the trail's end (at least during summer months). The trail will gain a bit of ele-vation and do quite a bit of dipping up and down before taking a more gradual descent, deep into the woods.

Soon you will loop northward and come to an intersection with the Ice Age Trail heading off to the east. You will want to stay left (west) and head back to complete the loop. It is on this north side of the lake that you will pass through remnants of the old Camp 4 log-ging camp.

You will climb slightly; the trail seems to be overall on higher ground on the north side of the lake. The woods also open up at this point; you will see more in the way of low woodland grasses and you will have longer views. You will cross several small coulees, however, which will mean dipping down again into wet creek crossings many times as you head westward.

Just about at the halfway point, you will again intersect with the Ice Age Trail, which will head off to the right (north). Stay left (southwest) as you go toward the parking lot. With less than 1 mile remaining, you will descend into thick woods and into a streambed and boggy area. Things get thick with undergrowth and very buggy in the summer, and the hiking will be tough and wet. Slogging along, you will turn southeast toward the lake before cutting back southwest, making a short climb, and—all of a sudden—popping out at the parking lot.

16

Rib Mountain State Park Loop

TOTAL DISTANCE: 3.2 miles

HIKING TIME: 1 hour, 30 minutes

DIFFICULTY: 4.5

VERTICAL RISE: 510 feet

TRAILHEAD GPS COORDINATES:
44°55'12.74'' N, 89°41'02.40'' W

A huge mound of quartzite, Rib Mountain has stood the test of geological time, and its peak is now the third highest point in Wisconsin at 1,939.5 feet. And as impressive as its height is its age—the mountain is dated at 1.6 billion years old!

Perhaps the most significant feature of Rib Mountain is located on its back side. The south side of the mountain holds a gem as valuable as the quartz below it: maples and their golden sap. Here can be found one of the most impressive stands of sugar maples in the state. And it is among these beautiful trees and along the southern slope of the mountain that this hike will take you.

As soon as you start mentioning large hills, mountains, and trails that meander along the sides of them, you're probably talking some serious elevation change. During this hike, you will begin at the top of Rib Mountain, perched more than 1,800 feet above Wausau. Before you know it, you will have descended to 1,330 feet before making the turn back up the mountainside.

The return ascent seems easy at first. But before too long, you will turn straight north and begin a major uphill scramble, climbing 320 feet in about 0.25 mile—almost 1 foot of climb per stride. And on top of that, the trail is a hodgepodge of loose rock—making a walking stick a must rather than an option on this great, sweeping trail on the maple-shrouded southern slope of Rib Mountain. At the top you are rewarded with a phenomenal view of Marathon County, high atop Sunrise Lookout.

HOW TO GET THERE

From the north or south, take US 51 to Wausau. Take the CTH N exit and head

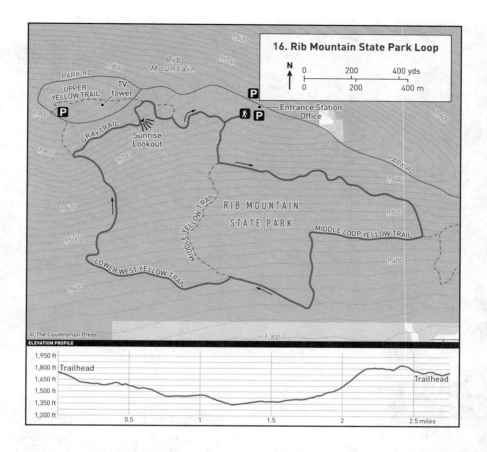

16. Rib Mountain State Park Loop

N

| 0 | 200 | 400 yds |
| 0 | 200 | 400 m |

Rib Mountain

PARK RD

UPPER YELLOW TRAIL

TV tower

P

Entrance Station Office

GRAY TRAIL

Sunrise Lookout

PARK RD

RIB MOUNTAIN STATE PARK

MIDDLE LOOP YELLOW TRAIL

MIDDLE YELLOW TRAIL

LOWER WEST YELLOW TRAIL

1,600
1,700
1,800
1,900
1,800
1,700
1,600
1,500
1,400
1,500
1,400
1,300
1,500
1,600
1,400

© The Countryman Press

ELEVATION PROFILE

1,950 ft				
1,800 ft	Trailhead			
1,650 ft				Trailhead
1,500 ft				
1,350 ft				
1,200 ft	0.5	1	1.5	2	2.5 miles

west to Park Road, 0.1 mile from US 51. Turn right on Park Road and take it for 1.9 miles up into the park. Pass through the park office checkpoint and the parking lot there and do a U-turn to the left to the lower parking lot just below the office. The trailhead is in the southwest corner of this lot.

From the west, take CTH B south out of Marathon City about 2 miles to CTH N. Turn left (east) on CTH N and go 9.5 miles to Park Road. Turn left and follow the directions above.

From the east, take WI 29 west from Wittenberg for about 25 miles to the Wausau area. Merge with US 51 north and take the CTH N exit. Turn left on CTH N and take it 0.2 mile to Park Road.

Turn right on Park Road and follow the directions above.

THE TRAIL

The hike follows a clockwise loop on the south face of Rib Mountain by connecting the Middle Loop Trail and the Lower West Yellow Trail; it eventually climbs back up a steep ascent to the Cobbler's Knob lookout. We nicknamed it the "South Face Loop." Ducking into the woods at the trailhead—which is marked by a yellow-and-gray blaze—a wide trail and dense woods welcome and envelop you as you begin your descent. The return trail of this loop will come up quickly on your right. Stay left and con-

COBBLER'S KNOB LOOKOUT AT RIB MOUNTAIN

GOLDEN MAPLE LEAVES BEJEWELING RIB MOUNTAIN IN FALL

tinue down the first really steep section. The trail will get a bit rockier, making for some slippery footing at times. You will also pass the Middle Yellow Trail turnoff; skip this and stay left, heading east now as the trail levels off for a while.

Eventually, the trail will come close to its easternmost point, where the Lower East Yellow Trail peels off to the left (east). Stay right and go south before turning to the west along another fairly level stretch of trail. Soon the trail will turn directly south and drop about 100 feet in just 0.125

mile before hitting its lowest point and turning northwest and beginning a very long uphill hike.

The climb is pretty slight at first, as you pass the turnoff for the Middle Yellow Trail. Stay left again, technically taking the Lower West Yellow Trail. From here you will meander among many maples, climbing slightly, and even descending a little at one point. Soon you will turn right (north) and start heading straight up the side of the mountain toward Sunrise Lookout. It's a bit of a surprise after all the pleasant rambling you have been doing so far. Have your walking stick ready for support on loose rock, and go slowly. A couple of benches offer places to rest along the way.

At the top, you will merge with three trails. The Red Trail will head to the left, the Gray/Yellow will go straight, and the Gray will go to the right. Take the Gray Trail (which will take you all the way back to the trailhead) to the right, along a narrower path than what you've been used to. This will take you toward the ridge of the mountain and up to Sunrise Lookout. The trail weaves between some boulders as it approaches the very rocky lookout.

After taking a much-deserved rest at the lookout, head northeast off the rock and continue on the Gray Trail east. You will eventually meet up with the original Yellow Trail at a bench. Take a left and head north to the parking lot.

Definitely one of the most scenic and challenging hikes in the state, this loop trail along the south slope of Rib Mountain makes for a great day's trekking. Enjoy the maples, especially in the fall, and don't forget to have a walking stick ready.

II.

NORTHEAST

Fallison Lake Nature Trail, American Legion-Northern Highland State Forest

TOTAL DISTANCE: 2.0 miles

HIKING TIME: 1 hour

DIFFICULTY: 1.0

VERTICAL RISE: Minimal

TRAILHEAD GPS COORDINATES:
45°59'54.98'' N, 89°37'4.94'' W

If there were ever a quintessential northern Wisconsin lake-country lake, encircled by an almost perfect trail and covered by a thick northern hemlock and hardwood forest canopy, then that lake would have to be Fallison and the trail would have to be the Fallison Lake Nature Trail.

On a cool Northwoods evening, with the sun low on the horizon, the lake shimmers like black glass. The trail itself almost looks like a movie set. A stand of old pines has left a thick carpet of auburn needles below, and the soft trail meanders between the tall trunks like icing surrounding the candles of a birthday cake.

In an area immersed in lakeshore development and paradoxically crowded remote roads, a visit to Fallison, tucked unassumingly off the beaten path, is a refreshing change. The lake isn't right off the road; instead the trail makes a short climb and then a descent before you get your first glimpse. You then pass behind trees as your view improves. Then you're guided into a bog along a long boardwalk before emerging, finally, to be rewarded with a view of the lake from the south shore.

While not necessarily long at all, the trail takes a while to finish. But it's not just the distance that will keep you coming back. It's the solitude, the scenery, and nature itself. The shoreline around the lake is a marvel of natural diversity, with hemlocks, old-growth white pines, sphagnum bogs, eagles, ospreys, loons, beavers, and more. In fact, on our hike, we were constantly stepping over long-ago-felled trees that had been partially dragged to the lake by a busy beaver.

HOW TO GET THERE

From the south, take US 51 north out of Woodruff about 4.5 miles to County

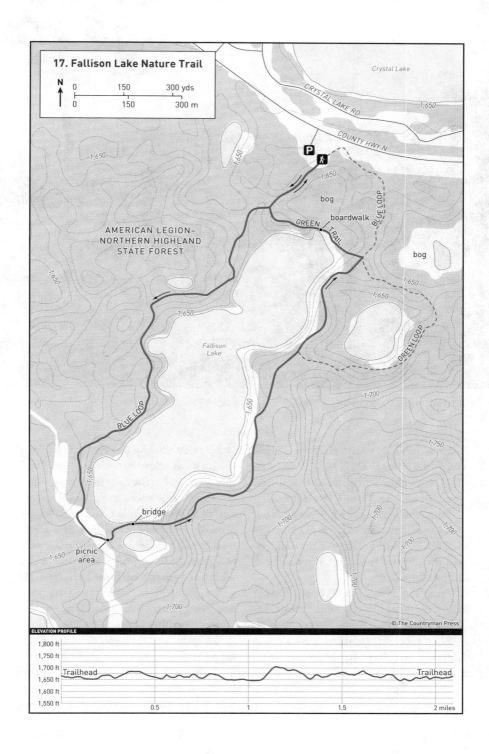

17. Fallison Lake Nature Trail

Crystal Lake

CRYSTAL LAKE RD

1,650

COUNTY HWY N

AMERICAN LEGION–
NORTHERN HIGHLAND
STATE FOREST

bog

boardwalk

GREEN TRAIL

BLUE LOOP

bog

1,650

1,650

GREEN LOOP

Fallison Lake

1,650

1,700

BLUE LOOP

1,650

1,750

bridge

picnic area

1,650

1,700

1,700

1,700

1,700

© The Countryman Press

ELEVATION PROFILE

Trailhead — Trailhead

1,800 ft · 1,750 ft · 1,700 ft · 1,650 ft · 1,600 ft · 1,550 ft

0.5 · 1 · 1.5 · 2 miles

FALLISON LAKE ON A QUIET SUMMER AFTERNOON

Route M (CTH M). Turn right on CTH M and go 2.6 miles to CTH N. Turn right on CTH N, and the Fallison Lake trailhead sign will be 2.4 miles on the right.

From the north, take US 51 south out of Manitowish Waters for about 12 miles to CTH N. Turn left on CTH N and go 4.1 miles to the Fallison Lake trailhead on the right.

From the east, take CTH N west out of Sayner for about 4.6 miles to the trailhead on the left.

For more information, contact the American Legion–Northern Highland State Forest in Woodruff.

THE TRAIL

This hike goes mostly along the Blue Loop, although we cut off from the Blue Loop and take the Green Trail back to the lot so as to cut between the bog and the north end of the lake for a great view.

Start by heading right (southwest) out of the parking lot and trail kiosk area. You'll head down some riser steps next to the bog before climbing back up to a small ridge on the north side of the lake. The return loop for the Green Trail will come up on the left; stay to the right and head counterclockwise around the lake on the Blue Loop.

The trail will take you away from the lake briefly, and then it will turn back and give you your first good glimpse from a boggy valley. From here, you'll climb a bit and pass a bench. Continue along the western shore, with a soft pine needle bed underfoot and towering pines overhead.

Soon enough, you will come to the southern tip of the lake. The trail will turn left (northeast) across a long boardwalk and over a large bog. Things are pretty overgrown here, and it can also get pretty buggy in warmer months. The trail will emerge from the bog and turn more northward, through a picnic area and past the hand pump. While things open up a lot here, and the trail is a little hard to find, simply stay near the lake. The trail will follow along the shore. Make sure to look up, too, because you'll find yourself surrounded by one of the greatest sights in the Northwoods: towering old-growth hemlock trees.

Coming out of the picnic area, you will pass over a small bridge, offering a great view of the lake from the southeast corner. This is a good place to take a break, snap some photos, and do some wildlife viewing. Don't be surprised if you see a beaver working feverishly on some important building project.

The trail will then start to wind along the eastern shore of the lake. After a short climb and descent into a valley, you will find yourself at the joining of the Green, Red, and Blue trails. Follow the Blue Trail toward the shore of the lake. A small peninsula makes for a great spot to view the lake.

From here, continue to where the

MEANDERING ALONG THE WOODED SHORELINE OF FALLISON LAKE

Green Trail heads west between the bog and the lake. This is definitely the way to go. There is a boardwalk leading to a short hillside that has a couple of benches looking out at the lake from the north shore.

Eventually, you will meet back up with the fork in the trail that you took originally. Head right (north) back toward the parking lot and trail kiosk.

18

Lost Lake Trail, Chequamegon-Nicolet National Forest

TOTAL DISTANCE: 4.5 miles

HIKING TIME: 2 hours, 15 minutes

DIFFICULTY: 3.5

VERTICAL RISE: Minimal

TRAILHEAD GPS COORDINATES:
45°53'7.77'' N, 88°33'45.17'' W

Tucked deep in northeast Wisconsin is heavily wooded Florence County, known for its trees, lakes, and trout streams. And nearly half of Florence County is publicly owned, making it a recreational paradise. Among the many campsites on picturesque, remote lakes in this area, there is Lost Lake Campground on the north side of the lake and the rustic Lost Lake cabins on the south, both offering a true Northwoods getaway (information about both are available on the Chequamegon-Nicolet National Forest website if you search for "Lost Lake").

In keeping with its name, Lost Lake is tucked very much away, far off the beaten path about an hour from either Florence or Eagle River. The small lake is flanked by one of the most impressive remaining old-growth hemlock forests in the state. These giants erupt out of the wet lakeshore soil and tower overhead like space needles.

Topping off this Northwoods retreat is a group of trails. Lost Lake Campground just happens to be sitting right on the path of the Perch, Lauterman, Ridge, and Assessor's trails. The trail highlighted here is the Ridge.

While pretty well marked, the trail sees limited traffic, meaning grasses can and do grow rather high in parts—so there is some bushwhacking required in the more open areas of the trail. While it would certainly be possible to strike off in the wrong direction, the general trail route is mostly intuitive. But be sure to have a good map of the area and a compass or GPS to get you back on track if it's needed.

This rolling hike takes you deep into the national forest, offering great views of glacial remains, seldom-seen hemlock and pine trees, and a great escape while visiting Florence County. And if you're looking for a rustic, old-time cabin experience, then the Lost Lake cabins are the place.

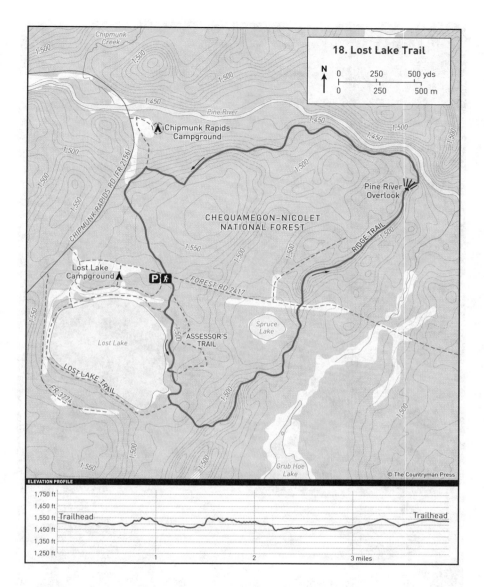

18. Lost Lake Trail

N
0   250   500 yds
0   250   500 m

Chipmunk Creek

Pine River

Chipmunk Rapids Campground

Pine River Overlook

CHEQUAMEGON-NICOLET NATIONAL FOREST

CHIPMUNK RAPIDS RD (FR 2156)

RIDGE TRAIL

Lost Lake Campground

FOREST RD 2417

Spruce Lake

ASSESSOR'S TRAIL

Lost Lake

LOST LAKE TRAIL

FR 3774

Grub Hoe Lake

© The Countryman Press

ELEVATION PROFILE

1,750 ft
1,650 ft
1,550 ft — Trailhead
1,450 ft
1,350 ft
1,250 ft

Trailhead

1   2   3 miles

HOW TO GET THERE

To get to Lost Lake Campground from the west, take WI 70 east out of Eagle River for about 29.5 miles to the junction of WI 70 east and WI 139 south. Continue on WI 70/139 for 2.8 miles. Turn left on WI 70 east and follow it for 3.7 miles to Forest Road 2450 (FR 2450) (Dream Lake Road). You will see signs to Lost Lake Campground. Turn right on FR 2450, which merges with Chipmunk Rapids Road, and follow it for 3.7 miles past Chipmunk Rapids Campground. The next turnoff to the left will be Lost Lake Campground (the cabins are the next left, but are down the road a while). Once you turn in here, and if you are not camping, drive past the campground entrance to the trailhead lot. Follow the

WINDING ALONG THE RIDGE TRAIL AT REMOTE LOST LAKE

gravel drive for about 0.5 mile to the Assessor's Trail trailhead parking lot on the right.

From the east, take WI 70 out of Florence for 16.5 miles to FR 2450. Turn right and follow the directions above.

From the south, take WI 139 north out of Long Lake for 5.7 miles to the junction of WI 70/139. Turn right on WI 70 east and follow the directions above.

For more information, contact the Chequamegon-Nicolet National Forest, Florence District Office.

THE TRAIL

A map on the kiosk at the trailhead provides a good overview of the hike. Take the Assessor's Trail south out of the campground parking lot, along the shore of Lost Lake. Be careful not to follow the Assessor's Loop. Instead, follow the sign to the Assessor's Pine, and then stay along the shore by the benches overlooking the lake. You'll continue back around the southeast corner of the lake, where there is a small bog—look for the wood duck nesting boxes. After hiking around the bog, you will find yourself amid some of the huge, 150-year-old hemlocks gracing this area.

Soon you will come to a trail intersection. One sign points left (northeast) and back to the Lost Lake Campground (it says 0.06 mile, but we think they meant 0.6) or, under the Ridge Trail heading, straight to the Pine River Overlook, Chipmunk Rapids Campground, or Lost Lake Campground 3.3 miles away. The latter is your trail.

Head southeast on this narrow trail, away from the lake and into a more mixed hardwood forest with more undergrowth. You'll encounter fewer hemlocks now, and more maples. The trail will turn northeastward as you begin a somewhat taxing climb up to the top of the trail's namesake ridge. After the long climb, you will find yourself hiking atop the ridge, probably a long glacial esker, with deep valleys on either side. But soon after, you'll begin a long and gradual descent as you work your way down to FR 2417.

You'll find that at FR 2417—not much of a road—you have the option of heading left and west along the road straight back to Lost Lake Campground (0.5 mile away) or crossing over and continuing on the Ridge Trail for another 2.4 miles. After crossing, head straight on the Ridge Trail and up another hill. This narrow ridge will lead you toward the Pine River Overlook.

A fairly indistinguishable overlook, you'll know when you've reached the river because the trail will turn abruptly left (west) and down along the edge of the river. This is the beginning of a lot more bushwhacking, so be prepared for some close quarters on the trail in the summer. Imagine your lawn's grass at home growing five feet tall, with not much of a path through it. That's what you may find here. While tight, the trail is pretty easy to follow— and undoubtedly some other hiker or deer or bear has been through recently, making a path through the tall grass and berry bushes.

Eventually you will turn southwest, away from the river, and make a long, slight ascent up an old overgrown logging road. The trail will be much easier to see and the hiking will be easier. You will come to a trail intersection. Head left and follow the trail into Lost Lake Campground or back to the trailhead parking lot. Or if you've nabbed a cabin, go back along the Assessor's Trail again to the south side of the lake.

19

Ed's Lake Trail, Chequamegon-Nicolet National Forest

TOTAL DISTANCE: 3.5 miles	

HIKING TIME: 1 hour, 15 minutes

DIFFICULTY: 2.0

VERTICAL RISE: Minimal

TRAILHEAD GPS COORDINATES:
45°28'11.91'' N, 88°47'29.17'' W

Who's Ed? We're not sure, but being the first to find a remote lake and being able to name it certainly has its perks. Actually, whether or not Ed is to be thanked for this beautiful area, the wide, sweeping trails that flow over this wooded landscape have their roots in early 20th-century railroad trails that undoubtedly carted timber and ore throughout the area.

Ed's Lake sits unassumingly between Crandon and Wabeno in lake country—and very near the Wolf River. While embedded in a relatively populated area of the north, Ed's Lake is a very quiet place—probably due to the fact that it sees more skiers than hikers. And it truly is remote when you compare it to some of the other trails in the book. This solitude is also the reason that it was here—out of more than 20 hikes in northern Wisconsin—that we saw signs of black bear like nowhere else. Several piles of scat led us along the trail and into a sunny opening blanketed with blackberry bushes. Later, while contemplating a trail intersection map perched atop a wooden post, we found ourselves needing to brush aside several locks of black hair in order to see the map. While it was a directional guide for us, somebody else apparently valued this post for its back-scratching attributes!

Ed's Lake National Recreation Trail is a sure bet for a nice Northwoods lake country hike and for scouting good Nordic ski trails for next winter. The impressive cherry-framed map at the trailhead marks the start of the Birch Trail, which heads west to the lake before looping back along an old rail bed. The namesake birch trees are more abundant along this trail than elsewhere in the state, and make for a beautiful white-and-brilliant-green backdrop to a great trail.

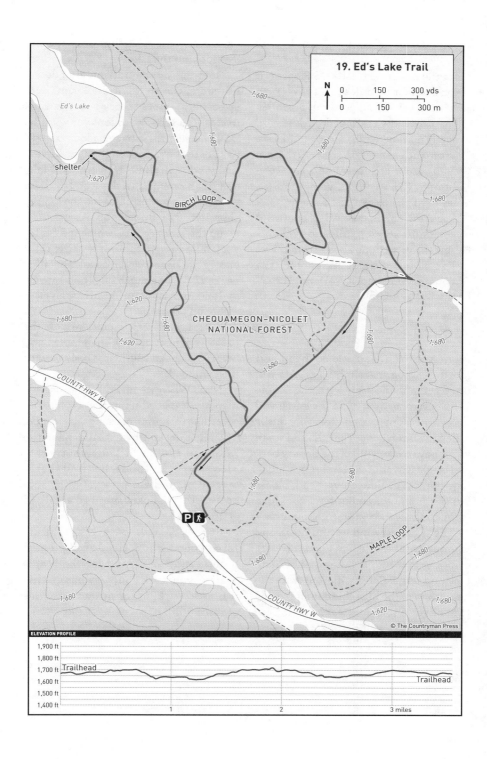

19. Ed's Lake Trail

Ed's Lake

shelter

1,620

1,680

BIRCH LOOP

CHEQUAMEGON–NICOLET
NATIONAL FOREST

1,620

1,680

COUNTY HWY W

MAPLE LOOP

COUNTY HWY W

© The Countryman Press

ELEVATION PROFILE

1,900 ft			
1,800 ft			
1,700 ft Trailhead			Trailhead
1,600 ft			
1,500 ft			
1,400 ft	1	2	3 miles

HOW TO GET THERE

From the northwest, take US 8 east out of Crandon for 1.6 miles to CTH W. Turn right on CTH W and go about 8.9 miles to the Ed's Lake trailhead parking lot, which is marked with a sign, on the left.

From the east, take WI 32 north from Wabeno 2.6 miles to WI 52 west. Turn right onto CH W, which you follow 5.5 miles to the trailhead on the right.

From the north, take WI 32 south out of Laona for about 9 miles to Wabeno. Follow the directions above from there.

For more information, contact the Chequamegon-Nicolet National Forest, Laona District Office.

THE TRAIL

From the trailhead kiosk, head left (northwest) on the Birch Loop. You will briefly share the trail with the Maple Loop before turning off to the left. It will become evident immediately why this is called the Birch Loop. The hills and small valleys are packed full of the papery bark and bright leaves of the birch. On a sunny day, the leaves dance overhead, blocking the sun and making for a cool hike through the woods in warmer months.

The trail will wind up and down and eventually take a turn to the left (west), bringing you into a valley full of hemlock and ferns. Quite different from the beginning of the hike this change seems to fit as you climb up toward the Adiron-dack-style skiers' shelter atop the hill overlooking the lake.

Continue on the trail, moving downhill along the shore of the lake. There are several spots where you can hike in closer to the lake to look for wildlife. Don't be surprised to see a loon on Ed's Lake or to spot a deer on the shore. Eventually, you will climb away from the lake and to an opening in the woods, where you have the option of taking the long or short leg of the Birch Loop. We went left along the longer route, which makes for a 3.5-mile hike in total. It was the right choice; we descended into a lush valley packed full of young maples and aspens, making for a sight unlike any seen elsewhere on the trail.

Eventually, you will emerge from the grass and meet up with the Maple Loop before you head southwest back toward the trailhead.

Note: When we hiked it, the trailside map kiosk placed us in the wrong spot according to the nail marking our location.

Continue southwest and past the return of the Birch Loop short trail. This section is a wide, flat trail that is leveled off and cut into the hills, suggesting that it must have been a rail bed at one time.

Soon you will pass the original Birch Loop turnoff. Head straight past both it and the turnoff for the Maple Trail as you work your way back to the trailhead parking lot through a series of rolling hills.

Dells of the Eau Claire Park Loop, Marathon County

TOTAL DISTANCE: 3.0 miles

HIKING TIME: 1 hour, 15 minutes

DIFFICULTY: 2.0

VERTICAL RISE: 50 feet

TRAILHEAD GPS COORDINATES:
45°00'14.45'' N, 89°19'58.83'' W

Six hundred million years ago. It's an amount of elapsed time that seems absolutely impossible for the human brain to truly comprehend. A hundred years seems long, and now you're thinking about 6 million times that! And since we're talking about hiking and two-legged travel, consider this: The first known humanoid types date back about 2.5 million years. Let's see, that still leaves us with 597.5 million years of a world devoid of anything that resembles the people carrying energy bars and happily hiking along in waterproof boots on the trails over the shelf of Precambrian rock at Dells of the Eau Claire Park. It's unfathomable.

A Marathon County park, the Dells of the Eau Claire is also a state natural area. In fact, with its many Civilian Conservation Corps (CCC)-built bridges, shelters, and paths (along with the large camping areas, ample parking lots, resident park manager, and beach), the place feels a lot more like one of Wisconsin's state parks than a county park—a true testament to Marathon County. Add to this the fact that the Ice Age Trail wanders through the park on its 1,200-mile thread through the state, and the Dells of the Eau Claire is without a doubt a place that truly defines Wisconsin.

The ancient rock here looks like it was dumped all over the place by dump trucks. Called rhyolite schist, it is an exceptionally hard and dense rock formed by metamorphosis. Later, it was thrust up into a vertical orientation, like a layer cake set on its side. The cracks you see are the planes of rock, which have split over time. The water at the Dells both smashes up against the rock and rumbles in a less inhibited way through the big cracks; huge whirlpools create such a thundering force that

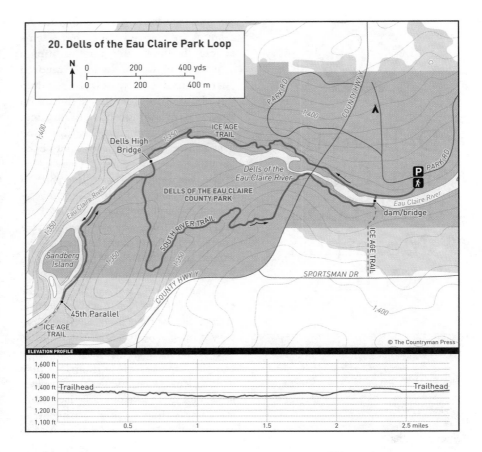

20. Dells of the Eau Claire Park Loop

N

| 0 | 200 | 400 yds |
| 0 | 200 | 400 m |

ICE AGE TRAIL

PARK RD

COUNTY HWY Y

Dells High Bridge

1,400

1,350

1,400

Dells of the Eau Claire River

PARK RD

P

DELLS OF THE EAU CLAIRE COUNTY PARK

Eau Claire River

Eau Claire River

dam/bridge

SOUTH RIVER TRAIL

1,350

1,350

ICE AGE TRAIL

Sandberg Island

1,350

SPORTSMAN DR

COUNTY HWY Y

1,400

45th Parallel

ICE AGE TRAIL

© The Countryman Press

ELEVATION PROFILE

1,600 ft				
1,500 ft				
1,400 ft Trailhead				Trailhead
1,300 ft				
1,200 ft				
1,100 ft	0.5	1	1.5	2	2.5 miles

they have ground potholes in the rock. Downstream, the water simply meanders along quietly.

This hike follows the Ice Age Trail past the Dells and along the rocky river's edge, across a huge CCC suspension bridge, through the quiet woods on the south bank of the river to the 45th Parallel, and back toward the Dells before peeling off into a wonderful section of northern forest—full of hemlock, maple, pine, and birch trees. Not an overly long hike at about 3.1 miles, it is incredibly scenic, and particularly so once you leave the more congested Dells area. Also, in the warmer months, there is a beach waiting at the conclusion of the hike upstream from the dam. And like many northern hikes, it's spectacular in the fall.

HOW TO GET THERE

From the west, north, and east, take WI 52 to CTH Y, just west of the village of Hogarty. Turn south here, follow this road 1.5 miles to the park, and turn left into the beach parking lot, where this hike begins.

From the south, take US 45 to CTH Z, about 3.5 miles north of Birnamwood. Turn left (west) and follow this about 7 miles to CTH Y. Turn right (north) here and take this about 1.5 miles to the park. Cross the bridge and turn right at the beach parking lot entrance.

CROSSING THE DELLS HIGH BRIDGE

THE TRAIL

This hike begins at the beach parking lot, just east of the dam. Start off by hiking toward the dam through the mowed grass—there's no formal trail here. At the dam there is a footbridge crossing, but don't cross (that's your return route); instead, stay straight and follow the trail into the woods, heading west on the north side of the river (the hike will be a counterclockwise loop) following the Ice Age Trail.

After a couple of hundred yards, the trail will come to CTH Y; cross the road here, being careful for traffic. You will emerge on the other side of the road directly above the Dells and the crashing water below. There are several places to take photos here and, as the park signage notes, it is prohibited to go onto the dangerous Dells' rocks—although you'll undoubtedly see people out there.

The trail continues along the river; stay with the Ice Age Trail (marked with yellow blazes) as it meanders along the river's edge and switchbacks at one point up a steep climb. The trail then descends back toward the river and will cross the 120-foot-long Dells High Bridge, 30 feet above the river—an incredible example of the CCC work projects of the 1930s.

After crossing, the Ice Age Trail will turn off to the right (west) and continue along the south side of the river; take this right turn and continue along the river. Soon after you turn right, you will come to another trail exiting off to the left (south). Ignore this trail for now; it is the South River Trail, which you will take on your return route.

This serene section of trail along the river is incredibly picturesque. There are towering pines and hemlocks over-head and the northern forest's trade-mark soft, piney bed underfoot. In the summer, the browns of the needles, the glistening of the river, and the bright greens of the woodland plants coalesce into a brilliant mesic mosaic on the river's edge.

The trail continues on, turning more southward and ambling up and down small rises, over rocks and roots, and being escorted by the glistening river. Eventually, you will come to a point of interesting significance—the 45th Parallel, or the point halfway between the equator and the North Pole. This milestone is rather unassumingly marked. Look for a roped-off section with a small sign stating that there are stone steps (really just a few stones) taking you down to a rocky shelf on the river's shoreline. Be careful here. If you've never spent time on shoreline rocks, you should know that they get slick, as slippery as ice, so tread carefully through any puddles on the rock shelf, in particular. It may require a big step to get out there. But it's a nice place to take a break and some photos. Just be careful.

From here, the Ice Age Trail continues south, following the river for a short distance before heading deeper into the woods and then popping out at CTH Z and, of course, continuing on for hundreds of more miles. But we decided to turn around here.

So backtrack along the river northward to the intersection with the South River Trail, just west of the bridge, turn right (south), and head deeper into the woods.

The trail will at first go deep into the woods away from the river, with a northern forest canopy overhead of the whites and brilliant greens of birch and maple trees in the summer and alive with color in the fall. Then there's the topography. Basically, you are rambling up and down a roller coaster of long, narrow glens. You realize that, instead of simply dipping down and going over the valley walls, the trail takes you along one ridge, across one end, and then back along the opposite ridge for a scenic tour of this ancient glacial landscape. Eventually, you will even pass a very old CCC stone shelter, looking like an ancient shack in the woods.

The trail will continue east and pop out at a parking lot. Turn left (northeast) and head through the lot all the way to the river and River Trail. You are now on the south side of the Dells—a bit harder

to see from here, but still audible. Turn right (east) and you will come to CTH Y again, this time on the south side of the bridge from where you crossed originally. Again, cross the road with care here.

Once across, you will find that the trail is wide and well established here as you head southeast along the south side of the river, making your way toward the dam. Once there, you will see that the Ice Age Trail heads right (south) on its long trek to the east. Turn left here and cross the bridge over the dam and you will return to your original starting point, just west of the beach and parking lot where you began.

Meadow Ridge Trail, Barkhausen Waterfowl Preserve

TOTAL DISTANCE: 3.1 miles

HIKING TIME: 1 hour, 15 minutes

DIFFICULTY: 1.5

VERTICAL RISE: Minimal

TRAILHEAD GPS COORDINATES:
44°35′54.06″ N, 88°2′16.76″ W

MAPS: USGS 7.5′ Green Bay West, Wisconsin; DeLorme Wisconsin Atlas & Gazetteer, p. 67 (D-8)

In an area most well-known as the home of the Green Bay Packers and as a deeply devoted industrial city, it may be easy to overlook the many environmental and natural areas Green Bay has to offer. But as with any major shoreline, wildlife abounds and relies on protected areas in order to survive and thrive. Included in this mix of natural areas around these parts is the nearly 1,000-acre Barkhausen Waterfowl preserve where wildlife exist in great abundance and variety.

Indeed, at the trailhead, a pamphlet entitled "Birds of Barkhausen" includes a checklist of much more than 300 bird species viewable here at some time during the year. From the common house sparrow to the common loon, the diversity is impressive. And while it marks the start of a wondrous 100-mile-long wetland, Barkhausen remains "Brown County's best-kept secret."

As commendable as the mission and success of Barkhausen are the more than 9 miles of skiing and hiking trails that allow visitors to explore the area. This hike takes you along the Meadow Ridge Trail, which starts at the Interpretive Center and winds its way past several ponds and prairies and into woods as it sweeps along the perimeter of the preserve. Its terrain is easy to hike, but the grass can be rather high. Fall hikes here are incredible, and the skiing is great for lovers of easy, flat terrain.

HOW TO GET THERE

From the south, take US 41 north from Green Bay to the Lineville Road exit. Head right (east) to Lakeview Drive (CTH J)—less than 1 mile after exiting—and take a left, heading north. The entrance to Barkhausen is 0.25 mile on the right.

From the west, take CTH M straight

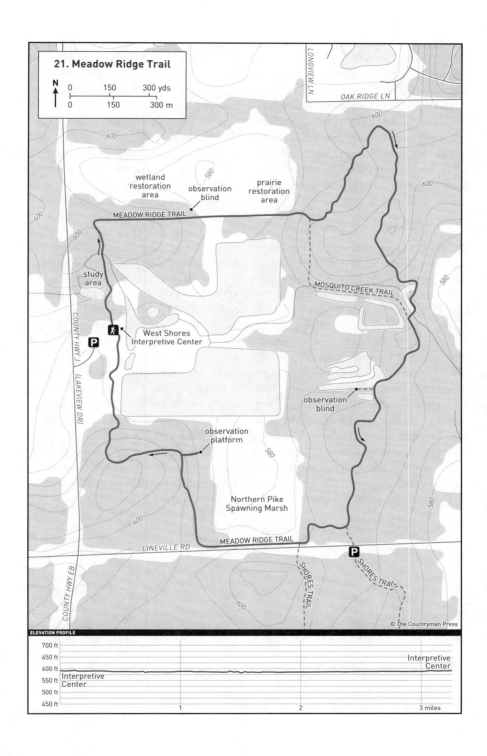

21. Meadow Ridge Trail

N
0   150   300 yds
0   150   300 m

LONGVIEW LN

OAK RIDGE LN

600

wetland restoration area

observation blind

prairie restoration area

600

MEADOW RIDGE TRAIL

600

580

600

study area

MOSQUITO CREEK TRAIL

580

West Shores Interpretive Center

COUNTY HWY J (LAKEVIEW DR)

P

observation blind

observation platform

580

Northern Pike Spawning Marsh

600

MEADOW RIDGE TRAIL

580

LINEVILLE RD

P

600

COUNTY HWY EB

SHORES TRAIL

SHORES TRAIL

600

© The Countryman Press

ELEVATION PROFILE

700 ft			
650 ft			Interpretive Center
600 ft			
550 ft	Interpretive		
500 ft	Center		
450 ft			
	1	2	3 miles

past US 41 to Lakeview Drive (CTH J), about 1 mile after passing US 41. Take a left, and the entrance to Barkhausen is 0.25 mile on the right.

From the north, take US 41 south to the Lineville Road (CTH M) exit. Head left (east) to Lakeview Drive (CTH J)—less than 1 mile after exiting—and take a left, heading north. The entrance to Barkhausen is 0.25 mile on the right.

THE TRAIL

The trail begins just west of the Interpretive Center and the trailhead is well marked with a large kiosk housing maps, bird guides, and a donation box. Head north, where you will pass between two ponds. Beside the pond on the left is a small study area for school groups and other educational programs. After passing the water, the trail—surrounded by several cottonwoods—will get pretty woodsy. After taking a turn to the east, you will emerge first next to a wetland restoration area and then into a sandier prairie area. There is an observation blind off to the left, perfect for bird viewing.

The trail continues straight along this route, with the trees on the right side of the trail and the prairie on the left. At the end of this stretch, the trail ducks back into thick woods, where you will leave the Mosquito Creek Trail and head left (northeast) while looping through the woods.

Eventually, you will emerge from the woods; the trail will open up into a sandy area and you will pass right beside yet another long pond, which almost looks like more of a creek. After crossing this, you will meet a trail off to the right, which leads to an impressive observation blind nestled right on the water.

Continue south on the trail toward CTH M. The Shores Trail will peel off to the left to cross the road, while you will continue right alongside it and past the Northern Pike Spawning Marsh, which is not quite visible through the thick grasses and tree line in the warmer months. But after turning north again, you'll reach another observation platform that provides great views of the large pond and the wetland to the east. The trail concludes by joining with and running alongside the park drive. Follow this straight north back to the trailhead and parking lot.

Tower Trail, Potawatomi State Park

TOTAL DISTANCE: 3.5 miles

HIKING TIME: 1 hour, 15 minutes

DIFFICULTY: 2.5

VERTICAL RISE: 130 feet

TRAILHEAD GPS COORDINATES:
44°52'34.13" N, 87°25'43.56" W

As the eastern terminus of the Ice Age Trail, Potawatomi offers excellent hiking through a variety of habitats and over varied terrain. The park—named after an early Native American culture whose name means "keeper of the fire"—is now a great recreational area in all seasons, visited by hikers and mountain bikers from spring to fall and by skiers in winter. And it's a very popular camping destination.

No matter the time of year, cars whisk past Potawatomi as vacationers blast their way across the Sturgeon Bay Bridge en route to the heart of Door County. But this park, nestled off the beaten path across from the city of Sturgeon Bay and right on the water, is certainly worthy of a visit—whether as a side trip or as a destination in its own right.

This hike, beginning on the Ice Age Trail and then joining the Tower Trail, takes you from the observation tower down toward the bay before winding back through the woods to the top of the old ski hill and back to the tower. Standing atop a 150-foot limestone bluff, the 75-foot tower offers an incredible bird's-eye view of the area. Much of Green Bay is visible to the west, as is the city of Sturgeon Bay to the north. It's even possible to see Lake Michigan, across the peninsula, to the east. In the winter, the ice covering Sawyer Harbor is peppered with ice-fishing shanties, and in the summer the water is full of passing boats and cargo ships.

This great hike offers a glimpse of Door County up close and up high. And if you are chipping away at the Ice Age Trail piece by piece, you'll certainly want to have hiked its eastern terminus.

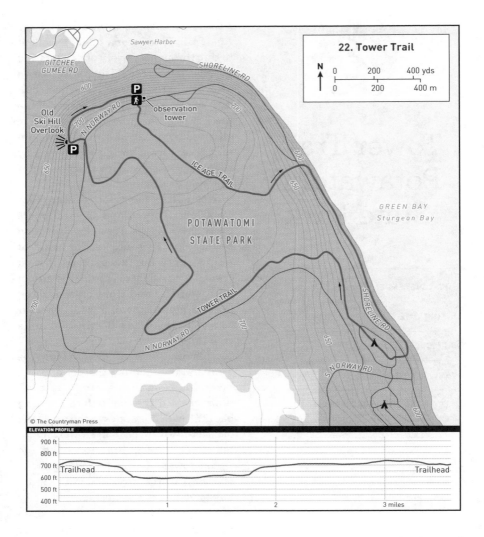

HOW TO GET THERE

From the north, take WI 42/57 south from Sturgeon Bay. About 3.5 miles after crossing the bridge, turn right (north) on CTH PD (Park Drive). Once on CTH PD, go about 2.5 miles to the park entrance on the right. It sneaks up quickly, and there are no signs aside from a small white board before the large entrance sign.

From the south, take WI 42/57 north. About 3.5 miles after the WI 42/57 junc-tion, turn left on CTH PD (Park Drive). Then follow the directions above.

THE TRAIL

Once in the park, wind your way past the campsites and up the hill to the lookout tower parking lot. This hike will go clock-wise, so use the trailhead just across the lot, past the rock and plaque marking the beginning of the Ice Age Trail. You will enter the woods quickly and begin to meander downhill toward the water. The trail winds between tall hardwoods in a forest with little undergrowth. There are some steep descents, so watch your footing and be careful in wet conditions. The trail will cross the road and emerge at the water. Several short offshoots allow you to access the rocky shore.

The trail then continues along the wooded shore, sheltered by cedars, before it turns right (west) and leaves the Ice Age Trail. After passing the road again, you will head back into the woods and begin an immediate climb back up toward the tower. The trail will cross a bike path four times as it, too, meanders through the same woods.

The trail will make a button-hook turn past a stand of pines and head more northward as it zigzags up toward the tower. The climb is relatively gradual, and you will also pass some very large white pines looming overhead in the shadows.

Toward the end of the hike, the trail will meet up with the road again. Although it looks as if you should cross the road now, turn right (north) and hike the trail alongside the road for a while until crossing it. Cross the road toward the mowed grass path that ducks into the woods on the other side. Off to the left are the old ski hill and a great view of the lake far below. A narrow trail leads you up to the tower, and just a short hike from here, you will pass through a wooded bluff and then up to the northwest side of the lot where you parked.

STURGEON BAY AT SUNSET

Whitefish Dunes State Park Loop

TOTAL DISTANCE: 2.8 miles

HIKING TIME: 1 hour, 15 minutes

DIFFICULTY: 1.5

VERTICAL RISE: Minimal

TRAILHEAD GPS COORDINATES:
44°55'37.46'' N, 87°10'57.38'' W

Among the most exceptionally rare habitats found near lakes are the shores themselves and their critically important sand dunes. These irreplaceable ecosystems support plant and animal life in unique diversity and abundance. So whether you're ambling along the sandy beach of Lake Michigan or hiking up "Old Baldy," a trip to Whitefish Dunes State Park offers a unique and varied hiking opportunity.

Like most of Wisconsin, the Door Peninsula was home to many early civilizations. In fact, while the beach at Whitefish Dunes may be peppered with sunbathers on a busy summer day, the crowd probably still pales in comparison to the congestion of early Native American cultures that called this area home for the summer. The plentiful fishing in both Lake Michigan and Clark Lake, along with abundant game for hunting and farming-friendly soil, created an ideal summer camp for those who lived here.

Today the residents of the park include a rich diversity of flowering plants, from wood anemone to wood betony. In the spring and fall, it is hard to hike without being distracted by a patch of milkweed, a harebell, or (if you're lucky) a dune thistle—all of which make for phenomenal photo opportunities, although they should never be disturbed.

This hike takes you past a re-created Native American camp, which offers a good look at what things may have been like several hundred years ago. The trail then takes a long ascent up into the dunes through a valley before turning west and taking you to the top of Old Baldy, the tallest dune at 90 feet above lake level. You then wind back through the flatter region of the park and into the woods before heading back to the

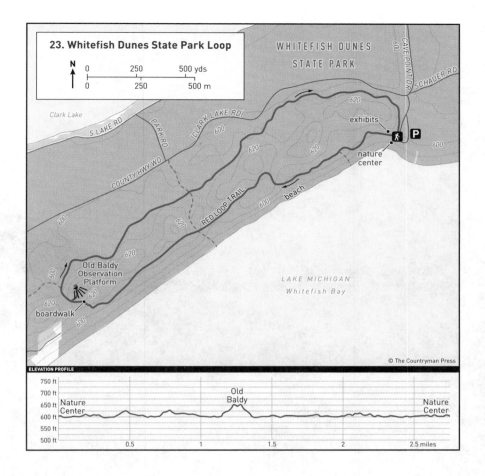

23. Whitefish Dunes State Park Loop

WHITEFISH DUNES STATE PARK

Clark Lake

exhibits

nature center

Old Baldy Observation Platform

boardwalk

RED LOOP TRAIL

beach

LAKE MICHIGAN
Whitefish Bay

© The Countryman Press

ELEVATION PROFILE

Nature Center — Old Baldy — Nature Center

trail's start. This is a great hike of minimal difficulty aside from the sometimes deep, sandy footing.

Some facts about visiting Whitefish Dunes should be kept in mind. This is an incredibly important ecosystem first and foremost; it doubles as a recreational area second. There are some priceless plant species located on the dunes that must not be disturbed. A second caution has to do with safety. Although there is a beautiful beach at the park, the coastline at Whitefish Dunes encourages rip currents that can pull a swimmer underwater and out to deeper depths. Unfortunately, swimmers have died here. Check

in with the park staff if you have any questions or concerns.

HOW TO GET THERE

From the south, take WI 57 north from Valmy about 1 mile to Clark Lake Road. Turn right and follow Clark Lake Road about 3.5 miles to the park entrance on the right. It's a quick turn into the park after a sign tells you to stay in the right lane.

From the south, take WI 57 south out of Jacksonport for 0.2 mile to Cave Point Road. Turn left on Cave Point Road and follow it for 3.2 miles to the park entrance on the left.

STORMY WEATHER PASSING THROUGH WHITEFISH BAY

THE TRAIL

This hike, the Red Loop Trail, begins just to the right of the nature center as you approach it from the parking lot. Head west, behind the center, starting a clockwise loop. Immediately to your right will be several interesting re-creations of early Native American settlements. The exhibitions are posted with informational signs. This is the only area like this on the hike, so it is worth taking some time here before moving on.

The trail, well marked with red blazes, then heads southwest up into the woods on a wide path. There is a gradual climb as you approach the beach access points, but the trail will then level off before making a long, easy descent. You'll pass the third beach access and a trail to the north; continue southwest to the turnoff for Old Baldy. This open area of the trail begins to offer good wildflower viewing in the spring and summer.

The turn to Old Baldy will take you up and down, and along several boardwalks, until you reach the main turnoff to the top of the dune—a short out-and-back trip that totals about 0.25 mile, all along wooden boardwalks. Don't miss the opportunity to see this side of the peninsula, and the lake, from such a high vantage point. While the western side of the peninsula has many dolomite cliffs and hills offering big views, this isn't true on the east. From the top of Old Baldy, you can see well out into the lake and north to the shoreline and bay at Jacksonport.

After heading back down to the main trail, you will turn northeast around the base of Old Baldy, where the trail will level off. The sandy prairie landscape at this point is very unique. It is full of bird life, and there are a variety of wildflowers in this area.

The trail continues through this prairie, with some very deep sand for footing, until it ducks into the woods. The trail gets a bit narrower, the footing gets more solid, and the air grows cooler in summer. Mixed hardwoods and some large pines greet you as you meander up and down rolling hills alongside CTH WD. You will eventually turn southeast, back toward the nature center, as you dip into a wet valley before emerging next to a fence leading back to the starting point.

24

Peninsula State Park Loop

TOTAL DISTANCE: 4.0 miles

HIKING TIME: 1 hour, 45 minutes

DIFFICULTY: 3.5

VERTICAL RISE: 180 feet

TRAILHEAD GPS COORDINATES:
45°9'46.01" N, 87°11'52.07" W

Peninsula State Park is one of the gems in the state's park and forest system. It holds the distinction of having the most campsites of any park in the system, and it features miles of hiking and biking trails (along with skiing and snowshoeing in the winter), a golf course, a beach, fishing, boating, and even a resident summer theater troupe called The Northern Lights Theater.

While the present is full of activity, so was this Green Bay peninsula's past. Formed by several advances and retreats of glaciers and ancient seas, the layers of exposed dolomite comprise the terraces of the shorelines and create microclimates and habitats for a diverse array of plants, animals, insects, and crustaceans. The same early Native Americans who settled near Sturgeon Bay and Potawatomi lived here as well. A camp at Nicolet Beach served as a base for fishing and hunting. And as the park guide notes, "The last hereditary chief of the Potawatomi nation, Simon Kahquados, was buried in Peninsula in 1931."

Since its establishment in 1909, the park has seen a constant stream of visitors and campers, and it has had a variety of uses. In the past it served as everything from a girls' camp to a World War I prisoner-of-war camp.

The trail detailed here, which we've nicknamed the Eagle Tower Loop, heads deep into the varied and old-growth woods of the park before descending down to the shore of Green Bay. It takes you along the limestone cliffs below the Eagle Tower before looping back up a serious climb to the tower parking lot. The hike is rather level and has stretches of easy hiking, but there are parts with loose, rugged rock and exposed roots—all of which is made even trickier if it's wet. It's not a hike for sandals and good boots are essential. A hiking stick

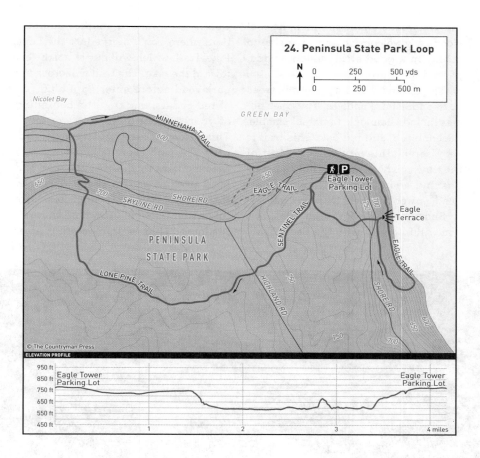

24. Peninsula State Park Loop

N

| 0 | 250 | 500 yds |
| 0 | 250 | 500 m |

Nicolet Bay

GREEN BAY

MINNEHAHA TRAIL

600

650

700

SKYLINE RD

SHORE RD

EAGLE TRAIL

Eagle Tower Parking Lot

Eagle Terrace

700

750

EAGLE TRAIL

PENINSULA STATE PARK

SENTINEL TRAIL

LONE PINE TRAIL

HIGHLAND RD

750

SHORE RD

650

700

© The Countryman Press

ELEVATION PROFILE

950 ft				
850 ft	Eagle Tower Parking Lot			Eagle Tower Parking Lot
750 ft				
650 ft				
550 ft				
450 ft	1	2	3	4 miles

will be of use, too, particularly for the last quarter of the hike, which includes climbing a 100-foot ascent in half a mile.

Note: The iconic Eagle Tower was closed in 2015 due to structural issues that were eventually determined to be non-repairable. The tower was deconstructed in the fall of 2016 and at that time the Friends of Peninsula State Park started a fundraising campaign to rebuild a viewing structure.

HOW TO GET THERE

From the south, take WI 42 north out of Fish Creek. (Don't take the main park entrance unless you're camping, or bumper-to-bumper traffic is your idea of summer vacation fun!) Head out of town on WI 42 for about 2.5 miles. The road will wind downhill to a northern entrance to the park, Shore Road, on the left—the sign will say PENINSULA STATE PARK GOLF COURSE. Take a left here and follow the road up to the Eagle Tower parking lot, about 1 mile after turning.

From the north, take WI 42 south out of Ephraim 3.5 miles to Shore Road. Take a right and follow the road about 1 mile to the Eagle Tower lot.

THE TRAIL

This clockwise loop starts on the Sentinel Trail just south of the Eagle Tower parking lot. At the trailhead kiosk, head into the woods. In the summer, the cool woods are welcoming as you're able to strike up a good stride along a wide, packed-dirt trail.

The diversity and ages of the trees in this forest are endless. The tree species include hemlock, tamarack, maple, beech, birch, and red oak. This trail is very serene in every season. Most of the time you hear nothing but squirrels dashing about, leaves shaking overhead, or woodpeckers tapping away.

Shortly after beginning the hike, you will intersect with the Eagle Trail.

Continue onward to another intersection, where you'll merge into the Lone Pine Trail, which will curve northwest toward the lake. The trail will cross the park road before entering a bluff full of red cedars, marking the beginning of your descent down to water level. This descent is steep and it can get slippery. The path eventually takes you to the next park road. Cross the road and head straight (north) alongside a road that leads through the campsites. Take this about 0.25 mile to where the trail resumes. This is immediately after

ROCKY TRAIL ALONG THE ROUTE TO EAGLE TERRACE

campsite number 842, and there is a sign marking the trail (the Minnehaha).

From here, you duck back into the woods on the Minnehaha Trail and head east alongside the waters of Green Bay on a packed dirt trail, with many exposed roots, bordered by cedars. On the left you will pass the rocky shores of Nicolet Bay, and on the right you will pass the group tent camping area. The trail narrows and becomes rocky and can be pretty slippery. The ascents are demanding, and the footing is very technical and challenging. It's along this stretch where the trail offers incredible views of the dolomite limestone cliffs, and you are truly hiking through some of the most incredible geological history in the state.

After passing a bench, veer left onto the Eagle Trail. Almost immediately, loose rocks—interspersed among tricky exposed roots—welcome you to this stretch of the trail. The first 0.25 mile is pretty level, with a few ups and downs. Soon you will pass the most dramatic cliffs and rock faces before entering again into the familiar cedar-lined trail resembling the Minnehaha. You will sweep below Eagle Terrace before making a turn right (south) and heading straight up the side of Eagle Bluff. While the trail will make a couple of switchbacks, you'll still be climbing a couple of hundred feet in less than 0.5 mile.

Eventually, you'll get to the last section of the ascent. It is more gradual and takes you northwestward, where you will pop out next to Eagle Terrace. Follow the trail to the terrace for a good water break, a rest stop, and the view. Directly behind you, you should see a series of stone steps leading up to a map kiosk and a park road. Take those steps and head straight past the kiosk, through a connector trail, across another park road, and back into the woods.

This small loop through the original woods makes for a great cooldown after the long ascent and will wind back to the original trail, the Sentinel, which you took from the parking lot. Upon merging with the Sentinel, take a right (north) and a short section of trail will take you back to your starting point.

Newport Loop, Newport State Park

TOTAL DISTANCE: 5.0 miles	

HIKING TIME: 1 hour, 45 minutes

DIFFICULTY: 2.5

VERTICAL RISE: Minimal

TRAILHEAD GPS COORDINATES:
45°14′5.79″ N, 86°59′19.88″ W

There exists, way out at the extent of the "thumb" that is the mitten shape of Wisconsin, a place of natural solitude offering a large quiet beach, hundreds of acres of quiet woods, and a swaying prairie.

Newport is distinctly serene, largely because it is the only formally designated wilderness park in the system. It offers more than 2,300 acres, 11 miles of Lake Michigan shoreline, and 30 miles of trails. The offerings at Newport include long loop trails suitable for hikers, mountain bikers, snowshoers, and skiers. And aside from its wonderful beach, the park is never overly crowded.

There are no drive-up campsites either, nor the commotion that comes with them. Instead, to reach Newport's sites you must pack everything in at least 1 mile via hiking trails that lead to quiet wooded campsites along the shores of Lake Michigan.

The park has commendably resisted pressure to become less pristine. Instead, on a sometimes-busy peninsula, Newport holds steady as a landmark to this unique and beautiful Wisconsin county.

This hike, the Newport Loop, takes you along the Lake Michigan shoreline, past Sand Cove and Duck Bay, as well deeper into the woods of the park along serene tree-lined trails and a blanket of woodland plants. The footing and trail conditions are generally very good, although there are roots and rocks that do make things a bit tricky at times.

HOW TO GET THERE

Take WI 42 out of Ellison Bay for 1.8 miles to CTH NP (Newport Drive). Turn right on CTH NP and follow it about 2 miles to the park entrance. Head past

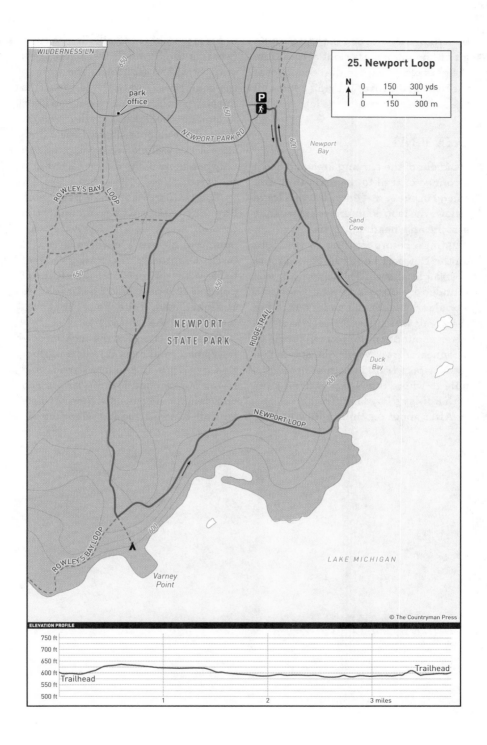

both the park office and the first parking lot on the immediate right across from the park office. Park in the second lot at the bend in the road. The trail begins off the southeast corner of the lot.

THE TRAIL

Head out of the parking area and down a connector trail to the main trail. You can go in either direction, but this route follows the loop counterclockwise. Take a right and head south for less than 0.25 mile before veering to the right on the Newport Loop (the return route is straight ahead). The wide trail, surrounded by birch and pine trees and woodland plants, meanders through the woods with little vertical rise or fall. After about 0.5 mile, you will come to a connector trail. Veer right, staying on the Newport Trail. Take this another 0.5 mile to where the Newport Trail joins with Rowley's Bay Loop Trail.

After about 0.5 mile, you will come to a merging of four trails. To the right (west) is the Rowley's Bay Loop Trail, straight ahead (south) is the trail to the campsites, and to the left (east) is the Newport Trail. Take a left and head alongside the lake, passing several more of the remote sites. These campsites are so secluded that you often can only see their paths disappearing into the woods.

The trail will continue past Duck Bay and Sand Cove, meandering through thick woods. Deer are very common, as are a diverse array of birds. Eventually, the trail will meet back with the original splitting-off point at Newport Bay. The beach lies straight ahead, while the parking area is just off to the left (west).

This hike is one of the most peaceful, remote, and relaxing hikes in Door County. While the county's roads and towns are clogged full of visitors and crowds in summer months, Newport State Park offers a welcome and serene retreat.

Fernwood Trail, Rock Island State Park

TOTAL DISTANCE: 3.5 miles

HIKING TIME: 1 hour, 30 minutes

DIFFICULTY: 2.0

VERTICAL RISE: Minimal

TRAILHEAD GPS COORDINATES:
45°24'34.10'' N, 86°49'46.36'' W

At the far northeastern tip of Wisconsin, there exists a 900-acre wooded island wilderness devoid of cars, roads, and even bikes. Is that enough to make you want to go? Not much more than about 1 square mile in size, Rock Island is actually covered in trails and is perfect for hiking—in addition to being a popular attraction for campers wishing to have a truly remote experience.

The island, undoubtedly as desirable historically for fishing, hunting, and shelter as it is today for tourism, was home to Native Americans long before European settlers saw its shores. The Potawatomi lived in small dwellings on the island and kept gardens in addition to gathering food. Excavations done in the 1960s and 1970s yielded tens of thousands of artifacts that have helped better understand the native people who inhabited this area. In addition to the Potawatomi, who were the main inhabitants, the Huron, Petun, and Ottawa cultures also called Rock Island home for short periods.

While no longer settled on the island, the Potawatomi were acknowledged when the first federally erected lighthouse in Wisconsin was built here in the early 1800s and named after them. Potawatomi Light still stands sentinel at the northwest corner of the island, above the dolomite cliffs and sandy shore. It's possible to tour the recently restored lighthouse during the summer months.

Perhaps the most noticeable structure on the island, however, greets you upon your arrival. As you step off the ferry you will find yourself at the dock of a massive stone boathouse, originally erected by Chester Thordarson, owner of the island between 1910 and 1945. While his plans for an island mansion

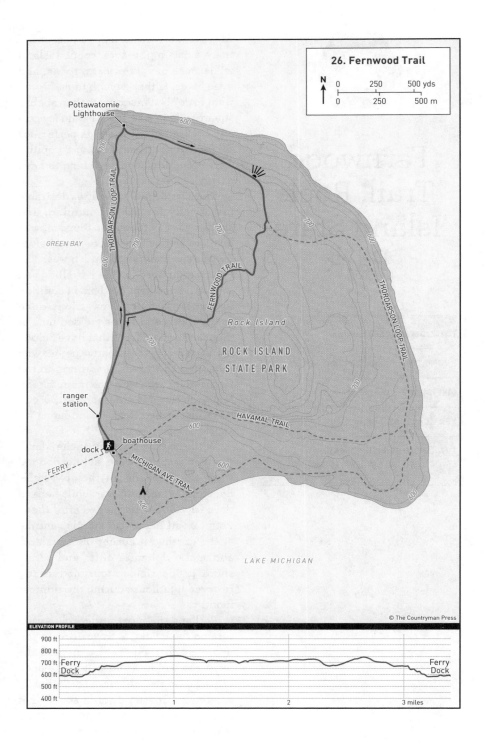

26. Fernwood Trail

N

| 0 | 250 | 500 yds |
| 0 | 250 | 500 m |

Pottawatomie Lighthouse

THORDARSON LOOP TRAIL

GREEN BAY

FERNWOOD TRAIL

Rock Island

ROCK ISLAND
STATE PARK

THORDARSON LOOP TRAIL

ranger station

boathouse

dock

FERRY

MICHIGAN AVE TRAIL

HAVAMAL TRAIL

LAKE MICHIGAN

© The Countryman Press

ELEVATION PROFILE

900 ft
800 ft
700 ft Ferry   Ferry
600 ft Dock   Dock
500 ft
400 ft
          1   2   3 miles

were never realized, he did manage to build this imposing boathouse. It served as home to his 11,000-book library and was the site of many summer parties.

Although the partying in the boathouse is a thing of the past, a trip to Rock Island is exceptionally enjoyable. It takes two ferries to reach the island from Gills Rock on the mainland, so if you're planning a day trip to Rock Island, you'll want to get there no later than noon, which means an even earlier ferry ride from the mainland to Washington Island. Check with both ferry companies before planning a visit to confirm times; be sure to build in at least a two-hour layover on Rock Island for hiking, exploring, and swimming at the beach. You can also camp on Rock Island. It might take some planning to get all of your gear over there, but it makes for a fun overnight excursion.

HOW TO GET THERE

First, take the Washington Island ferry from Gills Rock. Then, from the Washington Island ferry dock, follow Lob Dell Road/Detroit Harbor Road to Main Road for about 2 miles. Turn left on Main Road and follow it for 2.5 miles to Jackson Harbor Road. Turn right and take it for 3.5 miles to the Rock Island State Park parking lot. A 15-minute trip across the lake gets you to the island. All told, the trip can take one to two hours from Gills Rock.

For more information, contact Rock Island State Park at 920-847-2235 or find the park online (where you will also find ferry information to and from Rock Island). For ferry information to Washington Island, contact the Washington Island Ferry Line at 1-800-223-2094 or www.wisferry.com (this information, of course, is subject to change but a search

LOOKING THROUGH THE OLD WOODEN GATE ON THORDARSON LOOP TRAIL

HISTORIC STONE COTTAGE ON ROCK ISLAND

online should turn up the most up-to-date information). The bottom line is to plan for a day's worth of travel and visiting the island if you're coming from mainland Door County.

THE TRAIL

After hopping off the ferry at the boathouse, head north along the shore up toward the ranger's house (the small stone house atop the bluff to the left). The trail begins just to the right of the house and meanders up the hill toward the huge wood and stone gate, a relic from Thordarson's days. The majority of this hike follows the Thordarson Loop Trail, going clockwise around the northern tip of the island.

This western leg of the trail will take you uphill most of the way. During the gradual climb, the trail will converge with a service road from the right, and you will eventually pass the junction with the Fernwood Trail return route from the east, also on the right.

After a good, steady uphill climb, you will level off and eventually, about 1 mile into the hike, emerge at the Potawatomi Light. Until now, while the lake has been close by, it hasn't been very visible. This is a great opportunity to take a break, explore the lighthouse, and visit the beach down below.

After stopping, continue on the Thordarson Trail east out of the lighthouse area and uphill. Again, you will climb gradually as you wind eastward along the northern shoreline, the northeasternmost tip of the state. About halfway to the Fernwood Trail turnoff, you will come to a bench sitting high atop the northern shore and overlooking Lake Michigan and Saint Martin Island (Michigan) to the north. On a bright, sunny day, this opening makes for great viewing of the cobalt-blue water, bordered by emerald-green trees, and topped with pale blue sky.

From here, the trail rambles up and down before meeting with the Fernwood Trail turnoff to the right (southwest). Take this right-hand turn to loop back west to explore the center of the island. The trail will continue to climb very slightly, and soon you will find yourself immersed in the trail's namesake. Ferns blanket the ground of this cool, hardwood forest, making this remote hiking trail a serene trek.

Eventually, the trail will reach a high point on the island and begin meandering down toward the original intersection with the Thordarson Trail. At the junction, take a left (south) and head back toward the dock area, once more passing the junction with the access road on the left (but stay to the right). You will again pass the wooden gate and the ranger's house before arriving at the dock and the ferry trip back to Washington Island.

III.

SOUTHWEST

Perrot Ridge and Brady's Bluff, Perrot State Park

TOTAL DISTANCE: 3.0 miles

HIKING TIME: 1 hour, 30 minutes

DIFFICULTY: 4.0

VERTICAL RISE: 490 feet

TRAILHEAD GPS COORDINATES:
44°0'56.12'' N, 91°28'34.29'' W

The Mississippi River provides a lesson in geology unmatched in any textbook. Here you can actually hike on top of layer upon layer of dolomite and sandstone, the historical record of what happened here from the time of the ancient seas more than 600 million years ago to the second you put your foot on the trail.

This phenomenal natural area has been home to humans for thousands of years, including the first Native Americans, the French Voyageurs, the pioneer loggers, and now present-day anglers, hikers, canoeists, skiers, and campers. And the great thing about drastic elevation change is that it makes for great hiking.

This hike takes you up to both of Perrot's wonders—first Perrot Ridge at 1,153 feet, and then down a valley and back up again to Brady's Bluff at 1,166 feet. You will leave the parking lot, just a few feet above the river, and meander along the bank before beginning a long ascent en route to Perrot Ridge through a shaded coulee. Eventually, your scramble to the top of the ridge is rewarded with one of the most remarkable views in the entire state. You will not only see Minnesota across the wide Mississippi, but you will get a great view of where you're headed next—Brady's Bluff—to the west. Then you descend off the south face of Perrot Ridge, back into a deep valley, and begin a long climb up the north ridge of Brady's Bluff before a steep and long descent back to the river.

Note: If you're going to see a timber rattlesnake in Wisconsin, your odds are greatly increased by hiking at Perrot. They live in the rocky bluffs and, while extremely reclusive, they are seen somewhat regularly along the trails here. Check in with the park office for more information.

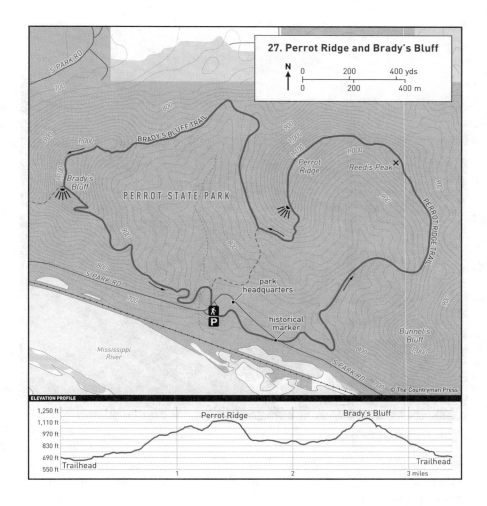

27. Perrot Ridge and Brady's Bluff

N

| 0 | 200 | 400 yds |
| 0 | 200 | 400 m |

S PARK RD

700

800

BRADY'S BLUFF TRAIL

900

1,000

1,100

Brady's
Bluff

PERROT STATE PARK

900

800

700

600

S PARK RD

Mississippi
River

park
headquarters

historical
marker

Perrot
Ridge

Reed's Peak ×

900

1,000

1,100

PERROT RIDGE TRAIL

900

800

Bunnel's
Bluff

1,000

600

S PARK RD

700

© The Countryman Press

ELEVATION PROFILE

| 1,250 ft |
| 1,110 ft |
| 970 ft |
| 830 ft |
| 690 ft |
| 550 ft |

Perrot Ridge

Brady's Bluff

Trailhead

Trailhead

1   2   3 miles

HOW TO GET THERE

From Trempealeau, take First Street west and go 1.5 miles to the park office. The parking lot/trailhead is just past the office, across the road on the left (south) side.

THE TRAIL

Take the Perrot Ridge Trail out of the southeast corner of the parking lot down toward the river. You'll immediately head into the woods and curve your way south toward the water. You'll soon emerge at the Perrot historical marker. Head diagonally (northeast) through this parking loop, across the park road, and up into the woods.

The trail will scamper down some stone risers into a little valley before the climbing starts. Huge, towering hardwoods loom overhead while a brilliant, emerald-green blanket of ferns covers the many little valleys as far as you can see in the warmer months. This area is pretty damp and cool in the summer, making it a bit cooler than the hot sun you'll experience on the ridge.

The trail continues upward until you

WINDING ALONG BRADY'S BLUFF

come to an intersection with a ski trail crossing. Stay "straight" (northwest) with the Perrot Ridge Trail. You will immediately make a rather rocky ascent toward a towering rocky bluff, Reed's Peak, but you will duck behind it on the north side, and the trail will level off and even descend a bit.

You will meander along the ridge on a narrow trail as you climb, more gradually now, toward the ridgetop. You don't really see it coming as you scramble up the rest of the way, since the ridge actually curves to the south like a boomerang. But you'll know when you're there. The river is now far, far below, and the view vast. A small bench at the tip of

the ridge is positioned to let you take it all in. It is one of those places that it is hard to believe exists in Wisconsin if you spend most of your time in the more easygoing, rolling areas of the state.

After a break, the descent lies ahead of you. Put your hiking cap back on, because things get tricky right away. The trail is rocky, sandy, and slippery, and it requires a lot of slow moving. A walking stick with a sharp point is useful, and you may need to incorporate a bit of sliding. This terrain doesn't last long, however, and soon you will be working your way steadily downhill. You will come to a long set of riser steps that make things easier, although they are sort of awkwardly spaced and a bit rough on rubbery legs—and can even be a bit slick from sand. In wet weather, they may be slick, too.

You will then merge with the cross-country skiing/mountain bike trail for a while. Take a right (southwest) onto this trail at the bottom of the steps. Eventually, this trail will peel off to the right (northwest), which is where you're headed (taking the trail to the left, or south, will bring you back to the parking lot).

The trail will transition into the woods and descend. Soon you will come to another intersection. Turn left (west) and immediately begin the ascent toward Brady's Bluff. The ascent is gradual at first, before giving way to a very steep and rocky incline with some tricky footing. This nice section of tough but rewarding trail leads you to the final stretch, curving south to the bluff. Soon you will turn out of the woods, make a final short ascent onto some sandy trail, and see an old stone shelter. You've arrived! The view is spectacular from here and this time you can see much farther in each direction—to Trempealeau Mountain across the valley to the west; to Winona, Minnesota, upriver to the northwest; and south downriver toward Trempealeau.

After a rest, you will begin the fun switchback descent off the front of Brady's Bluff, taking the trail to the east off the bluff, not the stairs to the west. The narrow, rocky trail will (heading west) first pass through some grass along this wide, exposed bluff before button-hooking back to the east and heading back into the woods. At one point, you will pass through a collection of old-growth oaks combined with shagbark hickories and cedars. The trail will eventually level off in a quiet valley just up from the park office and parking lot.

PERCHED ABOVE TREMPEALEAU BAY ON PERROT RIDGE

28

Bicentennial Trail, Hixon Forest

TOTAL DISTANCE: 3.7 miles

HIKING TIME: 1 hour, 45 minutes

DIFFICULTY: 3.5

VERTICAL RISE: 513 feet

TRAILHEAD GPS COORDINATES:
43°49'13.18'' N, 91°12'39.60'' W

If you live in Madison, you have the lakes and the trails around them. Milwaukeans have the River Greenway. Janesville has the longest urban section of Ice Age Trail in the state. The list goes on in terms of great natural escapes within urban settings in Wisconsin. A proud member of that group is La Crosse, where from downtown you can literally walk east on Main Street until it turns into, get this, Bliss Road, and hike up and into this city's urban escape, Hixon Forest, and its treetop companion, Grandad Bluff Park. A towering forested hillside, Hixon stands tall on the eastern edge of this great river city. And towering it is, with bluff tops that quietly stand watch more than 600 feet above the bustling city below.

The La Crosse Area Convention and Visitors Bureau writes that, in a cool partnership, the City of La Crosse has teamed up with the 7 Rivers Region Outdoor Recreation Alliance to build and maintain the trails at Hixon and to give an overall continuity to its trail development. This has produced the fairly new Vista Trail, which allows both hiking and mountain biking, along with three other trails exclusively for hiking. All told, there are nearly 10 miles of trails at Hixon; a visit in the fall of 2016 was accompanied by the chainsaws and brush clearing of a trail-building crew, so more trails seem to be on the way.

The trail highlighted here is the Bicentennial Trail, a 3.7-mile loop that begins with a steep, 1.25-mile-long ascent to a short spur trail and then a phenomenal overlook at 1180 feet, and then to two other overlooks, before a deep descent back to the trailhead.

Note: the kiosk and map call it 3.0 miles, but our GPS mapping shows it at about 3.7, so we're assuming that a former version of the hike was a bit shorter.

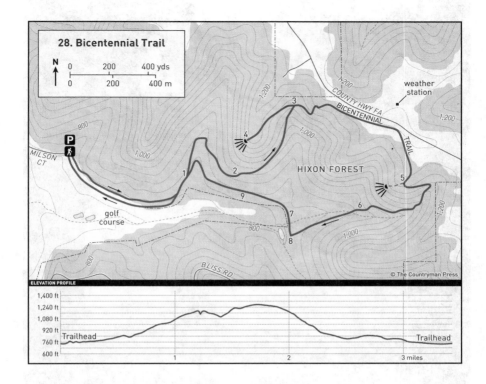

HOW TO GET THERE

Coming into La Crosse from US 90 on the north side of the city, take WI 16 south 4 miles, to a left on Bluff Pass.

Note: The traffic is heavy here at this curve, and this across-traffic left turn is tough. A better option is to go past Bluff Pass, stay on WI 16 for 0.25 mile, and then turn right, which leads into La Crosse Street. Then go almost one of these blocks and head back to Bluff Pass on the north side of WI 16, taking a right.

Either way, once you're on Bluff Pass, turn right on Milson Court and follow this around the corner into the parking area. The trailhead is on the right, or south, side of the lot. From the south, take WI 35 into La Crosse and turn right, east, on WI 16 (La Crosse Street). Follow this for about 1 mile, past the University of Wisconsin—La Crosse campus and take a left at the stoplight on WI 16. After 0.5 mile, take a right on Bluff Pass and follow the directions above.

THE TRAIL

The trail begins at a big trailhead kiosk with a huge map of the trails. For the most part, the trails are well marked; they even include numbered map posts for the first half of the hike (things get less reliable later on). There are also occasional posts with "Bicentennial Trail" signs on them.

You'll start by crossing a small wooden boardwalk. Then, into the woods you'll go: that's where you'll be for most of the hike. The trail is fairly level for the first 0.5 mile or so as you skirt the edge of the

OAKS ESCORT YOU TO THE OVERLOOK HIGH ABOVE THE MISSISSIPPI

bluff near the valley floor. There is a golf course on the right that's mostly hidden by large trees and is across a park road (which is actually your return route). Soon you will turn north and head deeper into the woods and go uphill a bit before doing a hairpin turn back southeast and downhill before leveling out. At map post #2, about 0.75 mile in, you will turn directly into the hillside and climb 200 feet in 0.25 mile.

After this climb, you will arrive at map post #3, where you will turn left and head southwest upward another 100 feet or so and then another 0.2 mile to the first, and best, overlook on the hike. A bench is located here for a great break on the edge of a great blufftop goat prairie. The trail continues a few more paces to a rocky ledge and an incredible view of La Crosse and the Mississippi River far below and La Crescent, Minnesota, and the western bluffs on the other side of the river.

After a break, retrace your steps downhill to map post #3, where you turned off, and head straight, southeast, to continue toward the east side of the forest. It seems like most hikers just go up and back so the trail will be more crowded with vegetation as you head this way, but this doesn't last. You'll actually dip down a bit and climb up before coming to another intersection. This trail intersection wasn't on any map as of fall 2016, and there was no map post. But, stay left and head east. You'll actually be near the road up here, CTH FA, but it's fairly quiet and sees limited travel.

Eventually, you'll emerge on the edge of the woods and see the National Oceanic and Atmospheric Association weather station radar sphere up ahead through the pines. Continue east and you'll pass another hilltop prairie and another great view to the southwest, this time just of the wooded valley and the Minnesota bluffs far off in the distance. You'll actually be near the apex of the hike at 1,236 feet; this is also where the second parking area and second trailhead is located.

The trail will duck back into the woods and head south on more of a narrow dirt and rock park access road. This will mark the beginning of a long descent back to the trailhead, and you'll soon pass a third vista. You'll also pass another trail that's not marked on any maps that heads northwest. Stay left though (looking downhill) and head east before coming to a buttonhook south and a steep downhill. The trail gets really rocky in this part, and a walking stick is really helpful—although that's optional for the college kids happily jogging past you.

You'll continue the long walk downhill, also passing a couple of single-track trails shooting off to both the north and south. One even has an old sign marking what must have once been an old route for the Bicentennial Trail. But stay on the access road and things will level out, as you take a long straight section to the tip of the golf course. A trail will head left (an access to the Oak Trail), but turn right, north, and follow the main trail back to the parking lot trailhead, about 0.7 mile from this right turn.

ENJOY A TREETOP REST ON THE BICENTENNIAL TRAIL

Jersey Valley County Park Loop, Vernon County

TOTAL DISTANCE: 3.1 miles

HIKING TIME: 1 hour, 30 minutes

DIFFICULTY: 2.5

VERTICAL RISE: 110 feet

TRAILHEAD GPS COORDINATES:
43°41'24.04'' N, 90°47'59.10'' W

As you roll down the coulees and climb the ridges along the roads of Vernon County, passing waving Amish farmers in horse-drawn buggies, life seems pretty darn simple. Particularly special is a little lake just outside of Westby with an excellent hiking trail looping around it. But it's not just this lake that is special, it is Vernon County's commitment to parks and forests that makes it stand out. Overall the county contains four parks encompassing nearly 1,000 acres, along with a 600-acre forest.

Indeed, this region is pretty hot these days on a few counts. It's the home of Organic Valley, the world's biggest farmer-owned organic cooperative. And then there's Viroqua, which has quietly become one of the country's most notable settling sites for likeminded folks committed to sustainability and connecting to the land. Known as the Driftless Area, the landscape is strikingly gorgeous. The moniker comes from the fact that the most recent glaciation spared this area, leaving it much hillier and rolling than areas of the state that were flattened by the glacier. Some of the best trout fishing in the country happens to be here, and the quiet, calm, artsy-craftsy mindset around here brings with it things like one of the best grocery cooperatives in the state, a wonderful bookstore complete with café, and a Waldorf School. But there's still a Dairy Queen and farm supply store. In fact, some of the most notable small-scale organic farms in the state are right here in the Driftless Area.

This hike takes you on a 3-mile tour around Jersey Valley Lake. While human-made, this lake doesn't look it. There is good marsh development, and the trees just seem to grow up out of the lake along the shoreline. Lakes

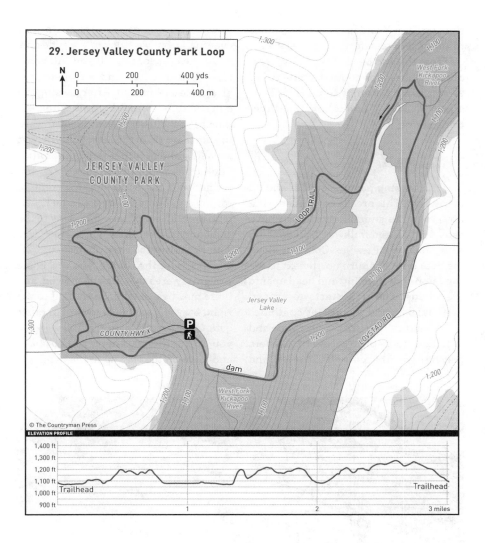

like Jersey Valley were made to control floods, a sometimes catastrophic problem in these tight valleys where water can build up an angry and devastating head of steam after big rains. These lakes give that water a place to go and a controlled way of corralling it.

After crossing the dam just past the parking lot, you'll head up the eastern slope of the lake on a heavily wooded hillside before descending to the northern tip of the lake and a wetland. From there, you'll button-hook back along the western shore and ascend to an overlook. You will then descend again to the boggy western tip before hiking through a pine plantation, across the park road, and down a steep ridge back to the parking area.

HOW TO GET THERE

From the west, take WI 27 north out of Westby for 2.5 miles to CTH X. Turn right on CTH X and follow it for 1.5 miles to where it enters Jersey Valley Park.

From the northeast, take WI 33 west out of Cashton for about 0.5 mile to WI 27 south. Go 4.1 miles to CTH X. Take a left on CTH X and follow the directions above.

THE TRAIL

Begin by hiking past the shelter and up to the dam. This area is covered in wildflowers in the summer. Look for phlox, aster, cattail, and milkweed, all dancing with monarch butterflies. Continue along the dam until you turn north next to the sandstone outcropping and head up into the woods. The trail starts to ascend very quickly, and the ascent continues for about 0.25 mile. The trail is wide and is actually more of an access road. There may be a trail that cuts off to the left, and

it works its way back to the main trail eventually, but we stuck to the wide one.

At the crest of the hill you will come to two farm gates and an open area alongside a farm field. After passing the gates and following the trail to the left (north) you will begin to descend toward the northern tip of the lake. You will pass a small stand of rather large pines after having seen mainly maple, oak, and walnut thus far. Soon you will come to the bottom of the valley and a lush wetland area. The trail may fork; stay to the right and go over the bridge, which was a bit rickety at the time of our visit.

Once over the bridge, you will come to a grassy area that may be mowed, and there may be a small loop trail off to the right. Stay left and head toward another gate. Once past the gate, the trail will take you up another ascent as you cut back and forth on the way up to the overlook.

JERSEY VALLEY ON A SUNNY FALL DAY

A TRANQUIL TRAIL ENCIRCLES THIS QUIET LAKE

The trail is narrower on this side and may be a bit more overgrown. The "overlook" is pretty much an overstatement unless you are here from fall to spring. Once the trees are leafed out, the valley is so overgrown that it is hard to oversee much. But the bench is a nice resting spot and is probably just past the halfway point.

From the overlook, you will turn away from the lake and head deeper into the woods before starting a pretty steep descent down toward the western tip of the lake, where you will emerge in an open wetland area. There may be a cutoff to the left, the Lower Lake Trail, but stay to the right and head uphill again. The trail will head straight west for a short time before making a buttonhook and coming back east, up along a ridge.

From here, the trail will make another turn west and then curve southward, taking you through a tranquil pine plantation, with soft needles underfoot; this area is very unlike the rest of the hike. Soon after, the trail will pop out at the road. Cross the road and head right, uphill on the side of the road, picking up the trail just on the other side of the park sign.

From here the trail will turn east and begin a long descent back to the lot. Be very careful here. The drop-off to the left (north) side of the trail is probably close to 100 feet and is just off the trail. Be extremely vigilant in this area, especially if you are with children.

Note: To avoid this part, simply turn left when you come out of the woods at the park road and head downhill alongside the road back to the parking lot. If you do continue on the trail, it will take you back to where you started at the parking lot, too.

Old Settler's Trail, Wildcat Mountain State Park

TOTAL DISTANCE: 2.5 miles

HIKING TIME: 1 hour, 15 minutes

DIFFICULTY: 3.0

VERTICAL RISE: 180 feet

TRAILHEAD GPS COORDINATES:
43°42′12.98″ N, 90°34′46.22″ W

Wisconsin is definitely known for its picturesque dairy farms and milk and cheese exports, but the state also just happens to be one of the largest producers of ginseng in the world. In fact, it was deep in the heart of the coulees and hills of the Kickapoo River Valley that ginseng grew in wild abundance throughout much of the 20th century. Thus, when Edna and Edward Lord showed up at Wildcat Mountain to escape lung problems in the city, ginseng turned out to be just what the doctor ordered. Eventually, the Lords and others started the Kickapoo Mountain Ginseng Company.

It's this sort of hunter-gatherer legacy of the Kickapoo Valley, as well as the fact that its rambling hills aren't necessarily ideal for farming, that make it perfect for outdoor recreation. Wildcat Mountain State Park, originally 60 acres, now covers more than 3,500 acres and offers miles of hiking and skiing—as well as access to one of the most popular and serene waterways for canoeing and kayaking in the Kickapoo River.

This hike starts at the north end of the Upper Picnic Area, just past the must-see Observation Point. The trail heads east and, after visiting the Taylor Hollow Lookout, it makes a steep descent down into the valley and meanders along several small coulees before looping around and heading back up to the picnic area.

HOW TO GET THERE

From the north and west, take WI 33 east out of Ontario for 3 miles to the park. Turn left onto the park entrance road and follow it past the park office to the north parking lot.

From the east, take WI 33 west from Hillsboro for 12.2 miles. Turn right at the park entrance road and follow the directions above.

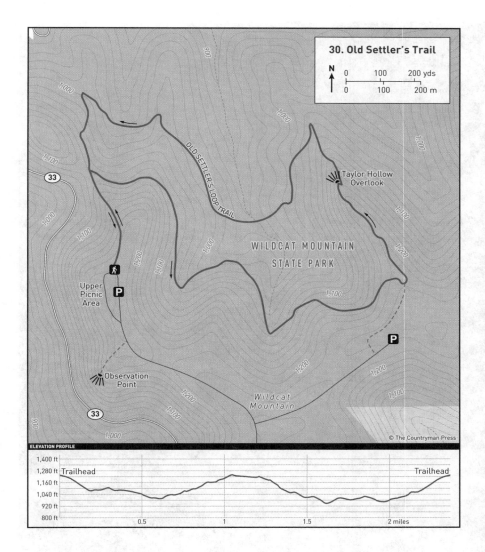

From the south, take WI 131 north out of La Farge about 10 miles to Ontario. Take WI 33 and follow the directions from the north and west above.

THE TRAIL

At the trailhead in the northwest corner of the Upper Picnic Area parking lot, head north on this connector trail. Soon, the trail will turn left and head down a long series of riser stairs, taking you deep into the valley on the north side of Wildcat Mountain and past rock outcroppings along the way.

You'll arrive at the intersection of the main Old Settlers Trail. Follow the arrow and turn right (east). Deep in the Wildcat Mountain valley, the trail will meander along the dense woods. You will pass over a bridge in an area that is bordered by ferns in the summer and is alive with color in the fall. Soon you will ascend up to the Taylor Hollow Lookout. After taking in

RUGGED RISERS LEAD DOWN TO THE OLD SETTLER'S TRAIL LOOP

the amazing view overlooking the Kickapoo Valley and the town of Ontario to the north, take the little trail heading steeply downhill southeast off the overlook. It will curve northward again and head down some riser steps into the valley.

You'll then pass a rock ledge and curve southwest, where you will be greeted by some old red pines as you descend even farther into the valley. The trail will continue back up alongside another ridge after you pass over a small footbridge. There is a rich diversity of trees, including maples, basswoods, hickories, oaks—

and even a large stand of Norway pines planted by a local school group.

The trail will turn south, away from the pines, and begin its long ascent to the ridge a couple of hundred feet above where you began. Eventually, you will come to the offshoot trail, leading back to the parking lot. Turn right, south, here and head back up the steep incline to the parking lot. And be sure to head over to the southwest corner of the parking area to the observation area there, which offers a sweeping view of the valley below Wildcat Mountain.

STONE TERRACE OVERLOOKING THE VERDANT KICKAPOO RIVER VALLEY

Wildcat Mound Loop, Black River State Forest

TOTAL DISTANCE: 4.0 miles

HIKING TIME: 1 hour, 30 minutes

DIFFICULTY: 2.5

VERTICAL RISE: 75 feet

TRAILHEAD GPS COORDINATES:
44°15'3.50" N, 90°35'53.00" W

Imagine a backcountry trail, deeply embedded under a canopy of hardwoods and conifers. Add some challenging and repetitive elevation changes, some high hilltop vistas, and a blanket of woodland plants flowering underfoot, and you've got Wildcat Mound in Black River State Forest. Unbelievably, this trail lies less than 5 miles from the busiest interstate highway in Wisconsin. But you'll be hard-pressed to hear a car or even encounter another person in the couple of hours you'll spend hiking the Wildcat Trail. And the treat of this hike comes atop Wildcat Mound, which is like looking out at the Blue Ridge Mountains from atop a North Carolina peak, with soft green valleys resting below curved hilltops.

To make matters even better for hiking, this area of the forest is dedicated solely to the silent sports. In very Midwestern-compromise fashion, the ATVs and snowmobiles have their own section. This area in particular is for Nordic skiers and hikers. And with a pass from the forest office, backcountry camping is allowed, as long as you set up camp off the trail 100 feet or more.

This hike takes you alongside the road northward before heading northwest and up into the sandy woods. You wind along a series of ups and downs before doing a button-hook turn and heading south, up to the first lookout, and then through a series of hills and valleys. The loop is about 4 miles, including hiking out to the overlook and back.

HOW TO GET THERE

From the north, west, or south, you will want to take I-90/94 to County Route O (CTH O) at Millston. Head east on CTH O less than 0.5 mile to North Settlement Road. (Signs for Black River State Forest

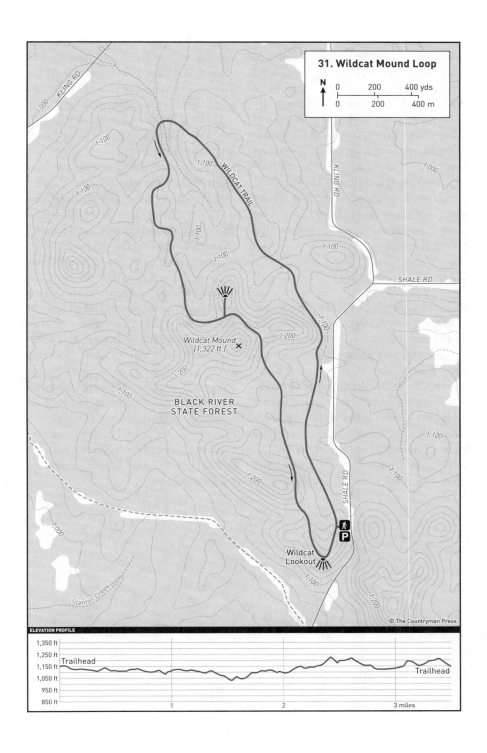

31. Wildcat Mound Loop

N

0	200	400 yds
0	200	400 m

KLING RD

WILDCAT TRAIL

KLING RD

SHALE RD

Wildcat Mound
(1,322 ft.)

BLACK RIVER
STATE FOREST

SHALE RD

Wildcat
Lookout

Stanton Creek

© The Countryman Press

ELEVATION PROFILE

1,350 ft		
1,250 ft		
1,150 ft	Trailhead	
1,050 ft		Trailhead
950 ft		
850 ft	1	2	3 miles

and Wildcat will be here as well.) Follow North Settlement Road for 3.3 miles to Shale Road. Take a left on Shale, and the trailhead will be after about 1.5 miles on the left. Park on either side of the road.

From the east, you are better off taking WI 21 or WI 54 to the I-90/94, and heading north or south as needed to the CTH O exit, and then following the directions above. The slippery gravel roads mentioned above can take a long time to drive, and they are pretty hard on your vehicle, so we suggest this option instead.

THE TRAIL

Head through the gate and up the access road until you reach the trailhead. At a fork in the trail, you will come to the first of the many map kiosks that make navigating here very easy. Turn right and head north. This is the opposite direction from the state forest map, which is the ski route, but a counterclockwise approach allows for a more gradual climb and offers a great overlook at the end of the hike.

As you approach the button-hook turn, the trail will be mostly rolling and you will find yourself traversing an old oak savannah. This opens up your view and makes it even easier to find that choice campsite in a clearing by a ridge. The turn southward is more gradual than it looks, but you will soon find yourself climbing your way up to the first overlook area.

It's often tempting to skip the overlooks, especially when they are on offshoot trails like this one, but this is worth it. The trail closes in to a single-track path and meanders among some big oaks toward the end of the ridge.

After visiting the overlook, head back to the main trail, turning left, south. You will be hiking alongside a large ridge as you begin the roller-coaster succession of hills and valleys on the way to Wildcat Lookout. You will pass the shortcut trail—designed to allow skiers the option of skipping the largest climbs—but you'll want to stay straight ahead and work your way up to the lookout. Shrouded in trees at first, you'll emerge from the valley to find both a great view awaiting you and a bench for a rest. The trip back to the road is a short one, and it's all downhill.

Roche-A-Cri State Park Loop

TOTAL DISTANCE: 3.7 miles

HIKING TIME: 2 hours

DIFFICULTY: 3.5

VERTICAL RISE: 330 feet

TRAILHEAD GPS COORDINATES: 44°0'4.66'' N, 89°48'45.22'' W

It may be hard to imagine, but much of the middle part of Wisconsin was submerged in a huge glacial lake about 15,000 years ago. Called Glacial Lake Wisconsin, it stretched from Wisconsin Rapids south to Baraboo and Roche-A-Cri Mound was essentially a rock island in the middle of the lake. Once the water subsided, the huge sandstone island was a several-hundred-foot-tall sandstone gumdrop resting in the middle of the rolling countryside.

Also noteworthy is the use of the mound by early Native American cultures living on the banks of Carter Creek as a 300-foot rock face to record their lives. While it is hard to know exactly how long ago the petroglyphs and pictographs were etched into and painted on Roche-A-Cri Mound, they are estimated to be as much as 1,000 years old. Demonstrating how important it has always been to humans to record their past and immortalize themselves, the rock also bears the names and dates—as far back as the 1800s—of early Wisconsin settlers and Civil War troops.

And it's easy to understand why people were excited to be in this area. The view of 10 surrounding counties from 300 feet above is exceptional, and the Top of the Mound Trail and Stairway escorts thousands of visitors atop Roche-A-Cri Mound annually. The climb is well worth it, especially on clear days. Crawling the steps to the top and emerging over the forested landscape below feels like poking through the clouds in an airplane. The view, which reaches more than 50 miles in every direction, is awesome.

The bulk of this 3.7-mile hike is flat and rolling. The toughest part is the hike to the top of the mound. But the view from the top is certainly worth the effort, and there are several places to rest on the way up.

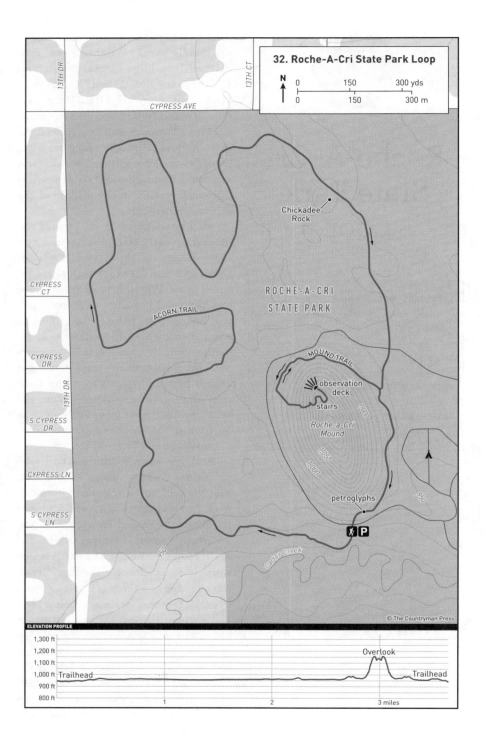

32. Roche-A-Cri State Park Loop

N

| 0 | 150 | 300 yds |
| 0 | 150 | 300 m |

13TH DR

13TH CT

CYPRESS AVE

Chickadee Rock

CYPRESS CT

ROCHE-A-CRI
STATE PARK

ACORN TRAIL

CYPRESS DR

13TH DR

MOUND TRAIL

S CYPRESS DR

observation deck

stairs

1,000

CYPRESS LN

Roche-a-Cri Mound

1,050

1,000

S CYPRESS LN

petroglyphs

950

950

Carter Creek

© The Countryman Press

ELEVATION PROFILE

1,300 ft			
1,200 ft			Overlook
1,100 ft			
1,000 ft	Trailhead		Trailhead
900 ft			
800 ft	1	2	3 miles

HIGH ATOP ROCHE-A-CRI MOUND

HOW TO GET THERE

From the north, take WI 13 out of Wisconsin Rapids for about 30.5 miles to the junction with WI 21. Continue on WI 13 south for 1.6 miles to the park entrance on the right. Go past the park office for 0.2 mile to the parking lot on the left, across from the petroglyphs.

From the west, take WI 21 east out of Necedah 13.5 miles to WI 13. Turn south on WI 13 and go 1.6 miles to the park entrance. Follow the directions above.

From the south, take WI 13 north out of Friendship 1.6 miles to the park entrance on the left. Turn left and follow the directions above.

From the east, take WI 21 west out of Coloma for 14.9 miles to WI 13. Turn left (south) on WI 13 and go 1.6 miles to the park entrance. Follow the directions above.

THE TRAIL

Head southwest out of the parking area and toward Carter Creek. At the creek, turn right, following the arrow pointing toward the kiosk. At the time we visited there weren't any signs for the Acorn Trail here, but this indeed

JUST 303 STEPS TO GET TO THE TOP!

is the beginning of it. Soon after this point you will pass an intersection with another trail from the left, but stay straight.

From here, the trail will begin its long ramble along mostly rolling terrain among oaks, pines, and maples. The trail is wide, flat, and a bit sandy, making it a great trail for Nordic skiing. There are many tree identification signs along the way, so if you're still working on the difference between a white and a black oak, you're in the right place. The park is full of both species, and the signs make identification easy.

The trail is very tranquil, and it takes you far away from any commotion at the campsites or the mound. Deep in the park, expect to see lots of birds and other wildlife. Don't be surprised to round a bend and find yourself sharing the trail with a deer.

Eventually, the trail will turn northward and pass through a pine plantation before turning east and then winding south toward the mound. Soon, you'll come to a fork, and the Chickadee Rock Nature Trail will split off to the right. Continue left (east) on the Acorn Trail. The trail will bend south and across the park road. Soon after the crossing, there will be an offshoot trail to the right to climb the mound. This out-and-back hike will take at least a half-hour to get to the top of the mound and back, and, after climbing 303 steps, you will be rewarded with arguably one of the best views in the state, making the trek absolutely worth it.

Once back down, join back up with the Acorn Trail where you left it and circle around the mound to see the petroglyphs and pictographs. There is an educational kiosk set up here to teach you about the etchings and pictures. After a visit here, head down the wooden ramp and back to your car in the lot across the road.

33

Mirror Lake State Park Loop

TOTAL DISTANCE: 3.5 miles

HIKING TIME: 1.25 hour

DIFFICULTY: 2.0

VERTICAL RISE: Minimal

TRAILHEAD GPS COORDINATES:
43°33'44.91'' N, 89°48'24.20'' W

Mirror Lake and its namesake state park are good examples of what brought people to this area for recreation in the first place. This region marks a transition to northern topography, where hiking means pine-needle beds and sand underfoot and sappy-smelling breezes in the air.

Because the lake is a designated no-wake zone, and the hikers and mountain bikers have their own separate trails, the hiking is very peaceful. And as is the case at many state parks, the hiking trails do not see nearly as much traffic as the other areas of the park. So, should you happen to find yourself in this neck of the woods looking for something more serene than much of the more-crowded Dells waterpark strip, this makes for a great escape.

This hike is a bowtie-shaped hike that combines the Northwest Trail and Newport Trail resulting in a 3.5-mile peaceful stroll through this great park. The hike takes you away from the commotion of the park's entrance and around a quiet wooded peninsula of hiking and skiing trails. The hike meanders along the shore of the lake before looping back through a warm, sandy prairie. Then, by turning left and adding the Newport loop, you hike along the eastern side of the lake and circle back through dense woods.

HOW TO GET THERE

From the north or northwest, take I-90/94 east to the Wisconsin Dells area. Take the US 12 exit and travel east on US 12 about 0.3 mile to Fern Dell Road. Turn right on Fern Dell Road and take it 1.5 miles to the park entrance on the right. Pass through the parking lot at the park office and at the stop sign turn left and follow the arrow for "Trail Parking." The bike/ski trail parking will be

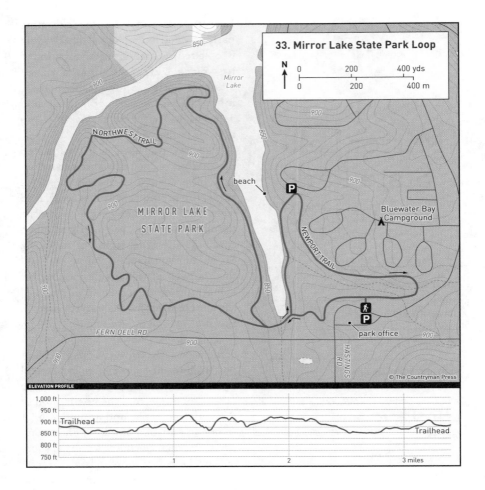

33. Mirror Lake State Park Loop

immediately on the right and the trailhead is located there.

From the east or southeast, take I-90/94 west to the US 12 exit. Take US 12 east and follow the directions above.

From the south, take US 12 west out of Baraboo for about 5.5 miles. Turn left on Fern Dell Road to the park entrance, which you will see after 1.5 miles, on the right.

THE TRAIL

There will be a kiosk marking the trailhead. Head into the woods and turn left,

following the arrow for the Newport Trail. The trail will bend around to the southwest and you will come to a trail intersection. Head straight and follow the purple Northwest Trail signs now as you pass by the southern tip of the lake and a marshy area. As you curve around the tip of the lake, stay right (north) on the Northwest Loop.

Immediately welcoming you will be huge Scotch pines along with some white pines, big white oaks, and towering cherry trees. The trail will pass directly across from the beach on the other side of the lake. You will turn to the left (west)

PASSING THE QUIET SOUTHERN FORK OF MIRROR LAKE

TRAVERSING THE TREE-LINED NEWPORT TRAIL

and dip down into a small valley and up the other side before curving north again and out into an opening with an old, overgrown stone foundation from an old house or barn. In the summer, the trail is bordered by spiderwort and other flowers taking advantage of the sun.

From here, the trail will buttonhook to the west and pass by a large opening in the woods. You will then climb out of this lowland, transitioning from dirt to a remnant of an old cement logging road. At the next trail junction stay to the right (southwest) and follow the trail on a long descent before winding back up southward, past a large rock outcropping and into a pine grove. The trail will then meander up and down and back and forth before emerging in a sandy prairie. There is a good wild-flower kiosk here, showing many of the flowers visible in the warmer months. From here, follow the connecting trail back past the southern tip of the lake and back to the Newport Trail, this time turning left, north, and continuing the original loop.

You will head along the eastern side of the lake and meander up and down a hill before arriving at the edge of a beach area. Follow the signs here to the right and then do a buttonhook east and then south back into the woods. This serene part of the hike passes by some big pines as you wind your way back to the original spur trail back to the parking lot. Turn left at the spur back up to the trailhead to complete this nice little hike at this great park on the doorstep to Wisconsin's Northwoods.

Devil's Lake, Ice Age Trail

TOTAL DISTANCE: 7.0 miles

HIKING TIME: 3 hours

DIFFICULTY: 5.0

VERTICAL RISE: 568 feet

TRAILHEAD GPS COORDINATES:
43°24'20.50'' N, 89°40'33.06'' W

Only 15,000 years ago, a great sheet of ice that once plugged both ends of the Devil's Lake Gap retreated, leaving behind a great glacial lake. At more than 40 feet deep, the lake is strikingly set apart by the 500-foot-tall surrounding bluffs. In fact, the elevation change is so dramatic here that there are different climates in different areas. In the cool, shady lowlands there exist several northern species of woodland flora, in contrast to the warmer, high elevations favored by dry-loving prairie plants.

The diversity of habitat includes 40 percent of the species of ferns and flowering plants found in Wisconsin, more than 100 species of birds, and several varieties of amphibians and reptiles—including the reclusive and poisonous timber rattlesnake (that's right, they're rare, but you'll still want to stay alert). Perhaps the most pervasive animals of note, however, are the human kind. The park's 400-plus campsites are almost always full on weekends during the summer and fall, and it is common to arrive at the turnoff to the main road only to see a PARKING LOT FULL sign posted, meaning hundreds of vehicles and thousands of visitors have arrived before you. In total, there are more than 1.5 million visitors annually, the most of any park or recreational area in the Wisconsin system. It is a number that seriously clogs certain hiking trails and oftentimes means that things get somewhat dangerous on those high bluffs, particularly for inexperienced and underprepared day hikers. Indeed, you may find yourself struggling past zigzagging lap dogs on long retractable leashes, large aimless groups, and exhausted once-a-year hikers who've simply had enough and literally plop down in the middle of a rocky trail with no shoulder for passing. Seriously, there are scenes on the

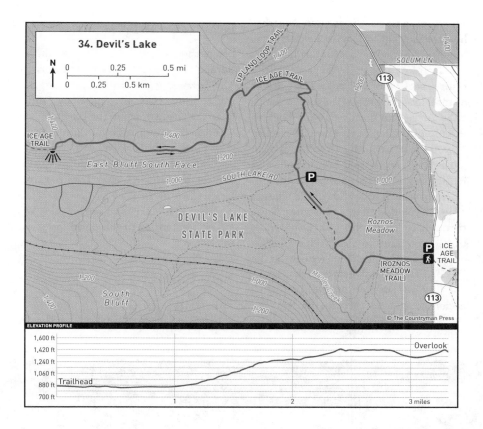

34. Devil's Lake

ELEVATION PROFILE

bluff-top trails here that resemble Black Friday at the mall. Sounds fun, eh?

Alas, the third edition of this guidebook brings with it a third attempt at hiking Devil's Lake, which both reduces the abovementioned congestion and dangers and still offers a great day hike. We believe we finally found it. Thanks, as usual, to the Ice Age Trail!

In the past we were lured into wanting to pass some of the major areas of interest in the park, but no more. The more you fall for that at Devil's Lake, the more you find yourself lured into a congested web of humanity reminiscent of a Niagara Falls overlook. To us, that's sightseeing. We were still looking for a quiet day hike at this Wisconsin geological treasure.

In this edition the hike is an out-and-back trip via the Ice Age Trail, starting from the actual valley where the glacier last sat and a trailhead on the far eastern edge of the park at Roznos Meadow. An expansive prairie with a little hilltop oak grove, the beginning of this trail offers a view and perspective from the ancient lake basin to the west that very few of those 1.5-million visitors ever see. From here, you'll head into the woods at the base of the East Bluff and steadily work your way up a nearly 600-foot ascent to the top of the south face via a steep stream coulee before eventually arriving at a quiet overlook of the valley below—a popular spot for mountain climbers but mostly off the radar of the mobs of tourists. Enjoy the view and a rest before turning back. What could be a jarring, dangerous, and somewhat disheartening trip to Devil's Lake is now, hopefully, a more peaceful day hike.

Also of note is that you can skip the prairie section of this hike and park at a small lot at the road crossing at South Lake Drive and do the out-and-back to the top of the bluff from here. By doing so, you shorten the hike from 7.0 miles to 5.0 miles. Also, there is hunting allowed in Roznos Meadow, although technically not within 100 yards of the Ice Age Trail. So you'll want to wear some orange through there in the fall. Otherwise, there is no hunting along the trail after crossing South Lake Drive (check out the Devil's Lake website—state parks always list this information on their websites under "activities and recreation"—or call the park office with any questions).

HOW TO GET THERE

From the north, take WI 113 out of Baraboo for about 6 miles to the Roznos Meadow Ice Age Trail parking on the right (about 0.25 mile past the South Lake Drive entrance to the park).

From the south, take WI 78 from Sauk City north 9 miles to WI 113. Turn left and take WI 78 north 2.5 miles to the Roznos Meadow Ice Age Trail parking lot on the left.

From the Merrimac Ferry, take WI 113 north 5 miles to the parking lot on the left.

THE TRAIL

The trail begins looking due west across Roznos Meadow at the lake basin

A VIEW DOWN THE ROZNOS MEADOW TRAIL TOWARDS DEVIL'S LAKE

straight ahead, the South Bluff to the left, and the south face of the East Bluff to the right like two great wooded wings floating up from the valley. Begin by heading into the meadow, an immense grassland prairie blanketed by bluestem. You'll see the small oak grove up ahead and you'll hike into it and duck up a small hill and turn southwest and up onto a sandy hill before hooking back to the northwest.

It is here, as you look toward the lake basin, that you're afforded one of the best views in the park. From here, continue northwest through the prairie, past an informational kiosk about the geology of the area, and then to the park road—South Lake Drive (the other small parking area is just to the right). Cross carefully and head into the woods now, on a single track. After passing a yellow blazed Ice Age Trail post and curving left, you'll begin the ascent.

The bluff side is full of hardwoods like hickories, oaks, cherries, and maples, and the canopy completely blocks out the sun. In the fall, the yellow leaves brighten the woods and the path is leaf covered. You'll bend to the north, head along the side of a small stream coulee, and actually cross the creek a couple of times during your long ascent up to bluff-top level.

After about 2.2 miles you will come to the intersection with the Upland Loop Trail and you will have actually covered much of your ascent by now, after having climbed more than 400 feet. Turn left here, southwest, joining the Upland Trail—a hiking and biking trail—for the last mile or so to the overlook. The trail is wider now, and you'll want to keep an eye out for bikes, although it's not necessarily a major thoroughfare.

You will eventually pass through two other trail intersections. Stay left, southwest, and continue to the overlook, all along the Ice Age Trail. In the absence of yellow blazes here, follow the telltale Ice Age Trail signs that are a rounded triangular shape and have a wooly mammoth on them.

Eventually making an abrupt turn south, the trail will go single track again, and a view up ahead will reveal the bluff edge and the South Bluff far off in the distance. It's a great place for a break, but be very careful near the bluff edges. People routinely fall at Devil's Lake and some are seriously injured or die. Enjoy the view from a few steps back and stay safe. If you're with children, keep them close. This is also a very popular place for rock climbers, so don't be surprised to see ropes that disappear off the face of the bluff. Obviously, don't throw anything off the bluff edge.

The great thing about using this as your destination and turnaround is that it's much less congested than the confluence of the trails a half mile west of here. After a break, turn around and retrace your steps back to the trailhead. And if you still want to visit the lake itself, there are beaches and picnic areas at both north and south shore visitor areas. But if you're looking for tranquility, you can simply quietly motor off down STH 113 once you're back at your car and head home.

Natural Bridge State Park Loop

TOTAL DISTANCE: 2.5 miles

HIKING TIME: 1 hour, 30 minutes

DIFFICULTY: 2.5

VERTICAL RISE: 320 feet

TRAILHEAD GPS COORDINATES:
43°20'41.77" N, 89°55'49.26" W

At the southwestern edge of the Baraboo Range—a 1.5-billion-year-old, 25-mile-long collection of several-hundred-foot-tall rocky bluffs and rolling hills—is Natural Bridge State Park and Natural Area. This whole region is not only geologically impressive, it's rather rare, with some of the oldest exposed rocks in the world. It's also where some of the most notable geological features of the entire range exist, including the expansive sandstone bridge at this quiet park that plays an important role despite being in the shadow of its bigger sibling state park, up the road at Devil's Lake.

The bridge itself is 25 feet wide and 35 feet tall and includes a 60-foot-wide and 30-foot-deep rock shelter underneath, making it not only a scenic place to visit today, but formally a protected home to humans. Indeed, archaeological work done here dates artifacts to 12,000 years ago. Also rather amazing are some of the animal remains found here, including those from elk, passenger pigeons, wolves, and mountain lions.

This 60-acre park is unstaffed, which gives it the feel of a quiet county park, and it's definitely worth a visit. And while it's most definitely overlooked for hiking—most visitors simply take the short trail directly to the bridge—the loop trail around the park is wonderful, with two climbs that combine for nearly 600 feet of elevation change and a great introduction to the upland woodlands that are protected here. The second climb takes you up to a south-facing bluff 250 feet above the trailhead and overlooks the verdant park valley below—a picturesque scene on a fall day. So, for a 2.5-mile hike this one not only feels longer, but it offers a great way to experience the rambling hilliness of the Baraboo Range and a close-up look at a rare and fascinating natural bridge.

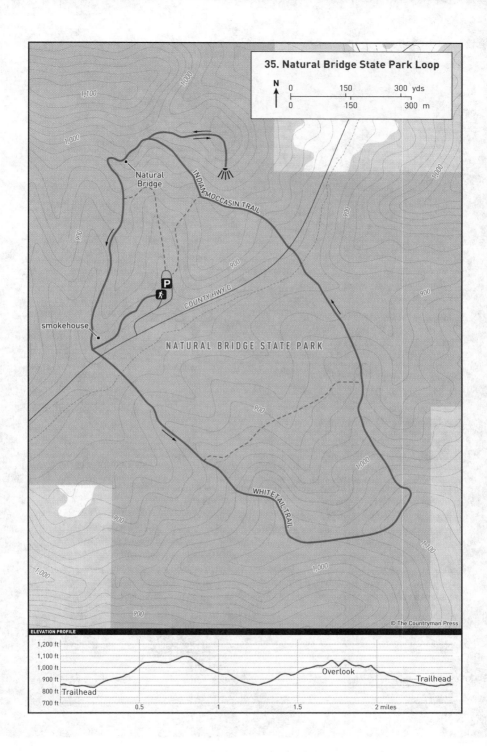

35. Natural Bridge State Park Loop

N

| 0 | 150 | 300 | yds |
| 0 | 150 | 300 | m |

1,100

1,000

Natural
Bridge

INDIAN MOCCASIN TRAIL

900

P

smokehouse

COUNTY HWY C

NATURAL BRIDGE STATE PARK

900

900

1,000

900

WHITETAIL TRAIL

1,100

1,000

1,000

900

© The Countryman Press

ELEVATION PROFILE

1,200 ft				
1,100 ft				
1,000 ft		Overlook	
900 ft				
800 ft Trailhead			Trailhead
700 ft	0.5	1	1.5	2 miles

THE BARABOO HILLS BLOSSOM WITH COLOR IN THE FALL

THE ROCKY AND REMARKABLE NATURAL BRIDGE

HOW TO GET THERE

From the east (including the northeast or southeast), take US 12 to CTH C about 8 miles south of Baraboo (or 8 miles north of Sauk City) and head west. Take CTH C 14 miles to the park entrance on the right (about 3 miles west of the town of Denzer).

From the west (including southwest or northwest), take WI 23 to CTH W, 9 miles north of the town of Plain. Head east on CTH W and it will turn into CTH D after 2.5 miles, staying east and then south. CTH D will merge with CTH PF. Stay straight, south, on CTH PF for 4 miles to CTH C. Turn left, northeast, on CTH C and go 1.4 miles to the park entrance on the left.

THE TRAIL

The trailhead is located at the southwest corner of the parking lot (not at the big map kiosk on the north end). The trail is actually kind of hard to see at first, but it is well defined once you walk down to that corner, essentially just across from where the last car could park in that corner of the lot. The hike is a combination of the longer Whitetail Hiking Trail loop, the Indian Moccasin Nature Trail, and an out-and-back to the overlook.

From the trailhead, head west onto a narrow, grassy path and into the wooded hillside. The trail will turn southwest in these woods, and you'll get a good view of the valley across CTH C to the south and the wooded hillside you're headed toward. Soon, you'll emerge at a trail intersection. Your return trail will come from the right, just next to the old stone smokehouse. Turn left though, and carefully cross the road.

The trail will cross an agricultural field briefly, which in fall offers bright hayfield greens and amber cornstalks, before heading back into the woods on this side of the road. And don't be fooled. While things have been fairly tame so far, you're about to climb. Indeed, this marks the beginning of a 300-foot ascent to the hilltop on this side of the road.

The trail is densely wooded with skyrocketing cherry trees—some of the biggest we've ever seen—as well as maples, hickories, and oaks. The trail is well established and is mostly single track. Not long after starting uphill you will come to a shortcut trail to the left, east. Stay straight and continue steeply uphill as you continue to climb along this long ridgeline. The trail is rocky with roots, and in the fall they're hard to see under the leaves. A walking stick is useful.

About 0.6 miles in, the trail will level out a bit and turn eastward before heading steeply up another ridge and eventually to the apex of the trail at about 1,150 feet elevation. The trail will turn to the northeast and begin the long, sometimes rocky, descent back toward the valley and road.

You'll emerge from the woods back into the farm field and cross the road at about 1.5 miles into the hike. Then you will head back into the woods and imme-diately resume climbing up this side of the valley. You'll pass a small prairie opening to the west of the trail and come to a trail intersection. This is coming from the parking area. Stay right and head northwest, ignoring what might look like the overlook trail offshoot to the right at 1.75 miles into the hike—this is a volunteer trail.

Keep heading northwest and you'll come to the back and topside of the natural bridge straight ahead. For now, turn right to take the trail to the overlook (there's no sign here saying that this is the overlook, but the turnoff is across from the split rail fence and right where the first of many informational kiosks on the overlook trail is posted). The trail will head southeast, continue climbing along a ridge, and then head up some riser stairs before leveling out and turning south to the overlook, which offers a great view from this Baraboo Range hilltop of the valley below and the hills to the south.

Turn back and retrace your steps to the turnoff, this time heading right, southwest, and you'll quickly emerge at the natural bridge, Wisconsin's largest such arch. The arch is actually pretty photogenic and there are some good angles for taking photos. There's also another informational kiosk here.

After a break, head down the riser steps and trail just right of the kiosk to the south. There will be another trail headed to the west, but ignore that. You'll pass two more trails, one to the right and another at a fork to the left (which heads immediately back to the parking lot), but stay straight and generally southwest and you'll continue to descend into the valley below, finally arriving at the old stone smokehouse. Take a left, and then head east on the spur trail back to the trailhead and parking lot.

36

Indian Lake County Park Loop, Dane County

TOTAL DISTANCE: 3.5 miles

HIKING TIME: 1 hour, 30 minutes

DIFFICULTY: 3.0

VERTICAL RISE: 200 feet

TRAILHEAD GPS COORDINATES:
43°11'22.04'' N, 89°37'16.47'' W

There are a few places near Madison that demand regular visits, particularly in the fall. With its rolling, tree-blanketed hills, a bucolic lake, and valley prairies, Indian Lake County Park is one of those places. And aside from birds singing, leaves rustling, snow crunching, or wind whispering, Indian Lake is a pretty quiet place. It is this serenity, and an abundance of excellent trails, that keeps regulars coming back. Oddly, though, this park is somewhat overlooked, especially considering it is reachable in minutes from Madison—perhaps a side effect of it being so close to Devil's Lake.

Like the venues of many hikes in this book, Indian Lake is also a remnant of the most recent Ice Age—both its water and its hills are the result. It isn't too far from here that the glacier stopped. So hiking these lushly wooded hillsides, amid picture-postcard Wisconsin farmland, is like hiking along the final scoopful of glacial terrain. In fact, some trails here—including this one—share their routes with the Ice Age Trail, which passes through from Table Bluff to the south and Lodi Marsh to the north. A few other notable aspects of Indian Lake are that there's a large dog park and a great sledding hill complete with a log cabin warming house at the top of the hill with a woodstove for all to use. There's also a tiny stone chapel built atop one of the hills here in 1857. Called St. Mary of the Oaks, it was built by a local man and his son in fulfillment of a vow he made after his family was spared from a diphtheria outbreak. To construct the chapel, they hauled several tons of stone to the hilltop, which also happens to offer the very best overlook in the park.

This hike follows the Red Trail and takes you deep into the heart of the hardwood forest and prairie on the park's longest trail before looping

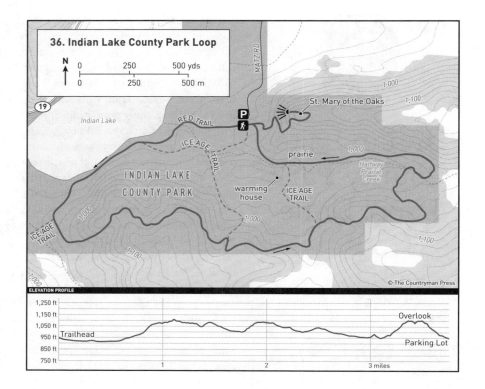

36. Indian Lake County Park Loop

ELEVATION PROFILE

back to the parking area 3.0 miles later (hiking up to and back from the chapel adds another 0.5 mile).

HOW TO GET THERE

From Madison, take US 12 west about 10 miles to WI 19. Take a left (west) on WI 19 and follow it to the park entrance, after about 2 miles on the left.

From the west, take US 14 east out of Mazomanie about 1 mile to WI 78. Take a left on WI 78 (north) to WI 19, about 1 mile. Take a right on WI 19 and follow it for about 8 miles to the park entrance on the right. (The first park entrance is the dog park and boat launch; take the second main entrance.)

From the north, take US 12 east out of Sauk City about 10 miles to WI 19. Turn right (west) on WI 19 and take it

for about 2 miles. The park entrance will be on the left.

For more information, contact Dane County Parks at 608-224-3730.

Note: If you're hiking with a dog, you need a county park dog tag.

THE TRAIL

The Red Loop trailhead is located at the south end of the main parking area. There may or may not be trail maps available, but there is usually a laminated map affixed to the kiosk. The trails themselves are well marked by both color-coded blazes and signs.

Follow the Red Trail right (west) out of the parking area. The trail itself is wide and is a Nordic ski trail in the winter, and so it makes for good side-by-side hiking with a companion. The rolling hike mean-

INDIAN LAKE IN EARLY FALL

ders through mixed hardwoods, with a stand of huge hickories and cottonwoods ushering you along the southern shore of Indian Lake. The trail passes a peaceful bench and overlook at one point before turning more southwest. The trail will lead you out of the woods and uphill into a grassy meadow (near the edge of the off-leash dog park area), following the path of the Ice Age Trail, which will veer off to the right (west) while you continue on the Red Loop south along the western edge of the prairie and through a valley.

The trail will take a dramatic turn east and head severely uphill from here. You will be faced with a very strenuous climb, difficult both for its vertical rise and its footing. The surface is basically a layer of

WOODEN RISERS LEAD UP TO ST. MARY OF THE OAKS CHAPEL

loose glacial litter ranging from golf-ball- to softball-size rocks, making the footing very tricky anytime but especially icy or slushy in late winter—a great candidate for hiking spikes.

Here the trail is heavily wooded again, and towering shagbark hickory and cherry trees that disappear above envelop you. Don't be at all surprised to flush a deer or flock of turkeys that have come to dine on fallen nuts in this woodland cafeteria.

Along this stretch your path will converge with the Green and Yellow loops. Just after joining the Yellow, the Red will turn off to the right (east) and make another uphill climb. You'll arrive high atop a ridge before beginning a long hike downhill into a deep valley on the eastern edge of the park. The trail will buttonhook to the west, taking you out of the woods.

The woodland landscape changes quickly as you turn west and pop out into an open prairie. In the summer, this area is covered in monarch-friendly milkweed, phlox, Queen Anne's lace, and yarrow. The trail will pass below the warming house log cabin and the base of the sledding hill. In the fall, the colorful trees blanket the edges of the amber prairie like a brilliant patchwork quilt.

After passing below the sledding hill, you will duck back into the woods once again. A short climb back into the open will bring you through a service road gate and back to the grassy picnic area next to the parking lot where you began. To add the climb to the chapel overlook, simply take the trail out of the parking lot to the east, up the wooden stairwells and boardwalks to the chapel 0.25 mile above.

Table Bluff, Ice Age Trail

TOTAL DISTANCE: 4.1 miles

HIKING TIME: 1 hour, 30 minutes

DIFFICULTY: 3.5

VERTICAL RISE: 100 feet

TRAILHEAD GPS COORDINATES:
43°8'38.46" N, 89°40'12.98" W

Certainly one of the best stretches of hiking in southern Wisconsin exists just west of Madison and northwest of Cross Plains. It is a part of the state's gem of a long-distance trail, the Ice Age Trail. Called the Table Bluff Segment (although Table Bluff itself is not yet annexed), this stretch of trail—out and back about 4 miles—takes you on a geological roller-coaster ride that includes multiple rigorous climbs and descents.

The hiking through the wooded areas of this trail easily rivals a hike along the Appalachian Trail. And if you're in training for a backpacking trip and you're within striking distance of this trail, welcome to your weekly practice facility.

What makes this trail great, however, is much, much more than simply its vertical rise. If you are at all interested in or appreciative of prairie restoration, you will be treated to one of the most magnificent prairies in the area. The list of species is endless and a midsummer hike is accompanied by a symphony of colors and textures, including the hard-to-find pale purple coneflower, rattlesnake master, compass plant, prairie smoke, and lots more. The woods are equally impressive, with oak groves dotting hilltops, along with shagbark hickories, maples, and basswoods, and woodland plants like may apples and spiderwort. And, of course, when we humans allow for and encourage restorations such as these, the wildlife will come. So birders will find a menagerie of birds ranging from herons in the wetland lowlands to pileated woodpeckers in the woodsy highlands.

Finally, it must be mentioned that while a large, 73-acre piece of this property is owned by the Ice Age Park and Trail Alliance (don't forget to become a member!), an even more substantial

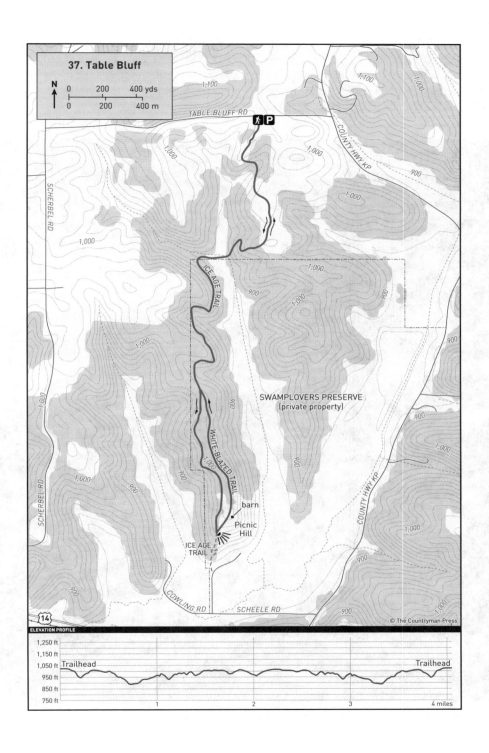

37. Table Bluff

N

0   200   400 yds
0   200   400 m

TABLE BLUFF RD

SCHERBEL RD

ICE AGE TRAIL

WHITE-BLAZED TRAIL

SWAMPLOVERS PRESERVE
(private property)

COUNTY HWY KP

barn

Picnic
Hill

ICE AGE
TRAIL

COWLING RD

SCHEELE RD

14

© The Countryman Press

ELEVATION PROFILE

1,250 ft
1,150 ft
1,050 ft   Trailhead   Trailhead
950 ft
850 ft
750 ft
                    1   2   3   4 miles

tract of this beautiful trail is owned by a private group known as Swamplovers, Inc., who have granted a permanent easement for the trail to pass through. This is a phenomenal testament to these very gracious landowners and stewards, who have done much not only to preserve this incredible landscape but also to share it with the public. Thank you, Swamplovers!

TABLE BLUFF IS BLANKETED IN BIG BLUESTEM'S COPPER WISPS ALL WINTER

HOW TO GET THERE

From the west or east, take US 14 to CTH KP, 0.5 mile west of Cross Plains. Head north approximately 2 miles and then left (west) on Table Bluff Road. The trailhead parking lot will be after 0.25 mile on the south side of the road. From the north or south, take WI 78 to head east on US 14, then follow same directions as above.

For more information, contact the Ice Age Trail Alliance at 1-800-227-0046 or find them online.

THE TRAIL

Starting at the main parking area on Table Bluff Road, the trail heads south into a mostly open prairie. You will meander eastward and head down your first descent past a small spring before buttonhooking back south and up to the property's north prairie. There will be an option to do a loop to the right (southwest), which is blazed with white blazes. We opted to stay left (southeast) and continue up into the incredible prairie. You will hook through the prairie, turning south, then westward, and finally into a hilltop colony of hardwoods.

In the woods, a long hillside switchback escorts you down into the main valley. A huge swath of marshland extends far to the south; you'll cross this opening and rejoin the woods on the other side of the valley and into the Swamplovers property. The change is seamless, with no change in trail quality whatsoever. The only issue of note here is that the agreement with Swamplovers stipulates that these landowners have permanent rights to use their land. This means that it is closed completely during the 10-day deer season in November and also that they have priority over hikers if they are using the trail for maintenance or recreation on their property. During dozens of visits, we've never had any

BREAKING TRAIL AFTER A FRESH WINTER BLANKETING

problems. In fact, we once stopped and chatted with a Swamplover who was hard at work cutting wood in a hickory grove and he was absolutely tickled that we enjoyed hiking there and graciously invited us to return frequently.

The trail through Swamplovers territory to the south crosses an impressive footbridge, which was constructed to traverse a washout area. These footbridges, by the way, are constructed by tireless volunteers of the Ice Age Trail Alliance, who make these trails possible. While this is a national trail, Congress simply establishes trails—it's up to the public to build them. So the human power and sweat equity comes from volunteers—and the great advocating force for building this wonderful 1,200-mile footpath in Wisconsin is the Ice Age Trail Alliance. Anyone can become a member and anyone can volunteer.

Up and down the trail goes through mixed hardwoods, and high points offer vistas of the valley below. Soon you will come to a fork in the trail—yellow blazes going straight/right (south) and white going left (east). They both end up in the same place. Going straight and following the yellow blazes toward the Goat Prairie on the south end of the property you'll arrive at one of the most striking views in southern Wisconsin.

At this point, the main (yellow blazed) trail will continue south and drop down to the valley below and to the southern parking area at Scheele Road (and you can do a down and up hike if you want). But to continue with the white blaze loop, this hike peels off to the left (east) toward the pole barn. There are some good little interpretive kiosks here, and it makes for a great place to take a break.

From the pole barn (looking north) you'll see white blazes along the logging road. This trail runs just east and parallel to the trail you came south on and back to that fork in the trail that allowed for this loop. Rejoin the main trail here and backtrack north along the trail you came on, all the way back to the parking lot.

Note: There is another option toward the end of the hike to turn left, but we prefer to backtrack through the steep switchback into the woods and up through that original Goat Prairie. It's up to you, though. The segment is dumbbell-shaped, so you can mix it up however you want and you'll always end up at the trailhead parking lot.

Blue Mound State Park Loop

TOTAL DISTANCE: 5.1 miles

HIKING TIME: 2 hours

DIFFICULTY: 3.5

VERTICAL RISE: 600 feet

TRAILHEAD GPS COORDINATES: 43°1'44.
92" N, 89°50'40.31" W

Looming high above its southwestern Wisconsin surroundings, Blue Mound is a geological monument. At just over 1,700 feet, it is the highest point in southern Wisconsin. And the park is complete with mature woodlands, prairie, highlands, cool valleys, sweeping vistas, dedicated mountain bike trails, hiking trails, a big open park space—once used for harness racing—on the mound's top, and a swimming pool (the only one in the Wisconsin State Park system).

The place is steeped in history. The mounds themselves—there are actually two, one in the park and one nearby within a small county park—are the result of a complex geological history. Essentially, the granite backbone of the mounds dates back more than 2 billion years. Over time, sediments of limestone and sandstone were left here by ancient seas, which came and went as the land here tilted back and forth. Much of this natural stone "capping" was washed away with ancient streams hundreds of millions of years ago, but the blue mounds were spared—and now the dolomite and shale remain, which you will hike over, through, and around during your rocky hike into the geologic past.

The route has been revised since the last edition of this book and the hike now starts at the swimming pool parking lot. This hike takes you on a comprehensive tour of the park, including a descent to the depths of the Weeping Rock Trail and all the way back up to the west observation tower. All told, it's a vertical drop—and subsequent ascent—of nearly 600 feet.

HOW TO GET THERE

From west or east, take US 18/151 to CTH F heading north. Turn left on CTH ID and take this into Blue Mounds. Turn right

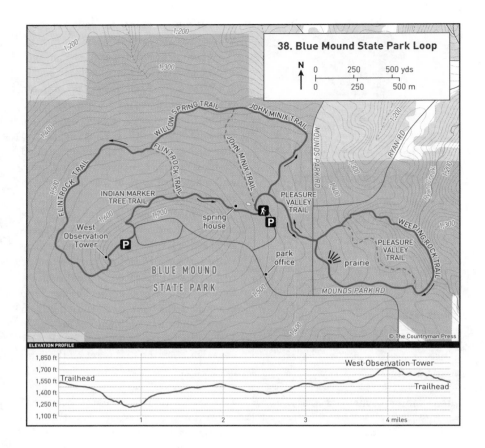

38. Blue Mound State Park Loop

ELEVATION PROFILE

on Mounds Road and take this about 0.5 mile to the park entrance straight ahead. After going through the entrance, take the first park road to the right, heading to the swimming pool lot. The trailhead is at the northwest corner of the lot.

From the south, take WI 78 to Mount Horeb and turn right on Main Street. Follow this route through town to the west. Main Street will turn into CTH ID as WI 78 leaves to the south. Stay straight and follow CTH ID to Blue Mounds, about 5 miles away. Turn right on Mounds Road and follow the directions above.

For more information, contact Blue Mound State Park at 608-437-5711 or look up the park online.

THE TRAIL

This hike is a big looping Figure-8 tour of Blue Mound that was concocted by looping together six trails—the Weeping Rock and Pleasure Valley trails in the lower eastern valley of the park with the John Minix, Willow Spring, Flint Rock, and Indian Marker Tree trails in the northern area. The hike starts at the big kiosk on the northwest corner of the parking lot near the Friends Shelter—look for the big hard-to-miss sign that says "Hiking Trailhead."

Head off past the kiosk up the black-top service road to the first trail intersection up ahead. Turn right onto the grassy trail and follow the signs for the

Pleasure Valley Trail to the right and downhill to the southeast, passing a mountain bike trail intersection and then crossing Mounds Park Road. Once across the road, go left on the Pleasure Valley Route and, soon after, take the Weeping Rock Trail into the woods to the left.

This is perhaps one of the most peaceful and quiet places in all of southern Wisconsin, and definitely at Blue Mound State Park. The trail will crisscross the creek several times via some fun and rather massive timber bridges (be careful if they're slick from moss or moisture).

Eventually, you'll enter a small prairie deep in the valley before the trail sends you clambering up a steep and rocky ascent for a test of the lungs before emerging back atop the valley and the edge of a prairie. Follow the Pleasure Valley Trail to the left and past a great hilltop prairie, erupting with color in the summer. At the top of the prairie, you're treated to a great view overlooking the rolling hills to the northeast.

At Mounds Park Road, turn left, west, and then back up the way you came originally. At the first main intersection, turn right and follow the John Minix/Willow Spring trail to the northeast. Eventually, you'll come to another intersection of trails, where the John Minix will head left back to the parking lot. Take the middle option and follow the Willow Springs/Flintrock/Ridgeview trail sign. The trail will arrive at another intersection, staying right to continue on the Flintrock Trail, which will take you on a long, gradual swoop around the western edge of the mound. After about a mile you will arrive at an intersection with a small sign that says "Picnic Area, .2 Mile." Take this trail that ducks up into the woods for another taxing climb up a rocky single-track trail that turns into a thigh-burning series of riser steps.

You'll emerge at the West Observation Tower, offering sweeping views to the west. After a visit, continue to the east. The trail is rather undefined in this mowed parklike area, but you'll see a blacktop trail headed east away from the tower. Head in that direction, hugging the woods on your left (the north side). You'll pass a drinking fountain and a small parking pull-off. Look for an offshoot trail to the left that can sneak up quickly, called the "Indian Marker Tree Trail." Head down this trail for some of the best hiking in the park—a geological roller coaster complete with huge boulders and rocky switchbacks.

You'll eventually pop out at the spring house, where you'll do a jog right and then left—just a few paces each—and head downhill to that blacktopped access road where you originally started 5 miles earlier.

Note: In the winter, many of this hike's trails become groomed cross-country ski trails. There are hiking and snowshoeing trails that are used all winter. Just ask at the park office for a winter trail map when you show up, and you'll be able to easily piece together a hike with spikes or snowshoes.

39

Pine Cliff Trail, Governor Dodge State Park

TOTAL DISTANCE: 5.5 miles

HIKING TIME: 2 hours

DIFFICULTY: 3.5

VERTICAL RISE: 190 feet

TRAILHEAD GPS COORDINATES:
43°0'40.06" N, 90°7'21.12" W

Governor Dodge State Park and the surrounding area holds the historical distinction of being the site of a lot of firsts. Some of the first early nomadic cultures moved here to enjoy the protection found in the fortress of limestone bluffs protruding through the earth and serving as brick walls. These cultures and later camps of Fox, Sauk, and Winnebago Native Americans used the area as a summer home.

Later came early European settlers, interested in mining the easy-to-find lead ore. It was these settlers who earned the nickname "Badgers," for their hard work, tenacity, and drive to go into damp, dark crevices in search of ore. Immigrants from Cornwall, England were particularly prominent in the area, and they are to thank for the Cornish pasty—a savory handheld meat and potato pie they would take into the mines—found in many regional bakeries today. A remarkable Cornish settlement, called Pendarvis, is preserved in nearby Mineral Point, a historic mining town now abuzz as a vibrant enclave of artisans and crafters.

This area is also the heart of modern-day Wisconsin. In fact, the first capitol—of the Wisconsin Territory, not the state—was in Belmont, 20 miles southwest of here. And the territory's first governor just happens to have been General Henry Dodge (1786–1867). Dodge was instrumental in establishing peace among the Native Americans, longtime residents, and incoming settlers in the area.

In terms of natural history, the park is particularly unique and important. The area was spared the advance of four large glaciers, which accounts for the still-preserved, 450-million-year-old sandstone bluffs you will hike past, as well as the only self-supporting stand of

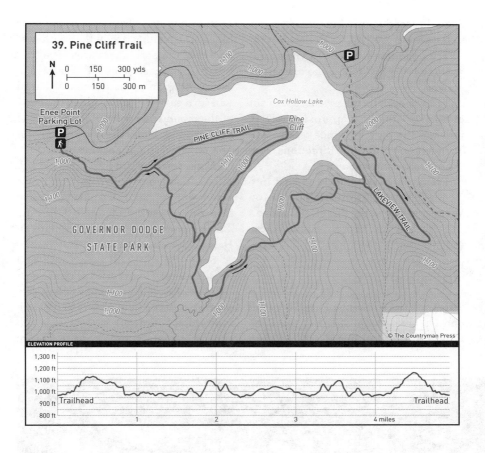

39. Pine Cliff Trail

N

| 0 | 150 | 300 yds |
| 0 | 150 | 300 m |

Cox Hollow Lake

Enee Point
Parking Lot

PINE CLIFF TRAIL

Pine
Cliff

LAKEVIEW TRAIL

GOVERNOR DODGE
STATE PARK

© The Countryman Press

ELEVATION PROFILE

1,300 ft
1,200 ft
1,100 ft
1,000 ft
900 ft
800 ft

Trailhead

Trailhead

1   2   3   4 miles

old-growth pines in southern Wisconsin. On this hike—the Pine Cliff Trail and the Lakeview Loop—you will pass gigantic space-needle specimens of white pines as you skirt the edge of a row of towering bluffs. With pine straw underfoot, ferns blanketing the understory, and the lake lapping the shoreline nearby, it feels as though you're in the middle of a northern Wisconsin wilderness.

Without question, this is a somewhat difficult trail, but it's not overly long. There are knee-bending sections that take you over rock and up, down, and through all sorts of terrain, and parts of it can be a bit overgrown in summer. But it's worth it. It takes you away from the crowded beach areas and into the quiet, limestone-shrouded valleys of this great park. Do note that the Pine Cliff part of the trail can be dangerous, with a lot of offshoot trails leading to the cliff edge. Stay back and keep children close by as you pass this section of the hike.

HOW TO GET THERE

From the east, follow US 18/151 south to Dodgeville. Take US 18 west (exit 47) toward Dodgeville and follow it for 1.7 miles to the intersection with WI 23. Turn right (north) on WI 23 and go 3.1 miles to the park entrance on the right. Turn right and follow the park road past the visitors center, turning right and following the road toward Cox Hollow

Lake. Proceed approximately 2.7 miles to the parking lot at Cox Hollow Beach.

From the south, take WI 23 north out of Dodgeville and follow the directions above.

From the north, take WI 23 south out of Spring Green for approximately 12 miles to the park entrance on the left. Turn left and follow the directions from the visitors center above.

From the west, take US 18 east into Dodgeville to WI 23. Turn left (north) on WI 23 and follow the directions above.

For more information, contact Governor Dodge State Park at 608-935-2315.

THE TRAIL

This trail, the combined Pine Cliff Trail and Lakeview loop, starts at the Enee Point parking lot, just down the road to the right after driving past the park office. The trailhead is in the southwest corner of the parking lot area. The trail begins by crossing a small footbridge over a creek and past a bench. The trail will turn east and follow along the edge of the creek and head uphill slightly as you meander along the edge of the first of many towering limestone bluffs.

Note: You may run into some old signage announcing the "White Oak Trail," which was the name of a past version of this trail—these days it's called the Pine Cliff on park maps but signs remain on the trail here and there.

Soon the trail will turn south and head up a very long series of riser steps that take you high up along a deep gorge to the top of the bluff above. You pass a footbridge boardwalk at the top as you turn east again and go over this large

PINE CLIFF POINT HIGH ABOVE COX HOLLOW LAKE (STAY BACK FROM CLIFF EDGES AND KEEP KIDS CLOSE!)

GOV. DODGE MICROCLIMATE MEANS NORTHERN-TYPE PINE FOREST IN SOUTHERN WISCONSIN

washout. The trail will climb slightly as you trek along this bluff and single-track trail. Soon there will be an offshoot trail to the right (south)—continue straight; the offshoot will be the trail you return on.

The trail continues along the bluff and then descends to the point of Pine Cliff. There are several volunteer trails that head out to the cliff, but the park is quick to note that the staff does not maintain these trails and hiking them is at your own risk. This is a rock cliff more than 100 feet above the lake, which is a really wonderful view, but also dangerous. Be very careful. If you stray off the trail you can happen upon a towering rock face with no guardrails really

fast. Falls are very possible, but also very easily preventable if you stay on the main trail. And so if you do bring children with you, keep them very close.

Leaving this point, veer off to the east and continue downhill as the already single-track trail closes in even more and the vegetation creeps onto the trail. There's definitely a need for a bit of bushwhacking in midsummer along here. The trail will skirt the edge of Cox Hollow Lake very closely and you can get a good look at the bluffs on the other side of this little bay—where you're headed next. The trail will climb again and head into the woods before popping out at a grass-covered access lane (not really shown on the park map).

Turn left here. You will emerge out of the woods into an open marsh and prairie, blanketed by a sea of the light purple joe-pye weed in the summer along with prairie coneflower and goldenrod. You do share a short section of this wide trail with a horse trail, so you'll want to be alert for passing horses—although you only share for 100 yards or so.

Soon you will leave this wide park lane, turning left, and heading back into the woods onto single-track trail along the edge of the lake again. You will slip between a towering limestone bluff next to you and a valley blanketed with ferns before crossing a small footbridge over a creek and buttonhooking to the northwest. The trail will start climbing markedly as you come up to a long, pointed cliff towering far above this south side of the lake. Again, there are volunteer offshoot trails here, and there are long drop-offs here as well—so be careful.

From here, the trail continues southeast and meanders through a beautiful section of trail past perhaps the most striking pines yet and next to yet another towering limestone bluff. The trail will pass around a quiet bay of the lake and come to the junction of the Lakeview Trail. Stay left and do the loop clockwise, passing along the edge of the lake on this eastern shore. Soon you will come to where the Pine Cliff continues on to the dam—turn right and stay on the Lakeview loop, which heads uphill to the southeast. You will emerge on the edge of a large prairie before descending to the south into a deep, quiet valley—and then turning back to the original turnoff from the Pine Cliff to the Lakeview.

Turn left at this intersection to backtrack the Pine Cliff Trail, following the same route. The only difference on the return route will be that after rejoining and leaving the horse trail at the southwest corner of the lake you round the bend to the northwest. This time, pass the single-track trail that you took from Pine Cliff and continue up the park access lane a few more paces. Take the offshoot trail to the right (east) here that will take you along this western route and back to the main trail, where you will veer left (west), take the long descent along the riser steps, and then head back to the trailhead parking lot.

Sentinel Ridge Trail, Wyalusing State Park

TOTAL DISTANCE: 5.0 miles

HIKING TIME: 2 hours, 45 minutes

DIFFICULTY: 4.5

VERTICAL RISE: 260 feet

TRAILHEAD GPS COORDINATES:
42°58'40.28'' N, 91°6'49.96'' W

When it comes to Wisconsin hiking, there are a few places you absolutely must visit and a few trails that you must hike at least once if you are able. Wyalusing is one of those places, and the Sentinel Ridge is one of those hikes.

It's all about the geology and hydrology at the confluence of the Mississippi and Wisconsin rivers, and the topographical result of what happens, over millions of years, when mighty rivers chisel the ground through which they flow. It is almost unfathomable to consider, for instance, as you stand perched 500 feet above the Mississippi on this hike, that the water used to be up here... way up here. Just under your boots. And as you descend deep down the Sentinel Ridge Trail toward the river below, the rock layers you descend into are actually taking you farther and farther back in time.

Wyalusing is a Native American word that means "home of the warrior." And, in fact, should you attempt this hike on a hot summer day, you'll undoubtedly feel like you are in engaged in a bit of a battle. It's a tough hike, due mostly to tricky footing and wild elevation changes—at least by Wisconsin standards. It's not just a single descent-ascent hike. The main descent along the Sentinel Ridge Trail is actually accompanied by a few ascents, before finally heading down rather quickly. Then, to top this hike off in lollypop fashion, it's best to add the Sugar Maple Nature Trail loop and a visit to Pictured Rock Cave.

It is a lot of up and down, and after any sort of rain, it is also slippery. But it is also one of the most remarkable hikes in this book and offers some of the most exceptional vistas along some of the most impressive trail. After doing the Sugar Maple Loop and going back up the Sentinel Ridge, you really get a

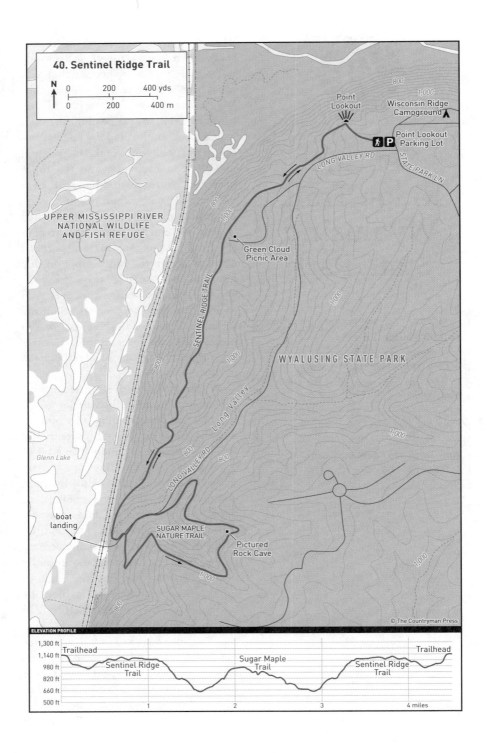

40. Sentinel Ridge Trail

N

| 0 | 200 | 400 yds |
| 0 | 200 | 400 m |

Point
Lookout

Wisconsin Ridge
Campground

Point Lookout
Parking Lot

LONG VALLEY RD

STATE PARK LN

UPPER MISSISSIPPI RIVER
NATIONAL WILDLIFE
AND FISH REFUGE

Green Cloud
Picnic Area

SENTINEL RIDGE TRAIL

Long Valley

WYALUSING STATE PARK

LONG VALLEY RD

Glenn Lake

boat
landing

SUGAR MAPLE
NATURE TRAIL

Pictured
Rock Cave

© The Countryman Press

ELEVATION PROFILE

1,300 ft	Trailhead				Trailhead
1,140 ft					
980 ft	Sentinel Ridge Trail	Sugar Maple Trail		Sentinel Ridge Trail	
820 ft					
660 ft					
500 ft		1	2	3	4 miles

sincere appreciation for this land and what it must have been like for Native Americans and early European settlers to clamber around this place, despite not having high-tech hiking gear and a reliable cache of drinking water. We joked at one point that this hike literally feels like you're hiking uphill both ways. The final stretch of trail is a steep ascent to the trailhead at Point Lookout.

This is definitely one of the top five hikes in terms of difficulty in this book. The midpoint reward is a visit to Pictured Rock Cave, which feels cooler in the summer than the rest of the hike and occasionally has a small waterfall trickling over its edge, particularly after large rains.

HOW TO GET THERE

From the east, take US 18 west to just outside of Prairie du Chien. Take a left (west) on CTH C. Follow CTH C about 3 miles to CTH X. Take a right on CTH X, and the park entrance will be after less than 1 mile on the right.

From the north, take WI 35 south through Prairie du Chien to the junction with US 18. Take US 18 east out of town to CTH C. Take a right on CTH C and follow the directions above.

From the south, take CTH X out of Bagley about 6 miles to the park entrance on your left.

For more information, contact Wyalusing State Park at 608-996-2261.

THE TRAIL

The trail featured here is a combination of the Sentinel Ridge Trail and the Sugar Maple Loop, with the trailhead at Point Lookout on the north edge of the park. Use the parking lot on the left, just past

TIMBER RISERS TAKE YOU UP AND DOWN SENTINEL RIDGE

the left turn for Long Valley Road, off the main State Park Lane as your starting point (this is also the parking lot for Point Lookout). There will not be any water at all on this hike, and the hike may take upward of three hours. You are mostly under tree canopy for most of the hike, although you will be exposed to the sun for a small portion.

Beginning at Point Lookout, you will head west and down quickly into the dense woods, high over the Wisconsin River. The trail is well established and wider than not, but you want to watch your footing. You will turn a bit southwestward and begin a long ascent through some mixed hardwoods and past some large pines. The ascent will take you through the edge of the Green Cloud Picnic Area (the park map shows you going below it on the western edge, but you actually share the parking lot road for a bit) until you get to the

PICTURED ROCK CAVE AFTER A SUMMER THUNDERSTORM

Passenger Pigeon Monument and the Indian mounds.

Soon after passing the mounds, the trail will transition to being more single-track and will start to wind downward. Continuing down the trail becomes much more solitary and technical—with rocks dotting the trail at times, large rock steps, and (if it's wet) slippery mud. You will come to a sliver of the ridge where it narrows to being just a few feet wide and the trail cuts right through the middle. It's at this point where there's a several-hundred-foot drop on the river side—so definitely be alert here. Soon you will come to a long stairwell that will take you quickly down, closer to the river level below. You will meet up with the ridge again, now lower and much more meandering. Eventually, you will pop out at the park road.

To the right will be the boat landing and dock. You will turn left and hike along the road for a few paces and cross, where you will access the Sugar Maple Loop on the south side of the road. Take the spur from the road up to where the loop goes either left or right. It seemed more natural to head straight and right (south), so we did the loop counterclockwise.

Heading south, the trail will switchback a couple of times before heading up a long, steep, straight ascent on a trail that now is more reminiscent of a logging road. You will eventually come to your offshoot to the left, which will take you east and then north toward Pictured Rock Cave. The cave spur trail, which was unmarked at our visit, is rather obvious. There are wooden railings taking you down the short descent into the cave. Once inside, you are treated to a significant drop in temperature on a hot day. It won't seem so at first, but get farther in and things cool off fast. This makes for a great place for a break before heading onward. This is probably a little more than halfway on this 5-mile hike.

Head back up the spur trail to the main Sugar Maple Loop and turn left (northeast); it will switch back to the west, taking you above the cave and over the small stream that trickles over its edge, particularly after a rainfall. You will meander along this nice stretch of trail in the woods, taking a switchback down to where you made the original split. Turn right (north) and head back to and then across the park road and back north up the Sentinel Ridge Trail and back to the trailhead.

Yellowstone Lake State Park Loop

TOTAL DISTANCE: 4.4 miles

HIKING TIME: 1 hour, 30 minutes

DIFFICULTY: 3.0

VERTICAL RISE: 140 feet

TRAILHEAD GPS COORDINATES: 42°46'9.74'' N, 89°58'18.87'' W

Known as the Driftless Area, southwest Wisconsin didn't receive the enormous amounts of meltwater that formed the lakes of the glaciated parts of the state. Instead, 455-acre Yellowstone Lake was constructed in 1949 and today, after winding down into the Yellowstone River Valley, you are greeted by a wooded lakeshore surrounding a glassy body of water. The scene is more reminiscent of the Northwoods than of southern Wisconsin farm country.

Also unique are some of Yellowstone's summer residents. The 968-acre park is blessed by a uniquely high concentration of bats. As the result of a project started in 1995, several bat houses serve as the summer residences for more than 4,000 brown bats that call the park home and seek to decimate the park's population of mosquitoes.

Since Yellowstone is such a popular park for water recreation, the many very good hiking and biking trails here get relatively less attention. Thus Yellowstone Lake State Park makes a great destination for a day's worth of hiking, skiing, swimming, fishing, or for a weekend camping trip, particularly in an area of the state that really is not known for its lakes.

This hike is a counterclockwise loop that is a combination of the outer parts of three of the park's trails: the Oak Grove, the Windy Ridge, and the Savannah.

HOW TO GET THERE

From Madison (and most points north, northwest, and east), take US 18/151 past Verona and toward Mount Horeb—about 25 miles or a half hour. Take the WI 78 exit and turn left, heading south toward Blanchardville, about 17 miles. In Blanchardville take a right on CTH F

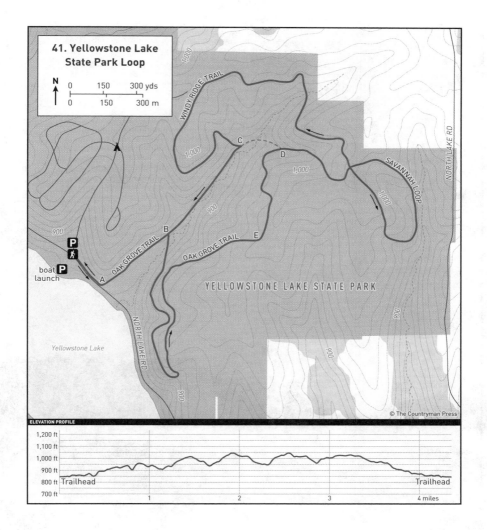

41. Yellowstone Lake
State Park Loop

(don't take the first one, wait until you've gone through downtown). After about 8 miles you will begin a marked descent. Be ready for the turnoff to Yellowstone Lake, on the left toward the bottom of the hill. Take a left onto Lake Road or look for the large park sign. Overall it's about 45 miles from Madison and takes 55 to 60 minutes at a relaxed pace.

From the south or southeast, take WI 69 or WI 81 to Monroe, following WI 81

northwest toward Argyle. From Argyle, take CTH G about 8 miles to CTH F. Take a right on CTH F, and the park entrance will lie about 2 miles ahead on the right.

From the west, or from Dubuque, take US 151 to Belmont. Take CTH G east out of Belmont about 19 miles to CTH F. Take a left on CTH F, and the park entrance is after about 2 miles on the right.

A SIGN OF AUTUMN: ASTERS ON THE SHORELINE OF YELLOWSTONE LAKE

For more information, contact Yellowstone Lake State Park at 608-523-4427.

THE TRAIL

Follow Lake Road past the park office to the large parking lot near the beach and boat launch. This hike takes you along a combination of the Oak Grove, Windy Ridge, and Savannah loops in an overall counterclockwise direction. Stationed at every trail intersection are easy-to-find and easy-to-read map kiosks.

From the parking area, cross the street and hike south alongside Lake Road. The start of the Oak Grove Trail will be on the left side of the road, about 100 yards from the lot. On the map, this is where the trail bends away from the lake at Point A (on the park map). After this, you're done with roads and you're off. Follow this trail to the first kiosk, Point B, and turn right (south), heading up a very steep 0.25-mile ascent, which offers a nice warm-up. As you crest the steepest part and get closer to the hairpin turn, some gnarly, old-growth burr oaks welcome you. Don't be surprised to find wild turkeys munching on acorns under these woody giants.

The trail will continue along the side of this large ridge. At the top, a good view of the lake offers a nice break before heading on. You'll pass a trail connector with the Blue Ridge Trail; stay left and continue on the Oak Grove Trail. You'll make a descent into a valley with a mixture of old-growth oaks, along with a stand of towering white pines. At Point D, hang a right and head between them onto the Windy Ridge Trail and up a challenging, sun-exposed hill.

The trail will turn left (north) and come to a turnoff for the Savannah Loop. Turn right (southeast) and head, counterclockwise, around this hilltop of tall prairie grasses. Return to the Windy Ridge and turn right (northwest), where a big oak welcomes you back to the woods and offers a nice spot to take a rest.

While the woods provide some good shade for a few steps, you'll emerge from them to look down at a long descent out into open prairie. In the spring and summer, this area is covered on both sides by a galaxy of shooting stars. Continue around the valley to the other side and into the woods. You'll come to a merging of trails, take a left (south), and head down a long descent to Point C. Take a right at the bottom of the hill and head into a cool, marshy valley, with limestone outcroppings covered in trees that seemingly defy gravity by balancing on the rock. Continue past Point B and head straight back to where you started at the park road.

Havenridge Trail, New Glarus Woods State Park

TOTAL DISTANCE: 5.8 miles

HIKING TIME: 1 hour, 30 minutes

DIFFICULTY: 3.5

VERTICAL RISE: 234 feet

TRAILHEAD GPS COORDINATES:
42°47'13.27" N, 89°37'50.86" W

The picturesque New Glarus region is exceptionally important from a geological and human settlement history perspective. The topography is hilly as a result of being spared from the most recent glacier, which barely made it this far, leaving untouched the rambling hills and valleys common in the southwest part of the state. Thanks to this topographical happenstance, it is also where abundant wildlife abound and thus where Native Americans also settled. The hilltop ridges encouraged these early inhabitants to create trails for hunting and defense against enemies.

One ridgeline trail became what would be considered a highway today, eventually becoming the "Old Lead Road," which European settlers used to haul lead ore via oxcart. The road became a thoroughfare of western settlement, connecting the Mississippi River to Lake Michigan.

History eventually turned ugly when European settlers clashed with Native Americans in the Blackhawk War, and again the trail was utilized to move troops and supplies. Today, while it may seem a bit odd to have a county road (which you will cross during the hike) running somewhat inconveniently directly through a state park, this road is actually the modern-day incarnation of that historic and important trail.

And so a lot has happened on this wooded hilltop of southern Wisconsin. Only the wise, old oaks, some more than 250 years old, have seen the most recent of it. But to hike this trail, and wind your way past the prairies and through the woods, is to know this place and this state a bit better.

This hike is the combination of two of the park's loop trails and a connecting trail: the Havenridge Nature Trail loop, the Vista Trail connector, and the Bison Nature Trail loop, for a total of 5.8 miles.

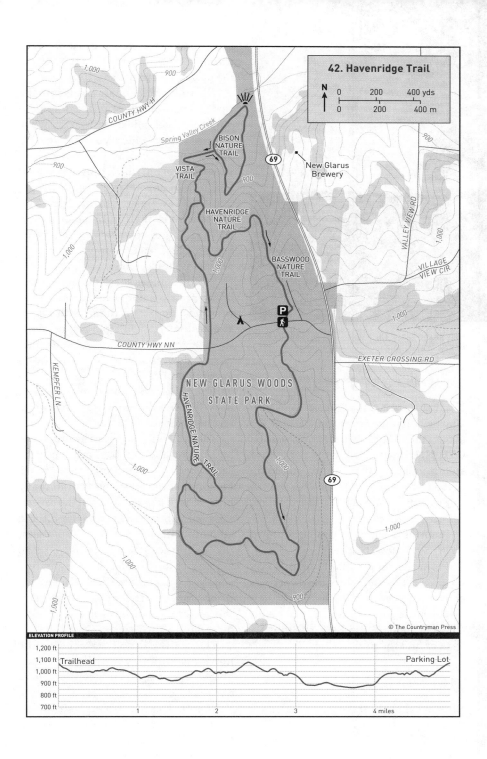

42. Havenridge Trail

N
0   200   400 yds
0   200   400 m

COUNTY HWY H

Spring Valley Creek

BISON NATURE TRAIL

VISTA TRAIL

69

New Glarus Brewery

HAVENRIDGE NATURE TRAIL

BASSWOOD NATURE TRAIL

P

COUNTY HWY NN

VALLEY VIEW RD

VILLAGE VIEW CIR

EXETER CROSSING RD

KEMPFER LN

NEW GLARUS WOODS
STATE PARK

HAVENRIDGE NATURE TRAIL

69

1,000

900

© The Countryman Press

ELEVATION PROFILE

1,200 ft				
1,100 ft	Trailhead			Parking Lot
1,000 ft				
900 ft				
800 ft				
700 ft				
	1	2	3	4 miles

COOL SHADE UNDER THE OAKS ON THE SAVANNAH LOOP AT NEW GLARUS WOODS

HOW TO GET THERE

From the west, take WI 39 into New Glarus, turning south on WI 69. Go about 1 mile out of town and turn west on CTH NN. Head through the park office station and park off to the left, just south of the shelter.

From the east, take WI 92 and follow the directions above.

From the north, simply come into town on WI 69. Follow the directions above.

From the south, simply take WI 69 up to CTH NN and follow the directions above.

For more information, contact New Glarus Woods State Park at 608-527-2335 or find the park online.

THE TRAIL

After checking in at the park office, park your car just west of the office in the first lot on CTH NN. The lot is on the right, and a pole barn shelter with picnic tables

is located there. Look for the Havenridge trailhead directly across CTH NN from the parking lot to the south.

The trail immediately heads into the woods and winds downhill before popping out rather quickly into an immense prairie, across which you will see WI 69. Past the highway you can see an active gravel pit, which provides a good look into what you are currently hiking over—a very thin layer of topsoil on top of a huge shelf of limestone rock. It's amazing to see how nature adapts, however, and sends deep-rooted prairie plants into the earth.

You'll meander south along the edge of the prairie before turning westward into the woods and then south again. The Walnut Trail will join you from the right. Stay to the left and continue south, mostly downhill, until you emerge in another prairie down in this southern valley of the park, where you will meet up with a small stream, turn westward, and head along the valley.

The trail will loop northward again and begin about a 0.75-mile gradual ascent back up to the road. Tall shagbark hickories tower over the trail in many places. As you near the top of the ascent, the trail will turn to the east a bit and connect with the Walnut Trail again; this time it will look more like a small logging road. Turn left here again and soon you will come to CTH NN. Be sure to look for cars. The speed is reduced in this area for them, but you still need to be careful.

The trail will now descend to the north again, and you will pass some of the park campsites, barely visible in the heavy woods, to the east of the trail. Yet another ascent greets you as you continue north before a button-hook turn at the top. Take the left turn on the Vista Trail to the north and down the long descent off the north side of the park's hillside. You will wind your way down and connect with the Bison Trail. Turn right down in the valley and meander along the edge of the woods and the huge prairie and follow this counterclockwise loop of this low valley. As you turn left at the farthest north point of the hike and start back toward the woods and Vista Trail connector, you are rewarded with a great view of the wooded park and hillside. You also get great views of New Glarus's Swiss-American settlement and the towering New Glarus Brewery—which almost looks more like a castle—perched atop a hill across the highway.

Back at the top of the hill you will rejoin the Havenridge Trail. A bench serves as a nice place for a break here. Staying left, or southeast, the trail will head downhill through more woods before turning east and northeast. A spur of a trail—unnamed—will head off to the south toward one campsite area. Stay to the left, northeast, and uphill . . . alas, again. The trail will loop around to the southeast again and head back downhill. You'll come to a somewhat tricky trail intersection where trails are crossing like an X. We stayed on a southeast trajectory and thus didn't take the trail to the left (northeast) or right (southwest), but basically stayed on our path "straight" (In reality, you can take either of the southern-pointed trails to get back to the trailhead.)

From here, you will make your final ascent and emerge at the edge of the parking area, where you will see the park office to the left and your parking lot straight up the hill.

Note: There is a Havenridge Trail guide, with numbered excerpts that correspond to numbered posts along the trail. The free guide is available at the park office and provides some interesting commentary on the area.

Magnolia Bluff County Park Loop, Rock County

TOTAL DISTANCE: 2.4 miles

HIKING TIME: 1 hour, 30 minutes

DIFFICULTY: 2.5

VERTICAL RISE: 145 feet

TRAILHEAD GPS COORDINATES:
42°43'48.81'' N, 89°21'23.79'' W

Off the beaten path for most hikers, Rock County is much more known as fairly flat farmland that most people simply pass through on the interstate. But Magnolia Bluff, as its name implies, offers a bird's-eye view of the area and long vistas of Green County to the southwest. As the second highest point in Rock County, it's certainly worth a visit for a scenic and short day hike.

Also notable is that Magnolia Bluff possesses its own climate. Due to the dramatic change in elevation between the north and south sides of the bluff, a microclimate exists. Within this zone is the only naturally occurring stand of white birch trees in the county. And the bluff is also home to the kitten tail, a plant on the state list of threatened species (so, be sure to stay on the marked trails around the bluff). Add some small prairies, a pond, a wetland, stands of pine trees, and a bluff-top grove of giant oaks, and the place offers great diversity for a small park in the middle of farm country.

Unique, too, is the fact that this park is only about a 30-minute drive from Madison, and it's just west of Janesville, yet it remains somewhat overlooked. Aside from great fall hiking and snowshoeing or skiing in the winter, the park would serve very well for those living close by who are training for a backpacking trip, thanks to its challenging footing and hilly terrain.

This hike is a 2.4-mile loop of essentially the outermost trails at the park. They aren't really named and some are shared with horses, while some are exclusively for hikers. To make the hike longer, loop through again and check out some of the other trails. Doing so would make it easy to spend a couple of hours here, hiking 4 or 5 miles.

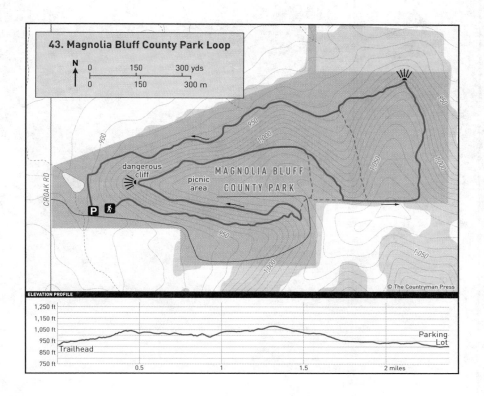

HOW TO GET THERE

From the north or east, take WI 213 south out of Evansville for about 2.5 miles to WI 59. Take WI 59 right (west) 3 miles to Croak Road. Take a left on Croak Road, and the park entrance will be after about 0.5 mile on the left. Park at the lower parking lot, immediately on your left after entering the park.

From the south or southwest, take WI 104 north out of Brodhead. After about 6 miles, it will merge with WI 59. Take the next right (east) on Finneran Road and the next left (north) on Croak Road. The park entrance will be after about 0.5 mile on the right.

From the west, take WI 59 out of Albany, going 3.5 miles to Finneran Road. Follow the directions above from Finneran.

For more information, contact the Rock County Parks Division at 608-757-5450.

THE TRAIL

The trail begins just off the lower parking lot when you first pull in—look for the hard-to-miss "Trail Start" kiosk, where there is a large map posted, and paper maps are available. One thing to note straightaway is that there's an off-shoot trail on some of the maps (absent on others) that does a little C-shaped wiggle straight north from this trailhead to the front of the bluff. This trail is poorly defined and ends up fraying into lots of volunteer trails below and onto the bluff face. Taking this route can lead to scrambling up onto parts of the bluff that have no guardrails and that

OVERLOOKING THE FARMS OF GREEN COUNTY: WISCONSIN'S SWITZERLAND AND CHEESE EPICENTER

don't seem to lead anywhere. Indeed, on a recent trip, we investigated these and found ourselves scrambling along a rocky ledge, thinking it was the trail, only to find that it led to a 20-foot drop. Scarier still: It was the trail.

The park should have never added this offshoot to the map and should post that the route is a volunteer one and is dangerous. Not only that, it takes hikers right into the protected area of the kitten tails. So avoid this trail from both the bottom of the bluff and once you're on top, where they have curiously added a trail taking hikers to that same, unprotected 20-foot drop.

Now, back to the start of the hike. Instead of going that direction, stay right at the trailhead and head east through a peaceful stand of red pines. You'll be hiking just below the south side of the bluff; on fall and winter days, much of the rock will be visible. The trail will wind its way uphill, making a big buttonhook left up to the bluff. The ascent is actually pretty steep, and the trail can be somewhat overgrown. But it will open up as you move on.

Eventually, you will emerge from the woods into the picnic area and the grove of huge oaks and the bluff overlook will be straight ahead. On a clear day, the view extends for miles, with much of Green County (Wisconsin's Switzerland) lying below. A wooden rail fence lines the top of the bluff, but as noted, there was a very curious decision to make a break in the fence and provide crude rock steps and a trail to get down onto the rock face that is often slick with rock dust. Those stairs lead down to a cliff face and a 20-foot-plus drop. So be careful, particularly with children.

Turning here to the right and doing a U-turn, the trail will continue back into the woods on the north side of the picnic area and head east. Follow this section of trail to the southeast and eventually to the first big stand of birch trees and then a stand of white pines, which will cause these farm country woods to make you feel like you're up north. Eventually, the trail will make a 90-degree turn and head north toward the far northeast corner of the park. You'll also be merging with horse trails here for basically the rest of the hike. At that corner, turn west and head downhill, passing two trail intersections before taking the third (you can go all the way down to the last turn, but this third turn offers better views of the east face of the bluff). Continue on this trail to an intersection on the far west side of the park, and then take a left and head south back to the parking lot, just below the bluff.

Lake Kegonsa State Park Loop

TOTAL DISTANCE: 2.5 miles

HIKING TIME: 1 hour to 1 hour, 30 minutes

DIFFICULTY: 1.0

VERTICAL RISE: Minimal

TRAILHEAD GPS COORDINATES:
42°58'48.58" N, 89°14'9.66" W

For thousands of years, the lakes and rivers of what is now the Madison area have attracted people. The Winnebago Native Americans who once lived in this area named this lake *Kegonsa*, which translates to "lake of many fishes." And when you see the lake covered with ice shanties in the winter, or the shoulder-to-shoulder anglers at the bridges in the summer, it appears the name is still fitting.

If you imagine Kegonsa without the cars and campers, or boats and motors, you can see why the native people would have found this area desirable. While the landscape has changed since then, there were undoubtedly similar shady woods and open prairies full of the game that the Winnebago and other nomadic cultures needed to make it through the long, cold winters and hot summers. In fact, the mark of one of these cultures lies indelibly along this hike in the area of the White Oak Nature Trail, in the form of effigy mounds—sacred burial sites that are often in the shape of animals.

Today the park offers swimming, boating, Nordic skiing, and hiking along the shores of Lake Kegonsa, part of the four-lake Madison chain. These lakes, like much of the surface waters of Wisconsin, are the remnants of the last Ice Age. Glacial debris dammed a large riverway, resulting in this string of lakes connected by the Yahara River.

This hike is a 2.5-mile combination of the Prairie Trail and White Oak Nature Trail loops and, as the namesakes suggest, it takes you around a large prairie restoration and through a great hardwood forest, made up primarily of giant white oaks. Both trails are groomed for Nordic skiing in the winter, when there's enough snow.

Note: Most of the park is open to dogs on leashes, but the White Oak Nature

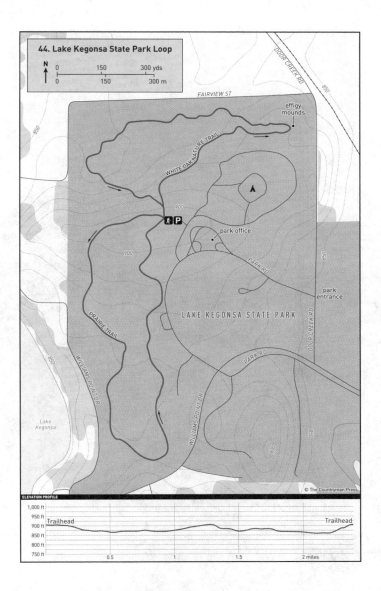

44. Lake Kegonsa State Park Loop

N

| 0 | 150 | 300 yds |
| 0 | 150 | 300 m |

FAIRVIEW ST

effigy mounds

WHITE OAK NATURE TRAIL

park office

PARK RD

PRAIRIE TRAIL

WILLIAMS POINT DR

LAKE KEGONSA STATE PARK

PARK RD

WILLIAMS POINT DR

DOOR CREEK RD

park entrance

Lake Kegonsa

© The Countryman Press

ELEVATION PROFILE

1,000 ft
950 ft
900 ft — Trailhead — Trailhead
850 ft
800 ft
750 ft

0.5 · 1 · 1.5 · 2 miles

Trail is closed to dogs. So, if you bring your dog, we suggest doing the Prairie Trail a couple of times. Or, you can get a park map and, if your dog is a swimmer, you can find the dog beach.

HOW TO GET THERE

From Stoughton, take North Page Street north out of town 2 miles to Williams Drive. Take a right on Williams Drive and stay on it for 4 miles until it comes to Williams Point Drive. Take a left on Williams Point Drive and the first right (approximately 1 mile) on Door Creek Road. The park entrance is immediately on the left.

From Madison, take US 51 south to CTH B just before Stoughton. Take CTH B for a little more than 1.5 miles to Wil-

HELIOPSIS TRUMPETS THE END OF SUMMER AT LAKE KEGONSA STATE PARK

liams Drive (a four-way stop). Turn left (north) on Williams Drive and follow the directions above.

From the north, south, or east and coming from I-39/90, take the CTH N exit and head south toward Stoughton. Turn right on Koshkonong Road (approximately 1 mile) and take it for about 0.5 mile to Williams Drive. Turn left (south) and take it for approximately 2 miles. Turn right on Williams Point Drive and follow the directions above.

For more information, contact Lake Kegonsa State Park at 608-873-9695.

THE TRAIL

This hike is a combination of two loops, the Prairie and White Oak nature trails, both done counterclockwise. After passing the park office, turn right, drive past the small parking lot on the left and take the next road to the left. This will lead to another small lot on the immediate left. There are restrooms and water here, and this is also the trailhead for the ski trails in the winter.

Looking to the west from this last lot, you will see a large, painted welcome sign and three trails (left, straight, or right). Take the trail to the left and head to a sign describing the prairie plants found here overlooking the immense prairie; this is the beginning of the Prairie Loop. Turn right (west) and begin the loop. Immediately, all sorts of prairie plants will emerge, including big and little bluestem, rattlesnake master, milkweed, and phlox. The trail travels along the western edge of the prairie, heading south just a couple of hundred feet from the lake, although it is hardly visible in the summer months. The first leg of the hike is a gradual downhill. Looking east across the prairie from here offers a great glimpse of what a truly healthy prairie ecosystem looks like. In these grasses are hundreds of species, including 60 species of birds, reptiles, spiders, butterflies, and mammals.

The hiking (and skiing) is relatively easy. After a long descent, you will turn and merge with a shortcut trail. Stay to the right and continue along another slight decline. The trail will then make a sweeping U-turn and head back north, passing a large stand of mixed hardwoods, great for shade in the summer and brilliantly colored in the fall. After passing the softball field and the other end of the shortcut trail on your left, continue on the main trail. This will take you along the park road and back to the beginning of the loop. Take a right (north) and head back to the parking lot area.

The White Oak Nature Trail is straight ahead. There are informative guidebooks available at the trail's start. The trail passes the light gray bark of several white oaks as it meanders eastward, past a couple of campsites, before making a U-turn left and eastward up a hill toward the effigy mounds. If you're not looking, or you don't have your trail guide, you'll miss them, off to the right. The trail then makes a slight dip and heads past some of the larger trees in the woods, passing a pine plantation, to begin its final ascent toward the end of the trail. A bench at the top is worth stopping at to look back over the valley you just traversed. It's a great view, and you may spot a deer or a wild turkey sneaking out the other side. The trail's end and parking lot are just a few yards from here.

Picnic Point Trail, University of Wisconsin

TOTAL DISTANCE: 4.7 miles

HIKING TIME: 2 hours

DIFFICULTY: 3.0

VERTICAL RISE: 200 feet

TRAILHEAD GPS COORDINATES:
43°5'04.08'' N, 89°25'43.39'' W

Most of the time, hiking means leaving town and heading out in search of a countryside trailhead someplace. So it's pretty hard to believe as you ramble along this lakeshore path—with a canopy of trees overhead, the water of Lake Mendota lapping the rocky shoreline next to you, and nothing but trail disappearing into the woods ahead— that you're in a city of 250,000 people. It's truly an urban oasis.

While open to the public, "The Point," as locals refer to it, was once a wedding gift from a Madison man to his new bride. They built a house and are responsible for the large stone wall at the entrance. After a house fire, they moved to nearby Shorewood Hills and eventually sold the property to the University of Wisconsin. A very popular place, The Point's main trail can get congested, particularly in the summer and fall. You'll find people reading, bird-watching, swimming, picnicking, canoeing, fishing, jogging, and strolling. On weekday afternoons in the fall, you'll even hear the sounds of the famous University of Wisconsin marching band from a nearby athletic field.

The Point itself is a peninsula that sticks out into Lake Mendota, the biggest of the Madison lakes—and offers prairie, wetland, and woodland habitats full of oaks, hickories, cottonwoods, and more. In fact, the entirety of the hike falls within the Lakeshore Nature Preserve, a 129-acre property closed to motorized vehicles and even bicycles, making it unusually serene for a place that is only minutes from downtown Madison, which is visible across the lake during a portion of the hike.

This hike (a change from the first edition of this book) now begins at the main parking area on University Bay

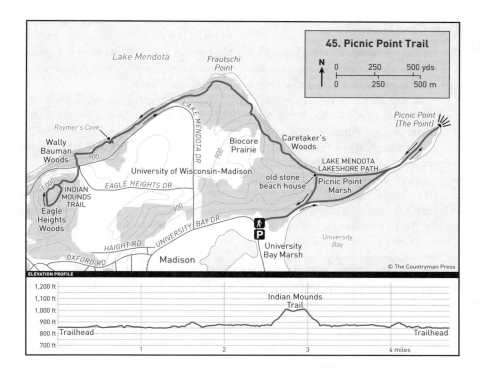

Drive, near campus. There are two parking lots, a small one on the trailhead side of the road and a much larger one on the west side of the road. Both lots are "pay and display" lots with kiosks where you buy a ticket for your car dash. They are free after 4:30 p.m. on weekdays and all day on weekends. If you do park at the larger lot across the road, be very careful crossing the road. Cars often come around the curve faster than the posted speed limit.

The new route is a 4.75 tour of the preserve, starting off with a southern view over University Bay, the university, and downtown Madison across the way and out to the tip of the point. Then the trail will loop back toward the main entrance, through the woods, past a prairie, and along a long shoreline trail on the north side of the property, across Lake Mendota Drive and uphill to the Indian Mound Trail in the Eagle Heights Woods before heading back.

HOW TO GET THERE

From the east, take University Avenue to the Babcock Drive exit on the right. Take Babcock to Observatory Drive. Turn left on Observatory and follow it 0.7 mile to Walnut Street. Turn right and follow Walnut 0.1 mile to Marsh Drive. Turn left and follow this 0.1 mile to University Bay Drive. Turn right and take University Bay Drive 0.3 miles to the trailhead parking lots.

From the west, take University Avenue to University Bay Drive. Turn left and follow it 1 mile (turning left at the top of the hill) to the parking lots and trailhead.

THE TRAIL

The trailhead is easy to find, thanks to the large kiosk near the large stone wall. The hike begins along the shore of University Bay and is very level at the beginning. This is the main trail to the tip of The Point, and it's wide and packed hard from the throngs of visitors who've come for decades. The basic gist of this hike is to follow this main trail to the tip of The Point along University Bay. Then, turn around and retrace your steps to the narrow isthmus near the tip, now veering right and taking the shoreline path on the north side of The Point to the west all the way to its end in Wally Bauman Woods, where you'll then turn south, cross Lake Mendota Drive, and hike up to the hilltop Indian mounds, where you'll complete a small loop and then head back to the trailhead.

Not long into the hike you'll be treated to great views across the lake to the University of Wisconsin-Madison campus. Wildfowl reside in the bay during the warmer months and it sees thousands of migrating birds in the spring and fall. In the winter, if the ice is frozen, this is an ice fishing hotspot.

You'll pass a couple of fire pit picnic areas and then start a gentle uphill, passing quietly by a large Indian Mound on the right. Coming off that small hill, you'll come out of the woods and head down into a valley and 40-foot-wide isthmus with a beach that drops down to nearly water level before climbing back up a small hill again. At the top of this hill is an old hand-powered water pump on the north side of the trail and a great overlook and stone bench on the east side, facing downtown and the campus across the bay.

Continue on to the tip of The Point, where there's been a lot of work done to make the north shoreline accessible. New stone steps will take you down to the shore, and there's also a great stone fire circle out here.

Note: Be careful taking the offshoot trail to the north side out here, particularly if you're with kids. The drop-off is right on the edge of the trail just past the bench over here, and it's 20 feet down to the shore.

Once you're ready, turn back on the main trail and retrace your steps about 0.25 mile back to the narrow isthmus and beach that you passed. Down near the beach on the northwest side, you'll see a trail disappearing into the woods here. Take that past the old rustic restrooms and down a long, sandy trail past towering cottonwood trees and the Picnic Point Marsh on the left and the sandy lakeshore to the right. The trail will head past the old stone beach house (your turnoff point on the way back); stay right along the shore and follow the signs for the Biocore Prairie and Frautschi Point. You'll head uphill into the woods again on a single-track trail, pass another steep trailside drop-off to the lake, and begin a series of ups and downs as you climb slightly. Runners love these trails, so don't be surprised if they come up from behind. Bikers are not allowed on the trails, but occasionally can't help themselves.

You'll pass through the Caretaker's Woods, packed with maples and ablaze with gold in the fall, before emerging at the Biocore Prairie. Turn right, and after a few steps, hop back into the woods, again following the signs for Frautschi Point. You'll pass a lot of offshoot trails along here, some leading to shoreline overlooks on the right and others coming from other parking areas on the left. Stay on the main trail, and after Frautschi Point,

THE ICONIC PICNIC POINT FOOTPATH IN FALL

continue on to Raymer's Cove. Along here there will be audio kiosks, too, where you can tune in with your phone to learn about the history of the area, like the tent colony that housed university students more than 100 years ago.

Eventually, you'll come to Raymer's Cove, a deep gorge. Follow the sign for the overlook, take the stairwell down to lake level, and then climb the switchback trail up the other side. From here you'll pass through the Bauman Woods

A NARROW ISTHMUS WIGGLES THROUGH LAKE MENDOTA AT PICNIC POINT

RAYMER'S COVE PRAIRIE GRASSES AND OAKS ERUPTING WITH FALL COLOR

toward your turnoff to the Indian Mound Trail. Ignore the first offshoot trail and wait until you come to a signpost with a sign warning against swimming. This is another cliff and a 30-foot drop down to the lake. Again, be careful here, the drop-off is just off the trail.

At this point, take the 90-degree turn left to the south and straight uphill toward Lake Mendota Drive. It's a rocky scramble and trickier with fallen leaves. A walking stick was optional thus far, but it would be pretty useful at this point. Be careful crossing the road. After you cross, you'll see the trail heading back into these woods—the Eagle Heights Woods—and you'll quickly come upon a trail to the right, where you'll find a map kiosk. Ignore this turnoff and go a few steps to the second one, marked by a sign for the Indian Mounds trail.

Follow this trail uphill and climb about 70 feet more in elevation to the hilltop woods where three large mounds rest. Take the loop around them clockwise, which offers a hilltop view of the lake in late fall and winter, when the leaves have fallen. Then, retrace your steps back down to the road, crossing carefully and then going downhill to the lakeshore trail and back east.

Follow your original route about 1.5 miles back to the old stone beach house where you will see a sign pointing to the right, south, to the "Picnic Point Entry." Take that route and pass straight through a trail intersection, through the dense woods to the other lakeshore where you'll meet up with the main trail. Turn right, west, and head back to the trailhead and parking lot.

IV.

SOUTHEAST

Mecan Springs, Ice Age Trail

TOTAL DISTANCE: 5.0 miles

HIKING TIME: 2 hours

DIFFICULTY: 3.0

VERTICAL RISE: Minimal

TRAILHEAD GPS COORDINATES:
44°3'29.28" N, 89°29'7.91" W

Wisconsin's Department of Natural Resources can easily be given partial or whole credit for achievements such as rehabilitating river and lake watershed habitats; reestablishing the bald eagle population from a point of near extinction; repurposing unused rail corridors as biking, skiing, and snowmobiling trails; and literally more exceptionally important initiatives than can be counted.

Indeed, there are incredibly hardworking folks who have fought to preserve this state's most precious resources—its natural resources—so that we don't make mistakes common in the past, so we have access to enjoy these resources, and so Wisconsin enjoys the significant economic benefits connected with them.

And as proof of all of this, as you stand near the parking area of Mecan Springs State Natural Area and look far down at the huge freshwater spring below, you are resting highly and mightily on a ridge of success. This remarkable and precious watershed contains Class I trout streams, which are some of the best in the state and hold self-sustaining populations of fish. Also calling this area home are bald eagles as well as the rare red-shouldered hawk.

The geology of the place was born from a huge glacial tunnel, which created the river and the long, tall gouge of the river valley. This hike follows the valley's south ridge along the Ice Age Trail and out to a spur trail overlook above a quiet bend in the river and back—approximately 5 miles of quiet, scenic hiking in total.

HOW TO GET THERE

From the north or south, take US 39/51 to the WI 21 exit at Coloma. Head east

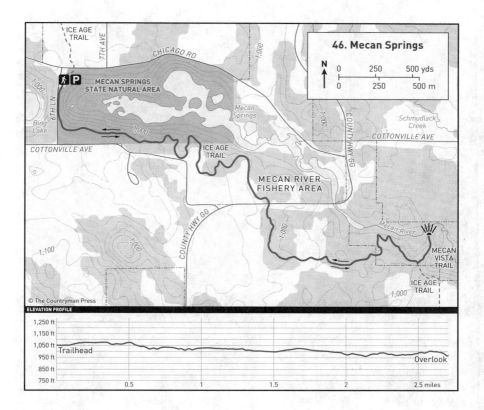

ELEVATION PROFILE

from here approximately 1 mile and turn left (north) on Sixth Avenue. After 1 mile, turn right (east) on Cottonville Avenue and 0.75 mile later a left (north) on Sixth Lane. The parking lot/trailhead will be in 0.25 mile on the right at the intersection with Chicago Avenue.

From the west and east, simply take WI 21 toward Coloma and follow the directions for east of Coloma on to Sixth Avenue above.

For more information, contact the Wisconsin State Natural Areas division of the Department of Natural Resources at 608-266-7012.

THE TRAIL

The trail starts off heading south along Sixth Avenue and along a stretch of large

pines above and, in the summer, berries below. You are high above the springs here, and on hot days this is a nice, breezy section. The trail turns to the left and climbs a bit as it meanders through more pines in a rather open woods, with a valley dropping off steeply to the springs. Soon the trail comes to a fun section with short grasses surrounding the single-track trail as it traces the valley's upper edge. The drop-offs to the left are rather significant as you hike atop this tall shelf high above the springs.

You will continue to trace this ridgeline around to the north, skirting close to a quiet road—Cottonville Avenue. Eventually the trail will make a long semicircular loop around an open prairie, duck into some woods, and emerge at the one road crossing on the hike

OAKS ESCORT HIKERS ALONG THE TOP OF THE MECAN RIVER VALLEY

at CTH GG. Cross carefully and duck back into the woods. The trail offers some steadily rolling terrain here as it passes through these quiet woods, eventually crossing through some open prairie again, past a hedgerow and a farm access lane, and back into the woods, where you will make your way toward the spur turnoff.

The woods are full of mature hardwoods here that you'll pass as you zigzag through them and up to the turnoff at the blue-blazed Mecan Vista Trail. Take this to the left (northeast) and follow along the top of this ridge, which juts out toward the river. There is a bench here, which makes for a good resting spot—and even in the summer, you're able to see far down to the river and into its clear waters below. In the fall, you're rewarded with a sea of color. This is a quiet and serene bend in a quiet river valley that makes for a nice opportunity to enjoy the woods.

Retrace your steps back from the spur to the main trail, turn right (west) back across CTH GG, go through the prairie, and finally along the long ridge above the spring and back to the parking area.

Hartman Creek, Ice Age Trail

TOTAL DISTANCE: 8.5 miles

HIKING TIME: 3 hours, 30 minutes

DIFFICULTY: 4.5

VERTICAL RISE: Minimal

TRAILHEAD GPS COORDINATES:
44°19'22.67'' N, 89°12'57.64'' W

The Waupaca area offers a great collection of lakes with all sorts of recreation and peaceful shorelines. Hartman Creek State Park provides an incredible variety of activities and offerings, including 7 lakes, 10 miles of hiking trails, 12 miles of biking trails (including 6 single-track mountain bike trails), a beach, 7 miles of horse trails, boating, paddling, fishing, skiing, and snowshoeing. And, perhaps most unique, is Campsite #102, a teepee!

In addition to all of this is some of the best Ice Age Trail hiking around. It's sometimes hard to find long, uninterrupted stretches of hiking trail in the southern part of the state. But Ray Zillmer, the father of the Ice Age Trail, had a plan for that (which we go into more detail about in the Kettle Moraine chapters). But to summarize, the idea was for a few-mile-wide, 1,200-mile-long park to wind through the state, marking the advance of the last glacier. Through the middle of this park a trail would meander. And not only would this serve to highlight the state's geological past and preserve exceptionally valuable natural resources along the way, it would just happen to offer some of the state's most striking landscapes in which to recreate—precisely what exists at Hartman Creek State Park and adjoining Emmons Creek State Fishery and Wildlife Area.

The following hike is a 8.5-mile trek through rare Karner blue butterfly habitat and oak savanna as it rambles up and down glacial hills and valleys and through quiet woods. Add to this the fact that the trail tread is exceptionally well maintained, and you're in for a grand day hike in the Waupaca Chain of Lakes neighborhood.

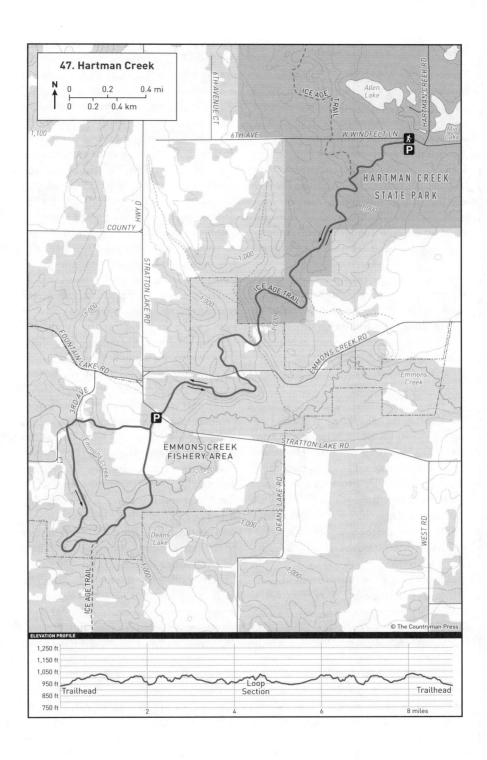

47. Hartman Creek

N

| 0 | 0.2 | 0.4 mi |
| 0 | 0.2 | 0.4 km |

6TH AVENUE CT

ICE AGE TRAIL

Allen Lake

HARTMAN CREEK RD

6TH AVE

W WINDFELT LN

Mid Lake

1,100

HARTMAN CREEK STATE PARK

1,000

COUNTY D HWY

STRATTON LAKE RD

1,000

1,000

ICE AGE TRAIL

1,000

EMMONS CREEK RD

Emmons Creek

FOUNTAIN LAKE RD

1,000

3RD AVE

Emmons Creek

P

EMMONS CREEK FISHERY AREA

STRATTON LAKE RD

DEANS LAKE RD

1,000

WEST RD

Deans Lake

1,000

1,000

ICE AGE TRAIL

© The Countryman Press

ELEVATION PROFILE

| 1,250 ft |
| 1,150 ft |
| 1,050 ft |
| 950 ft |
| 850 ft |
| 750 ft |

Trailhead

Loop Section

Trailhead

2   4   6   8 miles

HOW TO GET THERE

From the northeast, take WI 22 west out of Waupaca for 5 miles to Stratton Lake Road. Turn right (west) and go about 4 miles to the trailhead parking lot—to the left, just before the bend in the road.

From the northwest, take WI 54 east out of Plover 15.5 miles to County Route D (CTH D). Turn right (south) on CTH D and take it 3.5 miles to the junction with Stratton Lake Road. Continue straight on Stratton Lake Road for 1.1 miles to the trailhead parking lot on the right, just after the bend in the road.

From the south, take WI 22 east out of Wild Rose for 10.4 miles to Stratton Lake Road. Turn left and go about 4 miles to the trailhead parking lot on the left.

For more information, contact Hartman Creek State Park at 715-258-2372.

THE TRAIL

The trailhead includes an informative Ice Age Trail kiosk on Windfeldt Lane, not far after driving into Hartman Creek State Park and passing the office. The hike starts by heading through a mowed athletic field—but don't be discouraged, things improve quickly. This is actually an offshoot access spur that gets you to the Ice Age Trail proper in about 0.5 mile.

After hiking through the field, you will come to a turnoff to the right (west). This is well marked with both yellow blazes (the trademark Ice Age Trail marking) and signage. The trail will duck into the woods and skirt through a small apple orchard and head deeper into the woods along a single-track trail that winds its way uphill. After a short while you'll come to the intersection with the main Ice Age Trail, where you will turn left (south) and begin many miles of hiking along the trail. Not far from this turn, you will emerge into a several-acre prairie filled mostly with butterfly weed in the summer. The trail will wind along the eastern edge and you will come to the confluence of several trails—others of which are used for biking. Turn right at this intersection (west) through the heart of this prairie. The trail will wind south, back into the woods, and you will again cross a bike trail—a common occurrence on this hike since there are single-track mountain bike trails meandering through the area. Simply stick to the yellow blaze markings, and you'll know you're on the Ice Age Trail.

Eventually your trail will leave these trails and, still in the woods, you will pass nearby farm fields to the east before turning west and beginning a long climb deeper into the woods. You will emerge from the woods at one point to an opening on the edge of a long valley. This oak savannah is a wildlife paradise, where you may have your best chance of seeing a Karner blue. You will head down into this long, open valley, cross a hedgerow where a small tributary drains, and eventually meet the woods on the far west side—where there is another Ice Age Trail information kiosk.

The trail will head into the woods again, amid some young white pines, and meander south toward Emmons Creek Road. This narrow gravel road, with trees growing up to its sides and towering over, is hardly noticeable as you scamper across in just a few strides. The trail continues winding upward now after turning more westward along a long ascent. Eventually the trail turns south and emerges in a pine plantation that is inundated with towering pines that escort you to the next section and serve as a cool, breezy change of scenery.

You will cross Stratton Lake Road and

LONG, WINDING, AND TRANQUIL: THE ICE AGE TRAIL AT HARTMAN CREEK

head into a gravel parking lot. The trail will resume at the gate across the mowed trail entrance straight ahead. From the parking lot, head south among some tall prairie grasses to the fork in the trail. The return trail, the Ice Age, will be on the left; stay to the right to begin a counterclockwise loop. The trail will head out into the open—so on a hot, sunny day, it is pretty warm. You'll head toward a tree line, around it, and then you'll turn northwest and up into the woods along a single-track trail.

Soon the trail will turn southwest along a road and head down toward the creek. You will actually need to hop out of the woods and cross the creek using the road bridge on Third Avenue—a pretty quiet stretch of country road. Be careful on your way back into the woods on the other side, however. There are a lot of trails immediately next to the creek, used by trout anglers who access the creek here; go about 20 paces up the road, and the continuation of the trail proper will be marked on the left.

Head south and past a large fern bed. The forest will begin to transform to include more oaks as you hike, until you eventually emerge into an oak savanna. The trail will meander up and down this side of the creek for quite a while. Eventually, the trail will lead you down into a sandy valley, and soon you will meet up with the Ice Age Trail again, coming in from the right (south). Turn left, and you will join it as you hike through a marshy area, over a series of boardwalks, and across the creek.

After crossing the bridge, you will emerge from the woods out into a very impressive prairie, blanketed with black-eyed Susans in the summer. Also look for flannel plant, yarrow, blue vervain, knapweed, and lots of milkweed dancing with monarch butterflies. Head north—past the prairie and the agricultural field—back up to the parking area, cross the road, and retrace your original steps for 3.3 miles back to the trailhead.

Note: The only thing to watch for as you get to the conclusion of this long hike is the turnoff to the parking area, which is easy to miss after you've been trekking along for nearly 8 miles. There was no signage at the time we hiked it, but there was a bench and the trail, changing from wide to single-track, ducking off to the right into the woods. This takes you down through the woods, into the little orchard, and out into the original prairie. Turn left here and head back toward the parking lot/trailhead through the athletic field. (If you do happen to miss this turnoff, you'll hit Windfeldt Road, which is paved. You can simply turn right and hike along the road back to the parking lot/trailhead, about 0.25 mile. This is a quiet road within the state park.)

High Cliff State Park Loop

TOTAL DISTANCE: 4.8 miles

HIKING TIME: 2 hours, 30 minutes

DIFFICULTY: 3.5

VERTICAL RISE: 188 feet

TRAILHEAD GPS COORDINATES:
44°9'39.33'' N, 88°17'35.38'' W

A band of limestone stretches from Niagara Falls, New York, all the way through the upper Great Lakes, to Door County and then south—eventually forming the eastern shore of Lake Winnebago. By a twist of geological fate, the Fox River valley could have been more like Niagara Falls than you might think. This band of rock marks the sedimentary deposits of countless billions of calcium-rich organisms that died and layered, like calcium deposits in a teapot, the bottom of an ancient sea that covered much of North America, eventually forming limestone. To walk the bluffs at High Cliff is to hike over this sediment that was deposited millions of years ago.

Valued highly for its use as a building material, the lime was extracted as a powder by taking huge blocks of limestone and feeding them into a giant kiln. Exactly this type of operation once flourished at the foot of the cliff at High Cliff State Park. Imagine taking huge chunks, several tons each, out of a quarry 1,000 feet above water level and somehow negotiating them into the kilns below. Only the skeletons of these kilns remain, as crumbling structures at the foot of High Cliff and the start of this trail.

But European settlers weren't the first visitors to this area. Accessible as an offshoot of this hike are the Native American burial mounds found atop the cliff. Many of the mounds have educational kiosks in front of them, which share the history of these remarkable burial structures with visitors.

This hike combines the Lime Kiln, Indian Mound, and Red Bird trails and hikes to the park lookout tower as a destination. Starting at the Lime Kiln trailhead at lake level, you'll hike past the lime kilns and move along the Lake

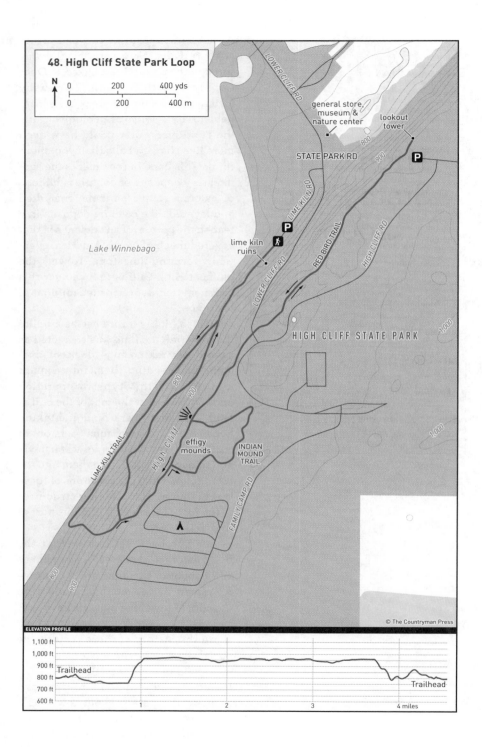

48. High Cliff State Park Loop

N

| 0 | 200 | 400 yds |
| 0 | 200 | 400 m |

LOWER CLIFF RD

general store, museum & nature center

lookout tower

STATE PARK RD

800

900

LIME KILN RD

RED BIRD TRAIL

HIGH CLIFF RD

lime kiln ruins

LOWER CLIFF RD

Lake Winnebago

HIGH CLIFF STATE PARK

1,000

800

900

LIME KILN TRAIL

High Cliff

800

effigy mounds

INDIAN MOUND TRAIL

1,000

FAMILY CAMP RD

800

800

© The Countryman Press

ELEVATION PROFILE

| 1,100 ft |
| 1,000 ft |
| 900 ft |
| 800 ft |
| 700 ft |
| 600 ft |

Trailhead

Trailhead

1   2   3   4 miles

Winnebago shoreline before an abrupt ascent to the edge of the cliff. In total, this hike will climb nearly 200 feet, most of it via this steep, short ascent. Once atop the cliff, you'll follow the Indian Mound Loop and continue along the cliff edge on the Red Bird Trail to the lookout tower before turning back and heading back down.

Note: You'll be hiking along a cliff edge, and while the trail is mostly back from the edge and tree lined, offshoot trails take you to abrupt drop-offs. Not only do you need to be careful if you choose to explore any of those trails, but if you're with children you need to monitor them very closely.

HOW TO GET THERE

From the north, take WI 55 south from Kaukauna about 6 miles to Spring Hill Drive. Take it for 1 mile, turn left on State Park Road, and go 0.5 mile to the park entrance. To get to the trailhead parking area, go past the main office and take a left at the stop sign. Just past the nature center/museum/general store, take a right into the long parking lot (follow the sign for the lime kilns) and park toward the end. The trailhead is next to the lime kilns at the far south end of the lot.

From the south, take US 151 out of Fond du Lac for approximately 16 miles to WI 55. (WI 55 will stay north, while US 151 will head due east.) Take WI 55 for about 11.5 miles to Spring Hill Drive. Turn left on Spring Hill Drive and follow it for 1.8 miles to State Park Road. From there, follow the directions above.

From the west, take WI 114 from Menasha about 7 miles to State Park Road. Take a right on State Park Road and take it to the park entrance on the right, about 3 miles. From there, follow the directions above.

From the east, take US 10 to WI 55 south. From here, follow the same directions as from the north above.

For more information, contact High Cliff State Park at 920-989-1106.

THE TRAIL

The Lime Kiln Trail begins by heading southwest out of the parking lot and past the old lime kiln ruins. Eventually you will get to where the return loop meets with the trail. Stay to the right, along the shore of the lake, for a counterclockwise loop. Almost all of this hike is wooded, and you are greeted right away by a mixture of hardwoods, especially towering maples and elms. You will come to a shortcut trail to the left (southeast) for the short loop turn-off, but stay on the long loop section along the lake.

After passing a series of boardwalks, the trail will come to a turning point, where there is a bench overlooking the lake. Turn left to the east and straight up the hill, a pretty taxing climb among some monstrous old cottonwoods.

The trail will head up a rocky ascent and squeeze between the cliff wall on one side and a huge separate spire of limestone on the other. Steps will take you up the final 30 feet to the top of the cliff. Straight ahead will be the campground. Take a left (northeast) on the trail atop the cliff and hike about 100 yards to the beginning of the Indian Mound Loop. Turn right to hike this loop counterclockwise as well. This very tranquil area offers an open forest floor, and you can easily see the mounds despite the many shagbark hickories growing up here. Follow the loop back around to where it

OVERLOOKING THE NORTHERN TIP OF LAKE WINNEBAGO ON THE RED BIRD TRAIL

will curve west past the upper parking lot and to the upper cliff trail.

Turn right here and continue northeast along the cliff top on the Red Bird Trail toward the Lookout tower. Note the caution signs about dangerous cliff edges. The trail is very flat here and follows a rock shelf but soon descends nearly 30 feet and intersects with the park road. Carefully cross the road and watch for cars. Once across you'll have a wide view of the long, open quarry across the road to the east. Continue across a wide, flat quarry shelf and eventually uphill into the woods and then past a couple of overlooks. About 0.8 miles after leaving the Indian Mounds, you'll come to a parking lot, and you'll see the lookout tower up ahead. For a great view above the treetops of Lake Winnebago far below, head up the stairs to the top of the tower.

After visiting here and enjoying the views, turn back and retrace your steps to the Indian Mound Trail, this time bypassing it and continuing straight southwest to where you came up the steps from the Lime Kiln Trail originally. This stretch will offer you all sorts of overlooks atop the cliff. Be very careful and stay on the trail. There are no protective barriers up here, and there is nothing but a sheer drop-off—close to 100 feet—between you and the valley below. At the steps, hike back down to the original turn-off for the return of the Lime Kiln Loop. Take a right and head northeast this time.

From here the trail gets markedly trickier. A series of valleys take you down and up several times, each climb seeming like the last. At one point, the trail will follow along a long boardwalk of steps downward, only to have you climb back up again. The trail is pretty slick here due to the moisture that gets trapped between the lake and the cliff among all the trees. And because the trail gets narrower and overgrown with more vegetation, loose rocks and roots are tougher to see. Eventually the trail will ramble downhill one last time as you meet back up with the original trail; continue northeast, past the lime kiln ruins, and back to the parking lot.

Point Beach State Forest Loop

TOTAL DISTANCE: 5.5 miles

HIKING TIME: 1 hour, 30 minutes

DIFFICULTY: 2.5

VERTICAL RISE: Minimal

TRAILHEAD GPS COORDINATES:
44°12′40.45″ N, 87°30′36.33″ W

Between shipping, sailing, and commercial and charter fishing, many people make their living or enjoy boating on the waters of Lake Michigan. And the Rawley Point Lighthouse is surely one of the many reasons that all of this boating is as safe as possible.

There has been a lighthouse here since 1853, but it hasn't always assured safe passage in the waters more than 100 feet below. Before 1894, 26 ships were caught up on this point. Today, like almost all lighthouses, the light here is affixed to a steel tower and is automated, turning on before dusk and turning off just after dawn.

Emerging from the woods and climbing over the dunes next to the lighthouse reveals a sight that is more seashore than dairyland, but that's the beauty of Wisconsin's diversity. A vast, sandy beach stretches in both directions, bordered first by bounding sand dunes and then by mostly coniferous forest. It is in this border habitat, in fact, that the rare dune thistle struggles to survive. Be sure to stay on the sandy paths and away from the vegetation out on the dunes—you may be crushing a threatened plant species.

The park itself is actually a forest unit in the Wisconsin park and forest system. And thanks to its great camping, miles of beach, wooded trails, and hiking, biking, swimming, skiing, snowshoeing, and more, it's a popular place. In fact, it also offers two of the fairly rare reservable cabins in the Wisconsin park and forest system. All told, Point Beach offers an opportunity to visit some stunning Lake Michigan shoreline, as well as a great opportunity for beach bumming—Wisconsin style.

This 5.5-mile hike is essentially the Yellow Loop and winds through the park just along the edge of the beach from

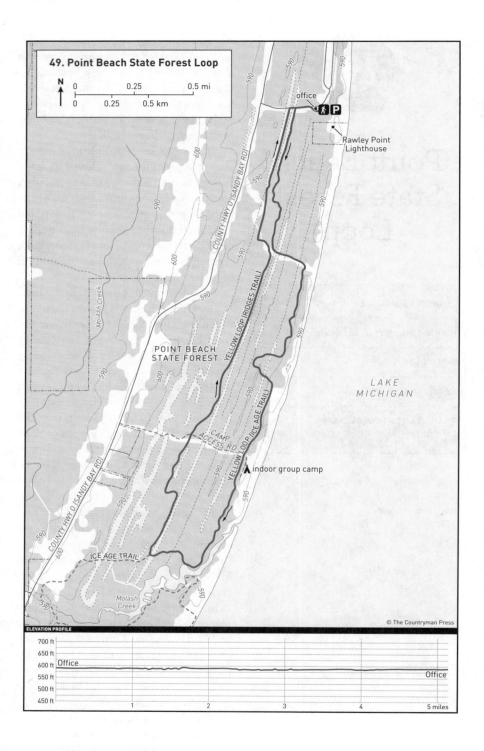

49. Point Beach State Forest Loop

N

| 0 | | 0.25 | | 0.5 mi |
| 0 | 0.25 | | 0.5 km | |

office

Rawley Point
Lighthouse

COUNTY HWY O (SANDY BAY RD)

YELLOW LOOP (RIDGES TRAIL)

POINT BEACH
STATE FOREST

LAKE
MICHIGAN

CAMP
ACCESS RD

YELLOW LOOP (ICE AGE TRAIL)

indoor group camp

COUNTY HWY O (SANDY BAY RD)

ICE AGE TRAIL

Molash Creek

Molash
Creek

© The Countryman Press

ELEVATION PROFILE

700 ft
650 ft
600 ft · Office
550 ft
500 ft
450 ft

Office

1   2   3   4   5 miles

LAKE MICHIGAN'S SERENE AND SANDY SHORELINE AT POINT BEACH

the visitors center and heads south to Molash Creek and back through the dense forest. Despite this area being full of visitors, it's possible to do this entire hike and barely see another person.

HOW TO GET THERE

From the north, take WI 42 south from Kewaunee for 16 miles to CTH V. Turn left (east) on CTH V and follow it for 2.5 miles to CTH O. Turn right (south) on CTH O to the park entrance on the left.

From the south, take I-43 south from Kewaunee for 16 miles to CTH V. Follow the directions above.

From the west, take CTH V out of Mishicot and go 6.8 miles to where CTH V ends. Turn right and take CTH O south. Take CTH O for 1.7 miles to the park entrance.

For more information, contact Point Beach State Forest at 920-794-7480.

THE TRAIL

If you pick up a map at the park office, you will see that there are Red, Blue, and Yellow loops. This hike is essentially all of the Yellow loop south of the park road. By doing so, you do not need to cross any roads, you stay clear of the crowded camping areas, and you only need to share the trail with bikes for a short while.

If possible, park in the small parking lot just past the visitors center. It is frequently crowded, but often people are inside the office for just a few minutes—so don't give up right away. Also, the grassy area seems to be an overflow parking area.

After lacing up, take the entrance road back past the visitors center, staying on the left-hand side of the road in the grass (against traffic). Just after passing the office, you'll see the trail heading into the woods to the left. Take a left and head south on the main combined trail of the Red, Blue, and Yellow loops.

About 0.5 mile into the hike, the Ice Age Trail will merge from the right. Soon after, the Red Loop will peel off to the right; stay left following the sign for the Blue Loop. You'll pass the access to the Ice Age Trail backpacking campsite and also the Kayak campsite, both essentially on the water, making for pretty cool campsites. There is an offshoot trail here and boardwalks that take you to the lake for more exploring, too.

The trail will continue to meander just inside the woods on the edge of the beach, and you'll ramble up and down rolling terrain on a wide trail. Eventually you will cross the road leading to the indoor group camp, and you'll actually hike along it for a while after it makes a 90-degree turn south. You'll pass the group camp cabins and, soon after, you'll come to Molash Creek, which is a pretty big flowage that forces a turn to the west. Soon after, you'll come to a trail intersection. The Ice Age Trail will continue left, south, and out of the park. Turn right on the Yellow Loop and head back north on the Ridges Trail.

This long section will take you past the Blue Loop turnoff; continue on until you come to the Yellow Loop sign and the sign for the park office. Take it to the right and back to the trail you started on, and head back to the visitors center road. Take a right at the road back to your car, the lighthouse, and the beach.

Horicon National Wildlife Refuge Loop

TOTAL DISTANCE: 4.5 miles

HIKING TIME: 1 hour, 15 minutes

DIFFICULTY: 2.0

VERTICAL RISE: Minimal

TRAILHEAD GPS COORDINATES:
43°37'48.69'' N, 88°40'9.60'' W

Looking out over the fiery-colored fall vegetation sprouting out of the Horicon Marsh on a cool October day with tens of thousands of geese dotting the sky above, you'd never guess what this place used to look like. At the turn of the century, the Canada goose population had been gunned down to almost nothing and after an unsuccessful attempt to dredge it and transform it into farmland, the marsh was a vast wasteland suitable for neither farmer nor goose. But things changed.

Recent annual censuses have recorded more than 250,000 geese in the 32,000-acre Horicon Marsh, which is a combination of both the Horicon National Wildlife Refuge and the Horicon Marsh State Wildlife Area. This internationally recognized bird habitat area is also the largest freshwater cattail marsh in the United States. More than 200 species of animals make the marsh home at some point during the year. Included are waterfowl and shorebirds like herons, mallards, sandhill cranes, teal, cormorants, and coots—in addition to all sorts of rare and important songbirds and raptors, hundreds of species of mammals, snakes, amphibians, and insects.

This hike is actually a combination of the Boardwalk, Egret, Red Fox, and Redhead trails. The longest, the Redhead, starts by taking you into the marsh and around a large pond before sweeping along the edge of an incredible prairie restoration on the Red Fox Trail—alive with color in the summer months. From there you join the Egret Trail and emerge from a hardwood stand to hike right through the marsh on top of one of the most scenic and amazing floating boardwalks around. From here you can get right up close to wildlife either flying by or wading below. The hike wraps up

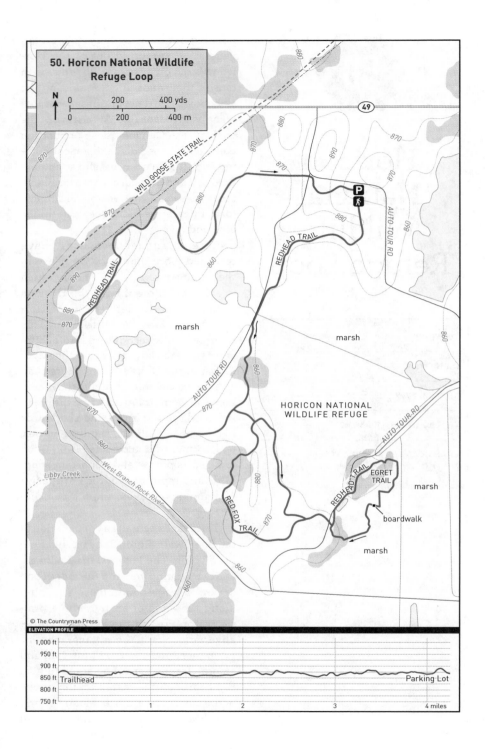

50. Horicon National Wildlife Refuge Loop

N

| 0 | 200 | 400 yds |
| 0 | 200 | 400 m |

WILD GOOSE STATE TRAIL

49

REDHEAD TRAIL

AUTO TOUR RD

P

REDHEAD TRAIL

marsh

marsh

REDHEAD TRAIL

AUTO TOUR RD

AUTO TOUR RD

HORICON NATIONAL
WILDLIFE REFUGE

EGRET
TRAIL

marsh

boardwalk

RED FOX TRAIL

marsh

Libby Creek

West Branch Rock River

marsh

© The Countryman Press

ELEVATION PROFILE

| 1,000 ft |
| 950 ft |
| 900 ft |
| 850 ft | Trailhead |
| 800 ft |
| 750 ft |

Parking Lot

1   2   3   4 miles

by tracing its way along the other side of the prairie and rambling up and down small hills alongside the woods on the banks of the Rock River before turning back to the parking area. It's a great hike that takes a little over an hour with blinders on—or much longer with binoculars, camera, and wildlife identification books in tow.

HOW TO GET THERE

From the south, take WI 26 north out of Burnett for 4.9 miles to WI 49. Turn right (east) on WI 49 and go 1.4 miles to the parking lot on the right (be careful, it comes up quickly soon after you pass the bike trail crossing). Follow the drive to the lot, veering left at the fork in the drive.

From the west, take WI 49 east out of Waupun for about 2.8 miles and follow the drive to the lot, veering left at the fork in the drive.

From the east, take WI 49 out of Brownsville about 9.2 miles to the parking area on the left. Turn left onto the drive and follow the drive to the lot, veering left at the fork in the drive.

From the north, take US 151 south out of Fond du Lac for 14.3 miles to WI 49. Turn left (east) on WI 49 and go 1.9 miles to the parking area on the right. Follow the drive to the lot, veering left at the fork in the drive.

MILLIONS OF WATERFOWL MIGRATE THROUGH THE 130 SQUARE MILE HORICON MARSH

For more information, contact the U.S. Fish & Wildlife Service office at the Horicon National Wildlife Refuge at 920-387-2658 or the Wisconsin Department of Natural Resources Horicon Service Center at 920-387-7860. Both organizations offer numerous educational programs throughout the year.

THE TRAIL

At the parking area, start hiking at the trailhead kiosk on the south side of the lot, heading south and starting a clockwise loop. After climbing a short hill along a wide, crushed-limestone trail, you will reach the crest to find one of many great views along this hike. In front of you will be standing water, and you will be greeted by the sight of a diverse selection of water birds in the warmer months. The view stretches in every direction. You will skirt the edge of this pond area by heading west to the auto tour road and then south alongside it. There is a rich diversity of wildflowers in this edge habitat. The trail will veer left into a small woods before emerging and coming to the intersection with the Red Fox Trail. Take this to the left, staying on a clockwise route.

This trail runs along a short hillside and skirts the edge of an immense prairie restoration. In midsummer, you'll be rewarded with a multicolored blanket of black-eyed Susans, wild bergamot, blazing stars, prairie dock, and a sea of prairie coneflowers and compass plants. This open habitat will transition dramatically as you cross the auto tour road and join up with the Egret Trail at a small T-shaped boardwalk. Head left (northeast) alongside the road and into the woods.

You will emerge from these woods to find yourself at the marsh's edge. There is an access trail to the left, but stay to the right and head south toward the boardwalks. The trail, once solid ground beneath you, will transition to a still solid but now floating surface. This boardwalk takes you past hopping frogs, honking geese, and any number of other birds. A large overlook gazebo provides a great spot for photos and wildlife viewing.

Note: In 2016, there was extensive work being done to the boardwalk, and much of it was inaccessible while it was being rebuilt and upgraded.

Continue on the Egret back to the T in the trail and take it left, across the road, and back to the Red Fox Trail. Veer left on the Red Fox this time, along the southern side of the prairie, and up a hillside. Looking northeast from here, you are treated to a great view of the marsh and much of the area that you have just covered.

The trail will now meander along and through a couple of large stands of oaks before taking you back to the intersection with the Redhead Trail. Take a left at this intersection and head west, across the auto tour road, and toward the Rock River. Eventually the trail will pass by an old stone fence and foundation before crossing the auto tour road, winding around a hillside, and jogging east back to the parking lot.

Parnell Tower Loop, Kettle Moraine

TOTAL DISTANCE: 3.5 miles

HIKING TIME: 1 hour, 30 minutes

DIFFICULTY: 3.5

VERTICAL RISE: 120 feet

TRAILHEAD GPS COORDINATES:
43°41'49.83" N, 88°5'21.29" W

With 30,000 acres comprising the northern unit of the Kettle Moraine State Forest, you would never know that it receives nearly 1 million visitors a year. The success of this area has its roots in a group of interested citizens, part of the Izaac Walton League, who sought to preserve this unique natural area close to Milwaukee. In fact, the group's leader, Ray Zillmer, thought that Kettle Moraine would draw people here just as the great national parks draw people to the West.

Today the area offers picnicking, biking, camping, skiing, hiking, horseback riding, hunting and fishing, snowmobiling, and all sorts of wildlife and plant viewing. There is an incredible diversity of life residing in the forests, prairies, and wetlands throughout Kettle Moraine North.

The northernmost of three hikes in Kettle Moraine North in this book, this loop hike takes you up to the 60-foot Parnell Observation Tower and along the Parnell Esker—one of the best and longest examples of the remnant of a meandering stream that flowed through a tunnel in the glacier, leaving sediment in its tracks. The trail is located toward the north end of Kettle Moraine North, offering a good view of the rest of the forest to the south. This loop, which joins up with the Ice Age Trail for a while, also passes one of the backpacking campsites in the park. These Adirondack-style shelters are available with reservations and are extremely popular for their seclusion. Anyone looking for a backcountry camping experience would find these shelters perfect for a weekend getaway.

Note: There are seven hikes in this book that are found in the various units of Kettle Moraine State Forest. The 56,000-acre forest stretches about 80 miles diagonally from just south of

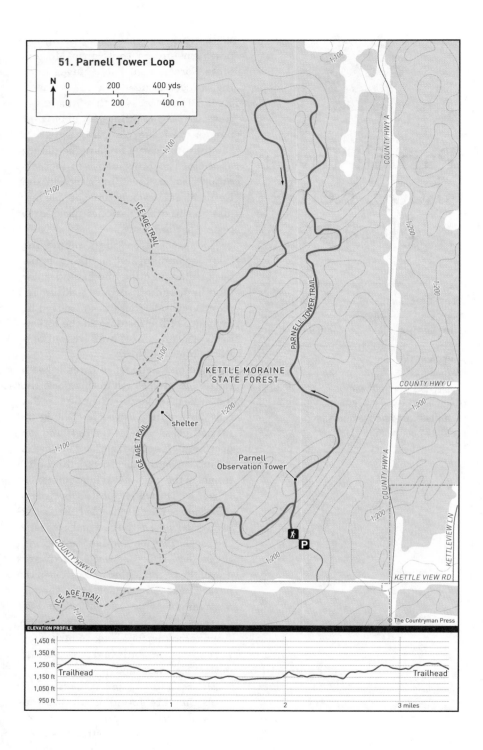

51. Parnell Tower Loop

N
0   200   400 yds
0   200   400 m

ICE AGE TRAIL

1:100

1:200

PARNELL TOWER TRAIL

COUNTY HWY A

COUNTY HWY U

KETTLE MORAINE
STATE FOREST

shelter

ICE AGE TRAIL

Parnell
Observation Tower

COUNTY HWY A

KETTLEVIEW LN

COUNTY HWY U

KETTLE VIEW RD

ICE AGE TRAIL

© The Countryman Press

ELEVATION PROFILE

1,450 ft			
1,350 ft			
1,250 ft			
1,150 ft	Trailhead		Trailhead
1,050 ft			
950 ft	1	2	3 miles

Elkhart Lake in Sheboygan County southwestward to just southeast of Whitewater in Walworth County. The four forest units, from north to south, are Northern, Pike Lake, Lapham Peak, and Southern. There are 250 miles of hiking trails combined in all of these areas, and the Ice Age Trail alone comprises about 72 miles of that. For the sake of this book and the titling of hikes, we use a generic "Kettle Moraine" identifier for those hikes found in any of these units (other than the hike at Lapham Peak, which is titled Lapham Peak, Ice Age Trail). There are several campsites within Kettle Moraine as well as remote backpack-only campsites along the Ice Age Trail. There are also wonderful visitor centers in Kettle Moraine. The Ice Age Visitor Center is just a few miles southwest of Parnell Tower on WI 67 and the Southern Forest Headquarters is located on WI 59 between the towns of Palmyra and Eagle.

HOW TO GET THERE

From the south or southwest, take US 45 north out of Kewauskum to WI 67. Turn right on WI 67 and take it north for about 13 miles. Turn right on CTH U and follow it for 2.3 miles to the Parnell Observation Tower parking lot on the left, just before the junction with CTH A.

From the north, take WI 57 south out of Kiel. Follow WI 57 for about 17 miles to CTH U. Turn right (west) on CTH U and follow it for about 7 miles to the Parnell Observation Tower parking lot on the right.

From the east, take WI 67 south out of Plymouth for about 6 miles to CTH A. Turn left (south) on CTH A and take it for about 2 miles to CTH U. Turn right (west) on CTH U about 0.25 mile to the

Parnell Observation Tower parking lot on the right.

From the west, take WI 23 east out of Fond du Lac about 15 miles to CTH U. Turn right (south) on CTH U and follow it about 8 miles to the Parnell Observation Tower parking lot on the left.

For more information, contact the Kettle Moraine State Forest at 414-626-2116 or the Henry Reuss Ice Age Visitors Center at 920-533-8322.

THE TRAIL

The trailhead is located at the far northern end of the lot. The trail begins rather brutally by taking you immediately up the first set of wooden riser steps toward the observation tower. After about 0.25 mile, the return route of the trail will appear on the left (west). Continue straight ahead toward the tower and up another long set of risers. Soon the tower will emerge in an opening. By heading up to the top, you can see for miles in every direction, and the lush woods of the forest blanket the hills around you.

Head back down and continue north through maples that offer cool shade in the summer, vibrant color in the fall, or stand like quiet stick people in the winter. The trail will wind its way, mainly downward, as it passes through the forest and meanders through glacial rock debris. As you hike along, the ridge will become more prominent—as will the drop-off, too. A shortcut trail will meet up with the main trail from the left (west); ignore this and continue on the main trail.

Eventually the trail will buttonhook to the left, and you will be met by a knee-bending descent into a deep valley. The trail will then curve back north before heading due west and out into an open prairie, full of phlox in the

PARNELL TOWER OFFERS VIEWS FOR MILES IN EVERY DIRECTION

summer. Watch out for the wild parsnip here—it comes very close to, and even encroaches on, the trail.

Note: If you don't know the menace that is wild parsnip, it's a tall—some-times 4 or 5 feet—celery-stalk-type plant with small yellow flowers. Touching this plant and getting its sap on you will combine with sunlight to cause a very mean rash. And this aggressive plant is spreading like crazy these days, particularly on roadsides, trailsides, and in prairies, so watch for and avoid it.

Once you're safely past that patch of wild parsnip, you will then climb up and down as you begin to head southwest toward the junction with the Ice Age Trail. A steep, rocky ascent will take you to an opening and a trail to the camping shelter, which is visible to the left. A bench with a view of the forest to the south is just up the trail.

The trail will meander down into a wooded valley before making a long, steep ascent. The Ice Age Trail will cut off to the right (south); stay left (east) to complete a windy ascent back toward the tower. Eventually, the trail will pop out just above the first set of risers from the beginning of the trail. Take a right (south) and head back down to the trailhead and parking lot.

52

Butler Lake Loop, Kettle Moraine

TOTAL DISTANCE: 3.1 miles

HIKING TIME: 1 hour

DIFFICULTY: 2.5

VERTICAL RISE: 100 feet

TRAILHEAD GPS COORDINATES:
43°39'47.16'' N, 88°8'12.14'' W

Back in the 1920s Ray Zillmer—essentially the father of the Kettle Moraine idea—would pack up the car, and he and his family would go off to explore the wild areas west of the Brew City. He would drive until he found the markedly different rolling terrain of what is now called Kettle Moraine. A world traveler and mountaineer, he simply adored this wild Wisconsin land, perhaps more than anything else on Earth.

Who knows why, but this hike just seems to epitomize what Zillmer saw and was thinking when he fought to preserve this rare topography. This loop, marked with purple blazes, meanders around the woods and prairie openings just southwest of quaint Butler Lake in the northern Kettle Moraine. We recommend doing the hike as a sort of figure eight, which finishes up via a more-than-1-mile stretch of Ice Age Trail.

It's a great area for doing a morning hike here and an afternoon hike at Parnell Tower (previous chapter) or the Zillmer Trail (next chapter), or to combine with taking your canoe out on Butler Lake.

Zillmer once wrote, "We spend a lot to go faster. Let us spend a little to go slower." The bottom line is that this Butler Lake hike is a great sampling of what he wanted us to experience—a trek in the woods with a picnic lunch to follow . . . to commune with nature, and to be better for doing so.

HOW TO GET THERE

From the north and south, take WI 67 to the intersection with CTH F in Dundee. Head east on CTH F approximately 1 mile to Division Road. Turn left (north) here and take it 1 mile to Butler Lake Road. Turn right (east) here and go just over 1 mile to the sign for Butler Lake on the right at the curve in the road.

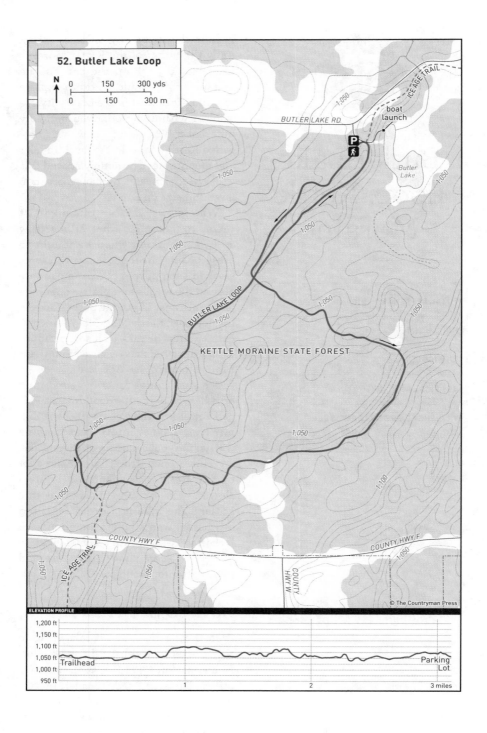

52. Butler Lake Loop

N

| 0 | 150 | 300 yds |
| 0 | 150 | 300 m |

ICE AGE TRAIL

BUTLER LAKE RD

boat launch

P

Butler Lake

BUTLER LAKE LOOP

1,050

KETTLE MORAINE STATE FOREST

1,100

COUNTY HWY F

COUNTY HWY F

ICE AGE TRAIL

COUNTY HWY W

© The Countryman Press

ELEVATION PROFILE

1,200 ft
1,150 ft
1,100 ft
1,050 ft
1,000 ft
950 ft

Trailhead

Parking Lot

1   2   3 miles

From the east, take CTH F and turn right on Division Road and follow the directions above.

For more information, contact the forest headquarters at 262-626-2116 or the Ice Age Visitors Center at 920-533-8322.

A VERY INVITING CANOE LAUNCH AT BUTLER LAKE

THE TRAIL

The trailhead is on the south end of the parking lot, marked by a large kiosk, and the loop is marked with purple blazes on posts. The hike starts out immediately in the woods on a wide path. Soon the trail bends east and turns north again and emerges into an opening.

The trail will turn southwest and head down into a lowland that in the summer can be rather boggy and mosquito filled. You will bend to the north and head up a steep hill and into a sandy prairie before peeling off to the northeast past a red pine stand and descending onto a ridge. Here the trail rides along a long ridge with young trees that is more open. The trail is tilted here, making the hiking kind of awkward.

The trail heads back into the dense woods and turns toward the intersection with the Ice Age Trail. Along the way you will pass an intersection with a snowmobile/horse trail, but ignore this and continue. Soon you will come to the Ice Age Trail, where you will turn right (northeast).

The trail tread is now much narrower on the more trademark Ice Age Trail.

You will go around a semicircle bend and turn more northeastward into an area of tall grass before heading back into the woods, thus beginning a period of up-and-down hiking—descending down into little valleys next to kettle ponds and ascending back up cone-shaped kames and rolling along long ridgeline eskers. Eventually, you'll intersect with your original, wide purple trail that you crossed in the beginning. Go straight across, still heading northeast and up a long hill to the tall point of the hike, overlooking Butler Lake to the east, and just above the parking lot to the west. There's a bench here to relax and enjoy the view before descending to the lake access road and turning left back to the trailhead. (The boat launch is to the right and offers a nice close-up view of the lake.)

53

Zillmer Trail, Kettle Moraine

TOTAL DISTANCE: 5.4 miles

HIKING TIME: 1 hour, 30 minutes

DIFFICULTY: 3.0

VERTICAL RISE: 100 feet

TRAILHEAD GPS COORDINATES:
43°38'32.60'' N, 88°11'26.94'' W

Wisconsin's own mountaineer, Ray Zillmer, was a Milwaukee attorney who worried that the world was getting too pampered by technology and too accustomed to the idea that "wilderness" only meant "out West." It was the 1930s, and Zillmer wanted to preserve what we had right here, in our backyards. He proposed a several-miles-wide, 1,200-mile-long park that would meander through the state marking the final advance of the most recent Wisconsin glacier 10,000 years ago.

Zillmer didn't quite get his whole wish, but Kettle Moraine was established and this northern section alone comprises 30,000 acres. Today for the cost of a state park sticker and some sturdy boots, anyone can visit this forest anytime.

Zillmer passed his dream along to others. The late Henry Reuss, who was a Wisconsin representative to Congress serving from 1955 to 1983, was a champion of the Ice Age Trail. Reuss, a decorated World War II veteran, fought hard for the further development of the trail and even wrote the book about it, *Along the Trail of the Ice Age*. Today, Wisconsin's congressional delegation still carries this torch by working hard to secure millions of dollars for the Ice Age Trail, which they all recognize as a crucially important conservation effort in this state that is great for Wisconsin's economy, too.

And so it is here, atop a hilly glacial remnant in the Kettle Moraine Forest, where you will find memorials to two of these heroes of Wisconsin's natural resources by way of the Henry Reuss Ice Age Visitors Center as well as the Zillmer Hiking and Skiing Trails.

The trails themselves are exceptional, particularly the Yellow Trail highlighted here—a 5.4-mile roller-coaster

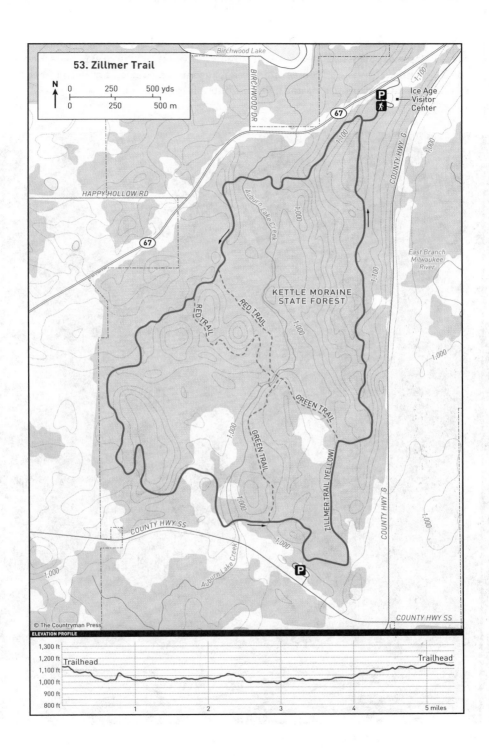

53. Zillmer Trail

N

| 0 | 250 | 500 yds |
| 0 | 250 | 500 m |

Birchwood Lake

BIRCHWOOD DR

Ice Age Visitor Center

67

COUNTY HWY G

HAPPY HOLLOW RD

67

Auburn Lake Creek

KETTLE MORAINE STATE FOREST

East Branch Milwaukee River

RED TRAIL

RED TRAIL

GREEN TRAIL

GREEN TRAIL

ZILLMER TRAIL (YELLOW)

COUNTY HWY SS

COUNTY HWY G

Auburn Lake Creek

COUNTY HWY SS

© The Countryman Press

ELEVATION PROFILE

1,300 ft					
1,200 ft					Trailhead
1,100 ft	Trailhead				
1,000 ft					
900 ft					
800 ft		1	2	3	4	5 miles

hike up and down and around just about every sample of postglacier geology you could imagine. The visitors center offers regular educational programs and exhibitions, particularly during the summer months. The trail is in great shape, and, because it is also used for skiing in the winter, it is rather wide.

RAY ZILLMER DREAMED UP A PARK WITH TRAILS LIKE THIS ONE, NOW HIS NAMESAKE

HOW TO GET THERE

From the north and south, take US 45 to go east on WI 67 approximately 2.5 miles to the Ice Age Visitors Center, just before CTH G. From the east and west, simply take WI 67 to the Ice Age Visitor Center, 1 mile west of Dundee. The trailhead is in the southwest corner of the large parking area.

For more information, contact the forest headquarters at 262-626-2116 or the Ice Age Visitors Center at 920-533-8322.

THE TRAIL

The Zillmer Hiking and Skiing Trails actually all share a trailhead off of CTH SS. But it is possible to hop on the Yellow Trail up on the north side of the loop, where it passes the Ice Age Visitors Center on WI 67, which is where we start the hike.

Head to the southwest corner of the lot where there will be a trailhead for a spur trail that will take you to the Yellow Trail loop, less than 0.25 mile away. This route is counterclockwise, so turn right onto the Yellow Trail and head uphill and into some prairie.

The trail will quickly turn left (southwest) and head downhill into the woods, and you will hike along a mixture of shade perennials like bloodroot and may apple in the summer. After ambling up and down some long rises and descents, you will come to a small stream with a large, wide bridge before going up a very steep ascent.

Eventually you will intersect with the Red Trail heading off to the left (southeast), as well as an access road going right (not marked on the park map); continue straight (southwest). You will share with the Red Trail for a bit before peeling off to the right (west) as it heads left toward the Zillmer Trail Shelter, a backpack-in campsite.

The trail will wind its way southward and into a large stand of towering red pines first, and then, eventually, into a stand of white pines. Eventually the trail will emerge from the trees into a more open prairie habitat abloom with prairie bergamot and milkweed in the summer, as well as dancing with butterflies.

From here, the trail will wiggle back and forth and eventually pass a small pond before making a turn and heading east. One thing not noted in the park map is a small parking lot off of CTH SS. This is not the main trailhead. Turn off to the left here (east) and go across a bridge and back up into the woods where you will soon join the Green Trail. Stay right (east) before turning south and heading into the main parking/trailhead area. It's kind of open here, and the trails somewhat scatter, but if you head out of this area to the east, you will again hook up with the Yellow Trail.

The trail will head through the pines and come to the edge of this plantation, where you will follow the trail to the left (north). There is also a trail that heads off into the prairie to the southeast, but ignore that. You will begin a long section of hiking northward, sharing again with the Green Trail. Eventually the Green will turn left (west) while Yellow will turn right (east).

The trail will resume several ascents and descents, and eventually you will find yourself atop a ridge. In the fall, the views from here are excellent. The trail will continue north and meander downhill and back to the trailhead and spur trail that will take you back to the parking lot.

54

Polk Kames, Ice Age Trail

TOTAL DISTANCE: 3.6 miles

HIKING TIME: 1 hour, 30 minutes

DIFFICULTY: 2.0

VERTICAL RISE: 100 feet

TRAILHEAD GPS COORDINATES:
43°21'10.48'' N, 88°16'15.99'' W

A good trail stands out. There's usually some sort of geological feature making the hike interesting, such as a waterfall, a steep-walled valley, a lakeshore. Oftentimes as hikers we don't really focus much on why these things are here or what brought them into being. Instead we know the *feel* of a good hike, and we simply enjoy it.

The Ice Age Trail is all about history—glacial history. And fortunately for the hiker, this means great terrain and phenomenal hiking. And the great thing for the Wisconsin hiker is that we have 1,200 miles marking the final push of the most recent glacier and a trail in the works that's celebrating it all.

Kames basically look like enormous gumdrops. You can relatively easily amble over, around, and betwixt them and not even know it. But if you stop and look around, and you're in the neighborhood of some of them, you'll see a series of conical hills, formed when a pocket or shaft developed in a glacier and sediment flowed into and filled up the void, like making a huge cast of dirt and rock. Once the glacier melted and retreated, what remained were the kames.

Here at Polk Kames, just outside of Slinger, is one of the finest preserved collections of this geological feature anywhere in the world. And thanks to the sale of this property by the Zuern family, a trail will toddle through it all and Wisconsin hikers will be able to enjoy it until, well, the next Ice Age, maybe.

This is a 3.6-mile lollypop hike that snakes its way west from the trailhead, through the woods, up across a farm field, and deep into a mysterious valley of kames. Then this hike continues on a white-blazed loop before heading back to the trailhead.

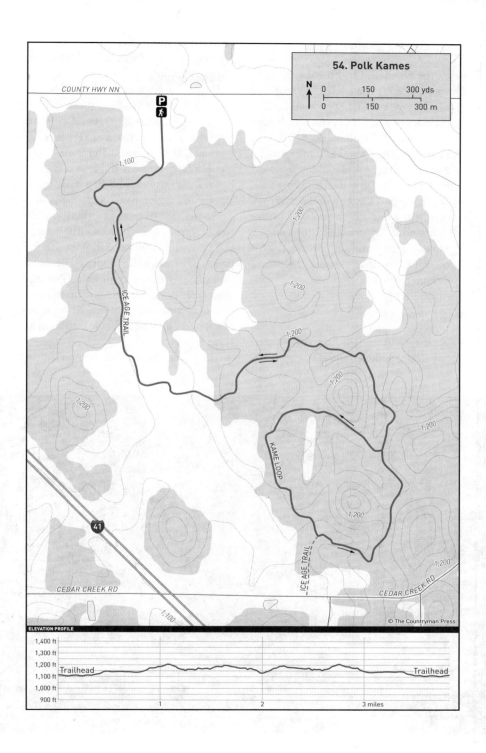

54. Polk Kames

COUNTY HWY NN

ICE AGE TRAIL

KAME LOOP

ICE AGE TRAIL

CEDAR CREEK RD

CEDAR CREEK RD

41

1,100

1,200

1,100

N

0   150   300 yds
0   150   300 m

© The Countryman Press

ELEVATION PROFILE

1,400 ft
1,300 ft
1,200 ft
1,100 ft
1,000 ft
900 ft

Trailhead

Trailhead

1   2   3 miles

HOW TO GET THERE

From the north and south, take US 41 to Slinger. Take WI 144 north 0.25 mile and go right on CTH NN. The trailhead is about 0.5 mile down on the south side of the road and is well marked.

From the west and east, take WI 60 to Kettle Moraine Drive on the south side of Slinger. Turn north here and it will turn into WI 144 as it crosses WI 175 downtown. Head north on WI 144 out of town and follow the directions above.

For more information, contact the Ice Age Trail Alliance at 1-800-227-0046 or find them online.

THE TRAIL

This section of the Ice Age Trail is part of the Cedar Lakes Segment and takes you on a short lollypop hike around Polk Kames. It runs from CTH NN on the north to Cedar Creek Road on the south.

Begin the hike at the CTH NN trailhead parking lot (in fact, there really is no parking on Cedar Creek Road, and as of this printing, it is asked that hikers not park at this end). The trail begins along a farm lane for the first 0.125 mile before ducking right (west) into the woods and down into a cool, boggy area.

Soon the trail crosses a small wooden footbridge, turns left (south) around the bog, and heads uphill past the first group of kames before exiting the woods straight out into a farm field. The path snakes through the field and up to a little stand of trees before heading back into the woods and then back into another farm field.

Soon you come to a hedgerow and

THE TRAIL TRAVERSES BETWEEN HUGE GLACIAL GUMDROPS AT POLK KAMES

enter a prairie. The trail climbs gradually here as it heads east. You'll round a bend, uphill and northeastward, and then you'll go into the woods again, where you'll find a little bench up here near a big maple.

The trail remains in the woods and goes deeper into this valley, turning right and southeast. As you look straight and to the right, you'll see the tall gumdrop kames poking out from the earth around you, and the trail will wind its way between several of them, passing through a small valley and next to a small pond.

Eventually you'll come to an intersection of the main yellow-blazed Ice Age Trail, which you've been on, and the white-blazed Kames Loop. Turn right here (west) and head uphill. The trail will switchback a couple of times on its way westward. Soon you will emerge at the edge of the woods, and another farm field and an opening offering a great view to the south, and on clear days you can see the Holy Hill shrine and its towering Romanesque church on the distant horizon.

Continuing on, the loop trail will meet back up with the Ice Age Trail—veer left here (staying east) and head around that same kame, eventually turning back north. Here you will pass between this kame you've been looping around and another one to the east, whose hillside is full of bright white birch trees. You will pass the original intersection with the Kame Loop that you took—stay right (northeast) and retrace your steps back to the trailhead.

55

Pike Lake Loop, Kettle Moraine

TOTAL DISTANCE: 4.7 miles

HIKING TIME: 2 hours

DIFFICULTY: 3.5

VERTICAL RISE: 230 feet

TRAILHEAD GPS COORDINATES:
43°18'30.49'' N, 88°19'16.31'' W

While it is a detached island from the main forest, the Pike Lake Unit of Kettle Moraine exemplifies why preserving places like this is so incredibly important. No matter which direction you approach it from, there is increasing human development. It's amazing, in fact, how the towns along here—once separated by defined blocks of farmland and woods—are now blended together by development. Today, however, amidst all of this human progress, is a wonderful lakeside park—full of picnicking, hiking, camping, and swimming opportunities.

Pike Lake, itself a kettle, is surrounded by a park with a beach, parking, a shelter, camping, and a newly built observation tower—offering views for miles atop 1,350-foot Powder Hill, a kame. Much of this loop trail borrows its course from the Ice Age Trail, which meanders through the park on a diagonal.

The trail starts at the beach area parking lot and heads straight up Powder Hill along the Ice Age Trail route to the turnoff for the Powder Hill Tower. A 0.5-mile, out-and-back hike takes you to the top of the tower and offers phenomenal views of much of Washington County and Pike Lake below. From here, the trail leaves the Ice Age Trail and heads east through mostly hardwood forest and past the campsite area, before turning north and then west for a long, rolling stretch through woods and some prairie to the trailhead.

The trail is very hilly at first, and moderately hilly throughout. And while the beach is bustling on warm summer weekends, the trails see limited use, making this a great destination if you're in the area looking for a great hike.

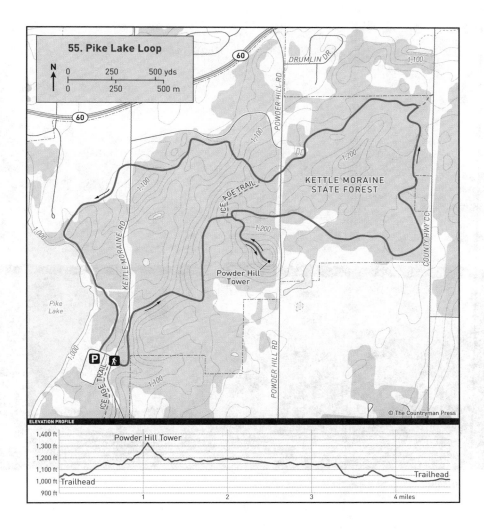

HOW TO GET THERE

From the west, take WI 60 east out of Hartford 1.6 miles to the park entrance on the right (Kettle Moraine Drive). Follow this drive for about 1 mile, past the visitors center, to the beach parking lot on the right. The trailhead is directly across the drive from the parking lot.

From the east, take WI 60 west out of Jackson for about 8 miles to the park entrance, Kettle Moraine Drive, on the left. Follow the directions above.

From the southeast, take US 41 north out of Menomonee Falls 9.5 miles to WI 60. Turn left (west) on WI 60 and go 3.5 miles to the park entrance, Kettle Moraine Drive, on the left. Follow the directions above.

From the north, take US 41 south out of Allenton 7.5 miles to WI 60. Turn right on WI 60 and go west 3.5 miles to the park entrance, Kettle Moraine Drive, on the left. Follow the directions above.

For more information, contact Kettle

LATE SUMMER SUNSET OVER PICTURESQUE PIKE LAKE

Moraine State Forest, Pike Lake Unit at 262-670-3400.

THE TRAIL

After crossing the road from the pleasant lakeshore and beach, you are engulfed by both the woods and the base of Powder Hill. The trail begins its ascent immediately as you head alongside the park road and wind along the west side of the hill. Eventually the trail will come to a bench and an offshoot to the south, which heads up to the tower.

When it comes to towers, the one on Powder Hill is pretty remarkable and offers a great view for miles.

After descending from the tower, head east, staying on the Brown Trail. The Ice Age Trail will turn off with the Orange Trail at this point. So, ignore that turnoff and stay east. You will pass Powder Hill Road, join with the White Trail, and hike along the edge of the camping area. Here you will meet up briefly with the Astronomy Trail—an educational trail that seeks to illustrate the size of the solar system and the planets through a series of models placed on posts.

From here, the Blue Trail will soon cut off to the left (north), while you will begin a gentle downhill alongside an open field to the right. The trail will make a sharp turn to the left and head north along CTH CC, still descending slightly. Soon you will turn west and meet up with the Blue Trail again, as well as meeting back up with the Ice Age Trail. From here you will pass the Powder Hill Road parking lot and cross the road. (Make sure to switch your mind from trail hiking back to road-crossing mode briefly—the cars may be coming quickly.) Then duck back into the woods.

The Black Forest Nature Trail will peel off to the right, but stay left and hike into a more open area before heading downhill and winding alongside a small pond before making a steep climb.

The trail will then merge with the Green Trail and head across Kettle Moraine Drive before emerging from the woods and into an open prairie. You will then merge with the bike trail for the remainder of the hike. The trail will meet up with the eastern shore of Pike Lake and go through a marshy area before ducking back into the woods, full of spruce and cedar, and emerging finally at the picnic area near the parking lot, beach, and trailhead.

Nashotah Park Loop, Waukesha County

TOTAL DISTANCE: 3.5 miles

HIKING TIME: 1 hour, 30 minutes

DIFFICULTY: 1.5

VERTICAL RISE: Minimal

TRAILHEAD GPS COORDINATES: 43°6'44.11" N, 88°24'32.25" W

Sometimes you just need a park. You want a place to play volleyball, toss a ball, have a cookout, meet with friends or family, and simply relax. Well, throw in some great hiking trails that double as ski trails in the winter, a couple of lakes with fishing, wetlands, waterfowl, wildflowers, and blazing fall colors—and you have Nashotah Park.

Nashotah is a very well-maintained and well-administered 450-acre park. In fact, the park almost has to be this way as part of the agreement the Gallun family made with the county upon signing the deed. They wanted to ensure that this area would be a home for native plant preservation and recreation. That was in 1972, and thanks to ever-growing Milwaukee suburbs, the decision to gift this land as a park undoubtedly saved this area from development.

This hike takes you along the Green Trail, the longest loop in the park, and shows off everything that Nashotah has to offer. Starting off at the westernmost parking lot, the trail goes south along a ridge and through a thick hardwood forest full of mature trees, offering great shade in the summer. The trail then turns west away from the lake and through a stand of pines before heading out into the open and through a large prairie. From here the trail meanders along the western edge of the park toward Grass Lake, before turning east and up and down a series of small hills back toward the parking area. But just before the lot, the trail turns north again and completes a 1-mile-long loop through the largest prairie of the hike—alive with wildflowers in the warmer months—then past the park office and back up to the parking lot.

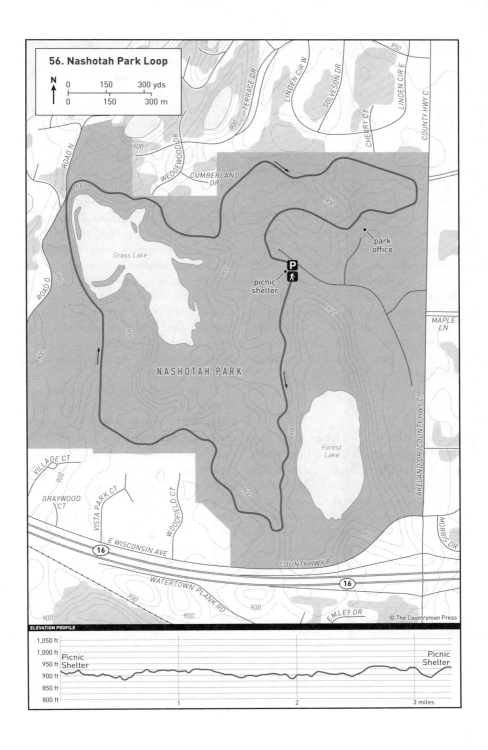

56. Nashotah Park Loop

N

| 0 | 150 | 300 yds |
| 0 | 150 | 300 m |

TERRACE DR

LINDEN CIR W

SOLVESON DR

CHERRY CT

LINDEN CIR E

COUNTY HWY C

ROAD N

WEDGEWOOD DR

CUMBERLAND DR

900

900

900

park office

Grass Lake

P

picnic shelter

MAPLE LN

ROAD O

900

900

900

NASHOTAH PARK

900

Forest Lake

LAKELAND DR (COUNTY HWY C)

VILLAGE CT

GRAYWOOD CT

VISTA PARK CT

WOODFIELD CT

E WISCONSIN AVE

16

COUNTY HWY R

16

MORRIS DR

900

WATERTOWN PLANK RD

900

900

900

EMLEY DR

© The Countryman Press

ELEVATION PROFILE

1,050 ft			
1,000 ft	Picnic		Picnic
950 ft	Shelter		Shelter
900 ft			
850 ft			
800 ft	1	2	3 miles

HOW TO GET THERE

From the south, take CTH C north from I-94 for 3.9 miles to the park entrance on the left. After passing through the park check-in, turn right and go 0.3 mile to the west parking lot.

From the east or west, take I-94 to the CTH C exit and follow the directions above.

From the west, take WI 16 east out of Oconomowoc 3.8 miles to CTH C. Turn left (north) on CTH C and go 0.7 mile to the park entrance on the left. Follow the directions above.

There is a daily use fee, per automobile, payable upon entrance to Nashotah. In 2011, this was $3 during the week and $5 on weekends. Annual passes are also available. For more information, contact the Waukesha County Park System at 262-548-7801 or online.

THE TRAIL

The hike follows the Green Trail and begins at the bottom of the hill on the south side of the parking lot, below the picnic shelter. The trail is very wooded here on the bluff above the lake. As you head south you will pass the intersection with the Red Trail, but stay to the left and continue along the lakeshore.

The trail will eventually head uphill and through a stand of large white pines. The stump of a fallen one was used to make a small seat. Turn west from here and head uphill through an open prairie to the Green Trail turnoff to the right (north). This section of trail takes you down through a deep valley prairie and up the other side, where the trail will head northwest and past the Tan Shortcut Trail intersection.

From here, you will head west and then curve north, past an old barn and down a long stretch of trail, until you come to the western shore of Grass Lake. You are very close to the western edge of the park at this point, and the trail actually runs parallel to CTH O over here. The trail will hook eastward at the northern tip of the lake and head down into a deep valley before climbing back up into the rolling prairie on the north side of the park.

While you may even see your car from here, you will turn off to the north again and make a long, sweeping loop through this great prairie, which is alive with birds and butterflies and aflame with wildflowers in the warmer months. Once you arrive at the northeasternmost corner of the park, the trail will turn south and then west and head up a steep hill, before passing the park office and dipping into the last valley. One final climb takes you up to the parking lot and trailhead above.

Lapham Peak, Ice Age Trail

TOTAL DISTANCE: 2.8 miles

HIKING TIME: 1.5 hours

DIFFICULTY: 3.5

VERTICAL RISE: 292 feet

TRAILHEAD GPS COORDINATES:
43°02'24.99" N, 88°24'10.45" W

While it may be hard to fathom these days, with real-time weather data literally at our fingertips, this is a very recent luxury. Instead, for much of history it was nearly impossible to know for certain what meteorological surprise was around the corner. And while not knowing about a pending storm is tough on anyone, it was especially life-threatening for sailors on Lake Michigan. But for decades during early European settlement, ships set sail without knowing for certain what the winds would bring or if a ship-sinking storm was barreling right for them.

This all changed in the 1800s with the work of one man, Increase Lapham, atop the tallest point in Waukesha County at 1,253 feet. It was here where Lapham received weather reports via telegraph from Colorado because much of the weather out that way would eventually dictate the weather in these parts. It was this idea of forecasting that eventually led to the establishment of a National Weather Bureau (now the National Weather Service) and was commemorated by the renaming of this hill, originally Government Hill, to Lapham Peak.

Just off one of the two most traveled interstate highways in Wisconsin, yet paradoxically quite serene, Kettle Moraine State Forest's Lapham Peak unit is as unique today as it was more than 100 years ago. But today's attraction is the exceptionally well-developed trail system traversing the hill and offering phenomenal hiking, mountain biking, Nordic skiing, snowshoeing, and a remote campsite accessible only by backpacking in along the Ice Age Trail, which meanders through Lapham Peak and is the featured trail for this hike. There's even a summer stage offering plays and live music located near the

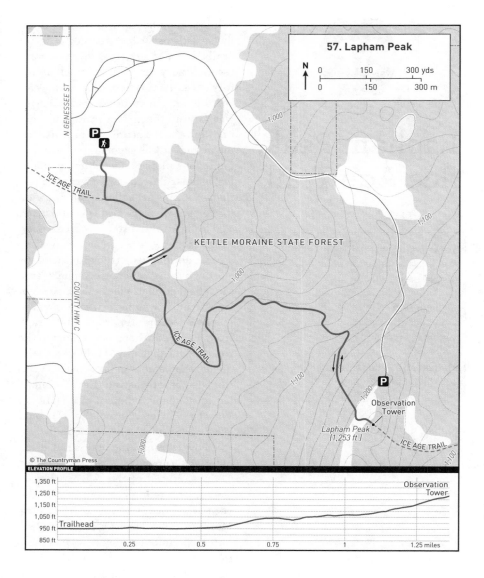

57. Lapham Peak

N

| 0 | 150 | 300 yds |
| 0 | 150 | 300 m |

KETTLE MORAINE STATE FOREST

ICE AGE TRAIL

N GENESSEE ST

COUNTY HWY C

ICE AGE TRAIL

Observation
Tower

Lapham Peak
(1,253 ft.)

ICE AGE TRAIL

© The Countryman Press

ELEVATION PROFILE

1,350 ft				Observation
1,250 ft				Tower
1,150 ft				
1,050 ft				
950 ft	Trailhead			
850 ft	0.25	0.5	0.75	1	1.25 miles

lower parking lot. In the winter months, the Nordic skiing here is highly coveted and includes a lighted ski trail for evening skiing and the woodstove-heated Evergreen Lodge.

This 2.8-mile, out-and-back hike leaves the lodge parking lot and takes a spur trail to the Ice Age Trail where it then follows a nearly 292-foot ascent up to the observation tower high above.

HOW TO GET THERE

From the south, take WI 83 north out of Wales 0.5 mile to US 18. Turn left (west) on US 18 and go 1.1 miles to CTH C. Turn right (north) on CTH C and go 1.8 miles to the park entrance on the right. Pass the park office and continue on the park road 0.2 mile, turn right, and follow this road to the Evergreen Lodge parking area. The trailhead is in the southeast corner of the lot—look for the Ice Age Trail sign.

From the north, take CTH C south 1 mile from I-94 to the park entrance on the left. Follow the directions above.

From the west or east, take either US 18 or I-94 to CTH C. Follow the directions above.

THE TRAIL

Follow the sign for the Ice Age Trail off the southeast corner of the parking lot. You'll see a blue blaze painted on the sign—Ice Age Trail spurs, or connectors, are painted blue (loops are painted white). Take this onto a wide trail that will pass an information kiosk about the

BOARDWALKS AND GOLDENROD ALONG THE BASE OF LAPHAM PEAK

THE LAPHAM PEAK TOWER HIGH ABOVE WAUKESHA COUNTY'S 83 LAKES

Ice Age Trail. Only about .25 mile in, the spur will come to a T intersection, with the main Ice Age Trail. Turn left, east, and follow the sign to the observation tower. From here, you'll be on the Ice Age Trail all the way up to the tower, so just follow the yellow blazes.

For the first part of the hike or so, the ground is pretty level. After that left turn, you'll pass by a large marsh and pond with a great observation platform just off the trail for seeing waterfowl and other wildlife. Continuing on the trail will mean turning south and swooping around the edge of the pond over a series of impressive boardwalks that were installed by the Ice Age Trail Alliance in recent years. The trail passes through a sea of wildflowers here during the warmer months before entering an oak grove.

You will pass one of the wide ski trails, head over another small boardwalk, and then pass a second ski trail, where you will then be enveloped by the woods again as you take your first few steps up onto the skirt of the hill. The ascent begins quickly as you meander east up the south side of a long valley before crossing a small rock bridge and buttonhooking back to the northwest and the other side of the forested valley.

Eventually you'll pop out of the woods into a hillside prairie and the trail will level out a bit. You'll pass a bench here before turning eastward toward the tower. You will head back into the woods and will pass the blue-blazed spur trail to the backpacking campsite. Veer right and follow the yellow blazes. The trail will curve again northeast along the top edge of another valley before swooping northeast and steeply uphill as it curves its way up toward the hill's peak.

You will pass some offshoot trails that head straight uphill to the east to the tower area. Stay on the Ice Age Trail and follow the yellow blazes as you head uphill and out of the woods. You'll cross over a wide access trail and head up a series of long riser steps to the tower above and your turnaround point.

Note: While the Ice Age Trail used to pass below the tower it now takes you right to it as it passes over the peak of the hill.

The view from the tower is an impressive one thanks to the already tall peak you've summited. The view to the east reaches all the way to downtown Milwaukee; to the north you can see the lake region; and to the southwest you will see the hilly, ribbon-like unraveling of Kettle Moraine forest extending toward Whitewater.

After visiting the tower, simply retrace your steps back off Lapham Peak, down the wooded hillside, and past the pond and marsh back to the trailhead below.

Scuppernong Trail Loop, Kettle Moraine

TOTAL DISTANCE: 5.5 miles

HIKING TIME: 2 hours

DIFFICULTY: 3.5

VERTICAL RISE: 110 feet

TRAILHEAD GPS COORDINATES:
42°56'26.02'' N, 88°27'40.81'' W

The Kettle Moraine State Forest includes more than 50,000 acres, making it the largest tract of public land in southern Wisconsin. The amazing part about Kettle Moraine is the fact that each one of those thousands of acres is within an hour's drive of the most populated areas of the state. Equally amazing is that much of the forest is set aside for the silent sports, including hiking, off-road bicycling, horseback riding, and skiing. On top of that, the scenery—as you stand atop an oak-covered bluff or meander through a pine-blanketed valley—is breathtaking.

Kettle Moraine State Forest's two largest sections are the Northern and Southern Units, and the Ice Age Trail runs throughout the entirety of both units for more than 60 miles. And in each unit there are trail areas designated for various uses, including mountain biking, Nordic skiing, horseback riding, and hiking. The Scuppernong trail area is designated for hiking and Nordic skiing only and offers more than 11 miles of trails that loop through the area's wooded glacial hills and valleys. The Ice Age Trail even passes through the area.

This 5.5-mile hike follows the Green Loop, the longest of the three loop trails available to hikers and Nordic skiers at Scuppernong, and it also heads out and back to an overlook offering a look through the treetops far off to the west of Kettle Moraine and Jefferson County farm country. The hilly trail weaves up and down and through a mixture of hardwoods and pines along a mostly wooded trail. While a Nordic ski trail, it isn't necessarily as wide and level as some, and the footing is a bit rocky and sandy at times. And, if you want to shorten things or add distance, it's easy to do here, thanks to the other loops.

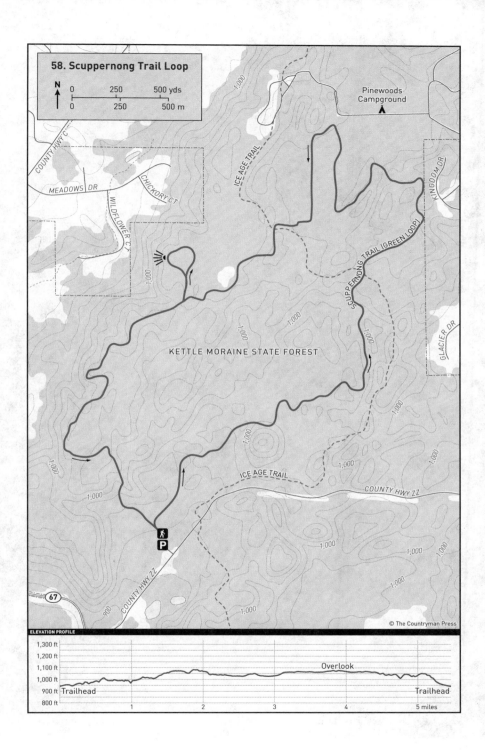

58. Scuppernong Trail Loop

N

| 0 | 250 | 500 yds |
| 0 | 250 | 500 m |

Pinewoods
Campground

COUNTY HWY C

MEADOWS DR

CHICKORY CT

WILDFLOWER CT

ICE AGE TRAIL

KINGDOM DR

SCUPPERNONG TRAIL (GREEN LOOP)

GLACIER DR

KETTLE MORAINE STATE FOREST

1,000

ICE AGE TRAIL

COUNTY HWY ZZ

COUNTY HWY ZZ

67

© The Countryman Press

ELEVATION PROFILE

| 1,300 ft |
| 1,200 ft |
| 1,100 ft | Overlook |
| 1,000 ft |
| 900 ft | Trailhead | Trailhead |
| 800 ft |

1   2   3   4   5 miles

LONG, LOOPING TRAILS BECKON HIKERS TO SCUPPERNONG

HOW TO GET THERE

From the south, take WI 67 north out of Eagle for 4.1 miles to CTH ZZ. Turn right and go 0.3 mile on CTH ZZ to the Scuppernong Hiking/Skiing Trail parking lot on the left.

From the east, take WI 59 west from Waukesha 8 miles to CTH ZZ. Turn right on CTH ZZ and go 4.5 miles to the Scuppernong Hiking/Skiing Trail parking lot on the right.

From the north, take WI 67 south out of Oconomowoc 11.3 miles to CTH ZZ. Turn left on CTH ZZ and go 0.3 mile to the Scuppernong Hiking/Skiing Trail parking lot on the left.

THE TRAIL

The trailhead is located in the northwest corner of the lot, and a large wooden map shows the three loop trails offered here. This trail, the Green Loop, basically follows the outer edge of all the loops and covers the most ground. The actual starting point is down the trail to the left of the kiosk, even though there's no sign pointing in that direction. The other trail to the right, between the kiosk and the bathrooms, is a park service road.

Upon starting, you will be greeted by a sandy path underfoot and pines overhead. The trail will take an immediate turn to the right, and you will head down a long, straight, and flat stretch, giving you a good warm-up for the hike. The trail will turn more northward from here as you pass through some oak and hickory trees. As you wind more eastward, you will climb your first hill before dipping down into a valley,

TALL WHISPERING PINES ESCORT HIKERS ALONG MANY TRAIL SECTIONS

a trend that will repeat itself several times on this hike.

Soon you will pass the turnoff for the Red Loop before descending toward the Pine Woods Campground. You will pass the Ice Age Trail before curving east toward CTH G. From here you will turn westward and zigzag down toward the grove of white and red pines next to the campground.

The trail will then turn directly north along a long stretch of logging road flanked by pines on the western edge of the campground. At the end of this stretch, you will come to an open area near the campground. Eventually, you will turn southwest and cross the Ice Age Trail and meet back up with the Red and Orange loops.

Soon you will come to the overlook loop turnoff. Take this to the right (north) and follow it to the overlook, which is on a high bluff covered in oak trees and offers a good view of the town of Ottawa to the north. From here, head back to the main trail, turning right and continuing along the Green Loop as it zigzags southwestward again. From here, it is mainly downhill back to the trailhead and parking lot.

59

Nordic Trail Loop, Kettle Moraine

TOTAL DISTANCE: 3.7 miles

HIKING TIME: 1 hour, 30 minutes

DIFFICULTY: 3.0

VERTICAL RISE: Minimal

TRAILHEAD GPS COORDINATES:
42°49'17.69'' N, 88°36'01.40'' W

When you look at the far southeastern corner of the state, bordered for about 70 miles by US 94 on the north and for 45 miles by US 90 on the west, it's a relatively small pocket by comparison with the rest of the state. So it's fairly notable, then, that a 22,000-acre, 30-mile-long forest exists here. And it's a place intentionally designed for recreation trails, camping, fishing, boating, biking, skiing, snowshoeing, and more.

Kettle Moraine is teeming with wildflowers, wildlife, trees, lakes, and rugged, gravelly glacial terrain. And it's also full of lots of trails. This hike focuses on one of Southern Kettle Moraine's great hiking and cross-country skiing trail areas, the Nordic Trail System, which offers nearly 23 miles along 7 different loop trails, a tidy trailhead parking lot complete with water, restrooms, and a warming house for the winter. There's even a sledding hill to cap it all off.

We find ourselves repeatedly coming to the Nordic trails for hiking. They are wide ski trails making hiking in small groups easier. And there are great swooping dives deep into valleys followed by steep climbs up to grand vistas, as the trails wind their way around the glacial landscape.

This hike follows the 3.7-mile Green Loop, the second longest trail of the Nordic Trail System and a rambling tour through burly hardwood forest, past a few prairie openings, through some stands of tall pines, and past a few hilltop vistas. You can also explore the other trails here if you want to add or subtract distance. Also, because it's a ski trail, it switches to skiing in the winter, but we find that southern Wisconsin skiing is rather sporadic most years. So much of the winter, these trails are still hiking trails until it snows. If you do come for

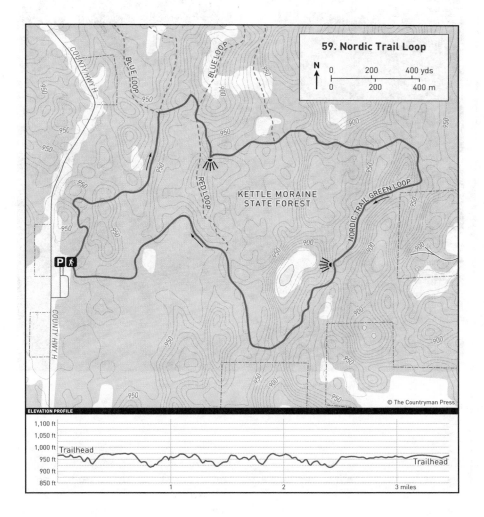

ELEVATION PROFILE

skiing and this loop is too hilly for your ski legs, there are other loops here that are tamer.

HOW TO GET THERE

From the west, take WI 12 out of White-water 7 miles to the town of La Grange. Turn left, north, on CTH H and take this 1.5 miles to the Nordic Trails parking area on the right. The trailhead is on the east side of the lot on the edge of the woods between the warming house and

the restroom building. From the south-east, take WI 12 out of Elkhorn 11 miles to La Grange and turn right, east, on CTH H and follow the directions above. From the north (or northwest via WI 59), take CTH H south out of Palmyra 4.5 miles to the Nordic Trails parking area on the left.

Note: The John Muir Trails parking area is on the west side of the road. You want the parking lot on the east side of the road. The John Muir trail system is a hotspot for mountain bikers.

GLACIAL HILLS AND OLD GROWTH TREES WELCOME HIKERS TO THE NORDIC TRAILS

THE TRAIL

There are map kiosks throughout the system and all of the intersections are well marked. All of the trails begin at the trailhead just east of the parking lot on the edge of the woods between the warming house and the restroom building where there is a large map on a trailhead kiosk.

Head off into the dense woods to the north following the Green Loop, which will share with several of the other colored loops for most of the whole hike as they come and go. The trail is a wide one that's clearly built for skiing, and it makes for great side-by-side hiking because of this. The trail tread is very good, although it can get gravelly and rocky at times.

Soon after heading away from the trailhead, you will go down and up a small hill and turn a corner to the east and descend quickly and climb again before turning north again and emerging from the woods into an expansive prairie opening with woods surrounding it. After 0.25 mile, you will come to a four-way intersection. Just follow the Green Loop arrow to the right, east, and head downhill for another .25 mile. The Blue Loop will take off to the northwest here and the Red Loop to the southwest, but stay on the Green Loop to the bottom of this valley, where you'll come to an overlook.

Soon the trail will turn east again and you will ascend, regaining the elevation you've lost so far by climbing 50 feet in 0.15 mile. The Blue Loop will rejoin you again as you continue your windy way eastward and past a huge oak tree overhanging the trail.

You'll eventually come to the midpoint of the hike, which also marks the farthest point east of the trailhead, and you'll arch around a corner to the south, then southwest past a stand of pines, and downhill to an overlook of a kettle pond below to the west and a hillside prairie opening.

The trail will head back into the woods as you amble up and down the several glacial hills and valleys west and then northwestward as you pass under maples that are alive with yellow in the fall. Eventually more trails will rejoin you as you head west back to the trailhead for a fairly level final 0.5-mile stretch homeward.

THE WIDE TRAILS ARE PREPPED EARLY FOR SNOW AND NORDIC SKIING

60

Richard Bong State Recreation Area Loop

TOTAL DISTANCE: 4.2 miles	
HIKING TIME: 1 hour, 30 minutes	
DIFFICULTY: 2.5	
VERTICAL RISE: Minimal	
TRAILHEAD GPS COORDINATES: 42°38'2.87" N, 88°7'26.28" W	

Wide-open vistas, full of wildflower-filled prairies, a lake, ponds, wetlands, and stands of hardwoods all assembled in the same place, is a scenario that is kind of hard to picture in far southeast Wisconsin. But with more than 4,500 acres set aside for wildlife, prairies, trees, and trails, the Richard Bong State Recreation Area is a welcome natural area in the most populated section of the state. The place is named for World War II ace fighter pilot and Congressional Medal of Honor winner Richard Ira Bong (1920–1945), a Wisconsin native.

But things weren't always supposed to be this way. In the wake of World War II, the land was slated to become a military airfield for fighter jets to use as a home base for defending the skies around Milwaukee and Chicago. Literally days before pretty much all of this area was to be paved and just after topsoil was removed, land was leveled, and wetlands were filled in—construction came to a halt. Thus, like a charred battlefield, the would-be Richard Bong Airfield was left for dead.

A subsequent initiative to turn the entire area into a modern, multiuse suburban development was thwarted, and the value of a large, contiguous tract of land in the southeast part of the state was realized. And today visitors are greeted with 16 miles of footpaths that wind through nature.

This hike follows the 4.1-mile Blue Loop, one of six loop trails here. The trail meanders through every environment the park has to offer: prairies, wetlands, woods, and lakeshore.

HOW TO GET THERE

From the north, take US 45 south out of Union Grove 3.1 miles to WI 142. Turn right (west) on WI 142 and go 3.9 miles

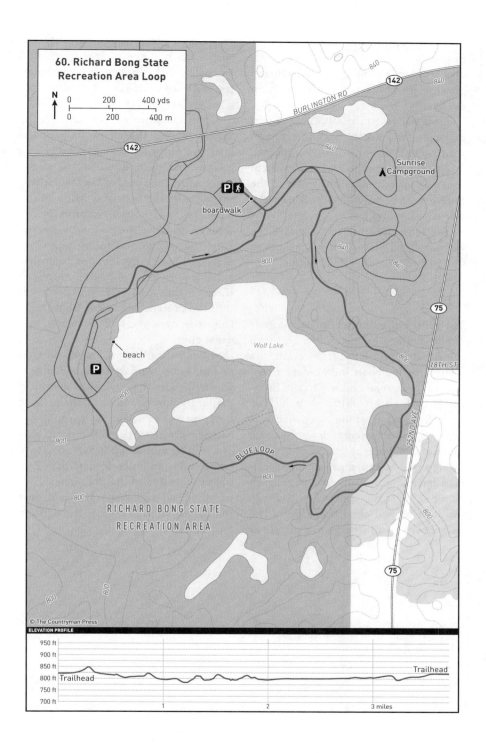

60. Richard Bong State Recreation Area Loop

N
0 200 400 yds
0 200 400 m

BURLINGTON RD

840

840

840

142

142

Sunrise Campground

boardwalk

800

840

840

840

75

18TH ST

beach

Wolf Lake

800

800

800

252ND AVE

800

BLUE LOOP

800

800

RICHARD BONG STATE
RECREATION AREA

800

800

75

800

800

800

© The Countryman Press

ELEVATION PROFILE

950 ft
900 ft
850 ft
800 ft Trailhead   Trailhead
750 ft
700 ft
              1   2   3 miles

to the park entrance. Turn left and, after passing through the entrance station, take another left and go to the trailhead parking lot about 0.25 mile down on the left.

From the west, take WI 142 out of Burlington 7.8 miles to the park entrance on your right. Follow the directions above.

From the east, take WI 142 east out of Kenosha approximately 17 miles to the park entrance on your left. Follow the directions above.

For more information, contact the Richard Bong State Recreation Area at 262-878-5600 or find them online.

THE TRAIL

The trail begins at the northeast corner of the trailhead parking lot. The trail immediately crosses a large wetland via a long wooden boardwalk before crossing the park road coming to the intersection of the start and finish of the Blue Loop. Take a left, going clockwise, and head up a slight ascent along the road. The trail will soon head toward Sunrise Campground and alongside a large prairie filled with colorful wildflowers in the summer. You will duck into the woods for a bit as you skirt the edge of the campground and emerge in a prairie as you climb your way up to the northeast corner of Wolf Lake, where you will find a bench and the intersection of several trails. All the trails are well marked, and it is easy to follow the Blue Trail.

Continue downhill and through the woods toward the eastern tip of the lake and alongside WI 75 very briefly before turning off and into the woods at the southern shore of the lake. Along this part of the trail you will find the most hills, although nothing is too strenuous. Soon the trail will emerge from the woods and turn northward, directly toward the shore and another small woods. The trail will buttonhook through this area and head back out into the prairie, ascending slightly. In this open area you will be treated to a great view.

Soon you will cross the horse trail and turn north toward the beach, where you will cross the park road and head along a ridge above the beach. From here, turn east and cross through yet another prairie area on the north side of the lake, crossing a gravel loop trail twice and heading back up to the original intersection of the Blue Loop. Turn left and head back across the road, over the boardwalk, and back to the parking lot trailhead.

Index

*Italics indicate maps and illustrations.